ENGLAND RUGBY

1871   2021

150 YEARS

Published in 2021 for the Rugby Football Union by Vision Sports Publishing Ltd

Vision Sports Publishing Ltd
19-23 High Street
Kingston upon Thames
Surrey
KT1 1LL
www.visionsp.co.uk

© Rugby Football Union

ISBN: 978-1913412-09-8

Written by: Phil McGowan and Richard Steele

Project editor and design: Doug Cheeseman
Editorial production: Ed Davis
Editorial consultant: Jim Drewett
Marketing: Toby Trotman
Production: Ulrika Drewett
Imaging: Jörn Kröger

RFU licensing manager: Tom Heeks
RFU editorial manager: Patricia Mowbray

Photography: World Rugby Museum, Getty Images, PA Images, Colorsport, Offside, Shutterstock, Priory Collection,
Garvin Davies, Frédéric Humbert collection, Simon Inglis, Marc Aspland
Memorabilia photography: Paul Downes, 3Objectives

Rugby Football Union
Rugby House
Twickenham Stadium
200 Whitton Road
Twickenham
Middlesex
TW2 7BA

Printed in Slovakia by Neografia

A CIP record for this book is available from the British Library

ENGLAND RUGBY

1871 2021

150 YEARS

Phil McGowan & Richard Steele

FOREWORD

By His Honour Judge
JEFF BLACKETT
President of the Rugby Football Union

These are extraordinary times. As I pen this foreword the world is still beset by the Covid-19 pandemic. Professional rugby and the Six Nations competition, which stopped abruptly in March 2020, was able to restart in the autumn and the 2019/20 season finally ended at the beginning of November 2020, since when we have enjoyed the Autumn Nations Cup. Community rugby also stopped suddenly and ended their season prematurely. Players started training under strict non-contact conditions and, subsequently, competitive grassroots rugby has had to be adapted to meet Government guidelines. This is a difficult period in our history, and a very unwelcome development just as we begin to celebrate our 150th anniversary.

In his foreword to the centenary book, the RFU President, Sir William Ramsay, wrote: "In reading this history, we realise how the game has developed and changed over the years, and how it has grown. Further changes are certain in the future, but through all time one sees the determination to retain our strict amateur belief, and this determination is still as strongly held as ever. Rugby Union football, as we know it, is not a job of work, but a game to be enjoyed in hours of relaxation, as a relief from the daily toil."

How times have changed. Twenty-five years after he wrote these words rugby union became a professional sport, and in the 25 years since then it has changed out of all recognition from the previous 125 years. Professional players are bigger, stronger and fitter than those who played in the amateur days. The game is faster; more spectators watch elite rugby; income generated by the game is enormous by comparison. And at the same time thousands of women and girls have taken up the sport, with their elite and international matches attracting ever more support and popularity.

But one thing that Sir William also said, and which remains a constant, is: "There is nothing I admire more than the vast amount of work put in, as a labour of love, by administrators all over the country, in order to further our cause. They must feel, as I do, that the final justification of the game is the firm and life-long friendships it produces, founded on healthy rivalry on the field in days of youth, and happy commingling afterwards." Today's volunteers are equally dedicated and without them the game would wither and die. I would like to pay tribute to all who give so much of their time and expend so much emotional energy so that our young men and women can continue to play the game that we all love.

This book celebrates the past 150 years – the growth of the game, the achievements of many individuals and teams, the growing pains of professionalism after the 1995 Rugby World Cup and the development of Twickenham into arguably the best dedicated rugby stadium in the world. At the same time, it provides us with an opportunity to look forward with hope and optimism and to renew. We aim to grow our community game, the bedrock of a successful sport, maintain an effective pathway for young men and women to become elite athletes, and to develop winning England teams. All this is set against our determination to make rugby union truly a sport for all – hence our focus on increasing diversity and inclusivity. And as we move forward I hope that all of us involved in the sport – from the minis and their parents, through the developmental year groups to adult players, coaches, match officials, administrators and supporters – continue to promote our core values of Teamwork, Respect, Enjoyment, Discipline and Sportsmanship.

I am immensely proud to be the President of the Rugby Football Union in our 150th anniversary season. It will long be remembered for the interruption to 'business as usual' because of the pandemic which has disrupted so much of our lives. But I hope it will also be remembered for a time of renewal and regeneration, when rugby led the way in adapting and thriving in modern society.

Jeff Blackett, December 2020

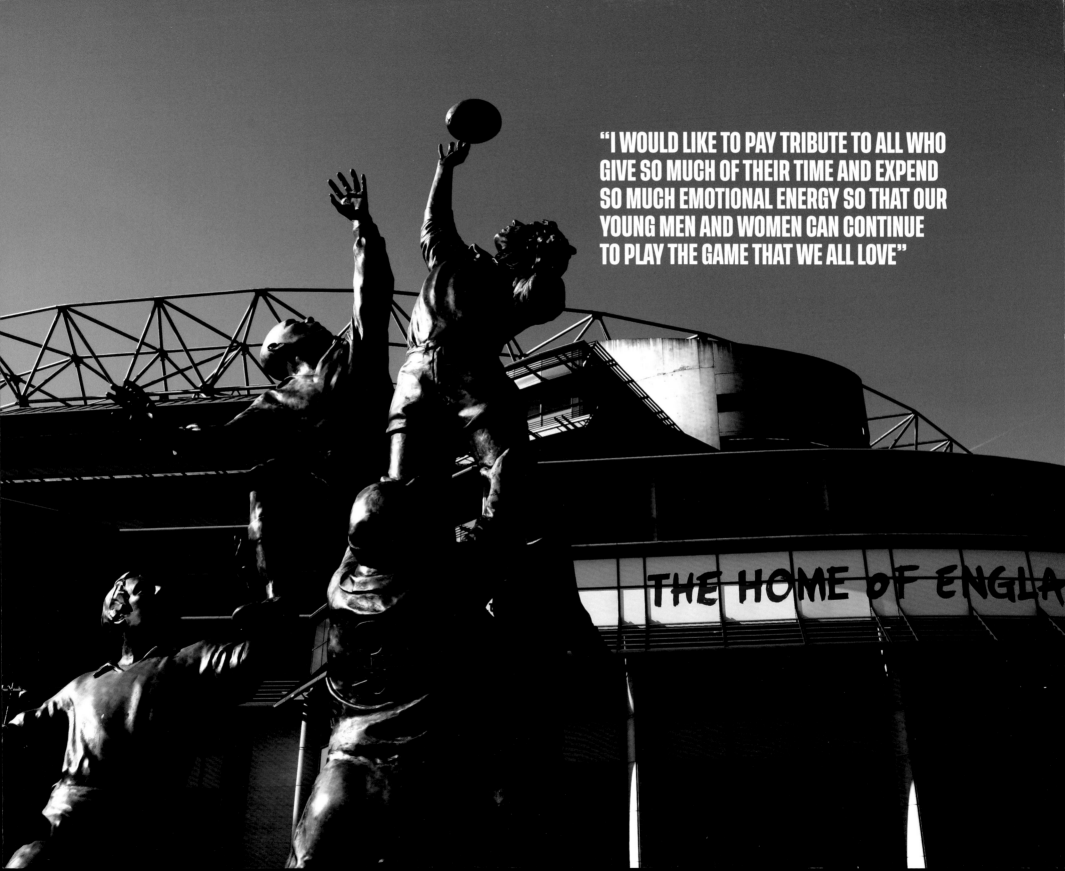

"I WOULD LIKE TO PAY TRIBUTE TO ALL WHO GIVE SO MUCH OF THEIR TIME AND EXPEND SO MUCH EMOTIONAL ENERGY SO THAT OUR YOUNG MEN AND WOMEN CAN CONTINUE TO PLAY THE GAME THAT WE ALL LOVE"

THE HOME OF ENGLA

CONTENTS

WELCOME

BILL SWEENEY

CEO of the Rugby Football Union

One hundred and fifty years of rugby union in England is a momentous landmark and is taking place during one of the most challenging times in our history. I'm sure we will be coming together in 2021 to celebrate in a way that only rugby can, welcoming a full return of rugby for community clubs and fans back into Twickenham Stadium.

The England men's and women's national teams are the performance pinnacle of our game and their success on the field helps to inspire the next generation of players, grow participation, excite fans and provide the majority of the funding for the RFU's investment into the whole of the game.

As with all clubs, our England teams have experienced many highs and a few lows along the way. Buoyed by our recent successes we are feeling confident about our next international fixtures and have high hopes for both our teams at the World Cups in 2021 and 2023. As I am writing this introduction, our women's and men's teams are ranked first and second respectively in the world, and have just both

been crowned as Six Nations champions, with the Red Roses claiming another Grand Slam.

Many of you will remember where you were in 2003. I was working for a sports brand with responsibility for the NZRFU sponsorship and some time after England won the World Cup I was at a dinner with Steve Hansen, then assistant coach of the New Zealand team, and a group of his players. He said: "You are the only Englishman here, congratulations, well done, you will never do it again. Your country is incapable of sustained success. You will win and you will drop off."

That comment has never left me and, as a nation, England is more than capable of lifting that trophy again. We have the best coaching team, fantastic athletes and the commitment and the passion from the fans. I am confident that we will fulfil our commitment to have consistently successful England teams.

It is a privilege for me to watch our England teams on the international stage, but I am equally passionate about the community game. It doesn't matter where you are in the country, rugby union values are the same and the atmosphere and spirit is the same. The camaraderie in a rugby club, the shared values, the respect and competition on the field, combined with what rugby does for its local community, is the most inspiring thing about our sport. Through this you develop both lifelong skills and friends. Our commitment is to make rugby union accessible to all and bring these opportunities to a more diverse group of players and volunteers.

I've played at four rugby clubs in three different countries and there is something unique and special about community rugby and the values of rugby union, it really is the lifeblood of our sport. If you don't have a thriving community game, then you don't have the pipeline of players coming into the game. You don't have players to go into the national academy high performance system and on to Premiership clubs and possibly reach the pinnacle of representing England.

When I joined the RFU I asked to

Below left: Owen Farrell and Katy Daley-Mclean with the respective 2020 Six Nations trophies

Right: The England team that won the 2003 World Cup in Australia in such memorable style

Far right: England's triumphant 2014 Women's World Cup winners arrive at Twickenham with the trophy

"IT IS A PRIVILEGE FOR ME TO WATCH OUR ENGLAND TEAMS ON THE INTERNATIONAL STAGE, BUT I AM EQUALLY PASSIONATE ABOUT THE COMMUNITY GAME"

meet the longest-serving employee to get some insights from her experience. The lady in question, Lisa Prior, told me the role was easy: "Fill Twickenham with winning England teams, take that money and invest it into the community game, develop the next bunch of England players, and do it again."

I started my rugby life at the age of 11 playing in Birkenhead School. Despite being moved to a footballing school, I never lost my passion for rugby and my first job after graduating saw me move to work in the oil industry. I joined Aberdeen Rugby Club and, within the week, I had a second family who welcomed me, even though I was English! When I transferred to the Middle East, I played for the Abu Dhabi Rugby Club for four years, including some time as their treasurer. When I returned home, I joined Rosslyn Park and enjoyed plenty of competitive fixtures and the spirit of a club with a great history. When children came along, like many of our players today, I came under a bit of pressure to play closer to home and I joined a more local club, the Weybridge Vandals. In every case and wherever I went in the game the camaraderie was just the same.

The recent challenges have shone a light on the spirit and strength of rugby union, but the community game is more than a game – it's a network, it's a family, a way of life and it will continue to thrive across England for the next 150 years and beyond.

Bill Sweeney, December 2020

1

LAYING THE FOUNDATIONS

1871-1888

FOOTBALL AT RUGBY

THE BIRTH OF THE RUGBY FOOTBALL UNION

Rugby football was one of a number of emergent football codes to be developed by schoolchildren at British public schools in the late 18th and early 19th centuries. It became known as rugby football because it was the game most associated with Rugby School in Warwickshire, whose pupils first codified the game in 1845.

Rugby School's football acquired many of its dominant features, such as running with the ball and tackling, in the first half of the 19th century. Later a simpler explanation of how the game came into being would be put forward by the Old Rugbeian Society crediting a former pupil of the period, William Webb Ellis, as having been the chief architect of the sport. Though not supported by contemporary evidence, the Webb Ellis myth continues to intrigue casual historians to this day.

The codification of rugby football and several others allowed football, in the second half of the 19th century, to transition from a children's game to an adults' game and the earliest football clubs came into being. Many of these clubs, such as Manchester Football Club, Blackheath Football Club and Richmond Football Club, played the game according to rugby rules. They soon ran into problems, however, as it became apparent that rules varied from one club to another.

To address this problem a Football Association (FA) was established in 1863. Its aim was to unite the codes and create a uniform set of rules that all would adhere to. It was only partly successful. After a serious disagreement over the validity of hacking, more than half the club representatives, led by a Mr Campbell of Blackheath FC, withdrew their support for the association.

The FA persevered and shortly established association football. Those who had opposed continued to play a version of the game more closely akin to the rules as understood at Rugby School.

In 1870 football enthusiast and innovative administrator Charles W Alcock arranged an *international* football match between Scotland and England in London. It ended in

Previous pages: The England side that faced Scotland at Raeburn Place, Edinburgh, on 27 March 1871

Above left: Football at Rugby, from The Graphic, 7 January 1870

Above: Football Rules from Rugby School, 1845

a tie so another game was arranged, which England won. Scotland was incensed – not by the result but by the nature of the contest.

Their frustration was two-fold. Firstly, the players representing *Scotland* were in fact drawn almost exclusively from the London area and didn't reflect the burgeoning football culture that had developed in the north. Secondly, and perhaps most pertinently, Alcock's men were playing the *wrong* football.

'Almost all the leading clubs play by the Rugby code and have no opportunity of practising the Association game even if willing to do so' – AH Robertson, F Moncreiff, B Hall Blyth, JW Arthur and JH Oatts, 1870

A challenge was subsequently issued and signed by the captains of five leading Scottish football clubs that a representative English side meet them to contest a football match. If accepted they would convene at Raeburn Place in Edinburgh where the contest would take place. Crucially the game would be played in accordance with the rules of Rugby School.

'An opinion had for some time prevailed among supporters of Rugby football that some code of rules should be adopted by all' – E Ash and B Burns, 1870

South of the border, wheels were already in motion. On 4 December 1870, four days before the Scots had issued their challenge, a letter, written by Edwin Ash and Benjamin Burns, had been printed in the

Above: Algernon Rutter, the first President of the RFU

Below: Pall Mall Restaurant and the plaque that now marks the site

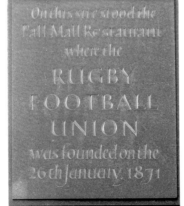

WITH SCHOOLBOY ENERGY AND YOUTHFUL ZEAL, IT WAS A MEETING OF YOUNG MINDS, ABOUT TO BEQUEATH A BIG LEGACY

Times newspaper inviting representatives of football clubs to a meeting in which a code of practice would be established to bring unity to the handling code.

The call was answered by representatives of 21 London-based clubs and on 26 January 1871 they assembled at the Pall Mall restaurant. There were 32 people in attendance and the minutes record that Algernon Rutter was appointed as President, Edward Holmes as Chairman and Edwin Ash as Honorary Secretary and Treasurer.

The first point of business was to confirm that the formation of a football society was desirable. This being unanimously supported, it was then proposed by Arthur Guillemard of the West Kent club that the society be called the Rugby Football Union (RFU), which was also carried unanimously. Two hours later the meeting was adjourned, Ash recorded their deliberations by hand in the minutes and the RFU came into being.

It would be a further five meetings before the Laws of Game were settled and approved, but before then it was necessary for a side to be selected capable of meeting the challenge of the Scots. For this they looked to Rugby School. A team of 20 was chosen to represent England. Of them, 11 were former pupils of the school. These included England's first captain Fred Stokes, Arthur Guillemard and John Clayton, whose jersey is the only one to have survived from the first match and is now on display in the World Rugby Museum at Twickenham.

They also selected themselves. Stokes' had been the first voice heard at the inaugural meeting, as representative for Blackheath, while also present were Reginald Birkett of Clapham Rovers, Alfred Davenport of Ravenscourt Park, Benjamin Burns of Blackheath and Guillemard of West Kent. All played in the first international Test match.

In contrast to later years, the average age of those present at the first meeting of the RFU was 23. With schoolboy energy and youthful zeal, it was a meeting of young minds, about to bequeath a big legacy.

Less than three weeks after their first meeting, a side travelled north to Raeburn Place, Edinburgh. The story of English rugby was about to begin.

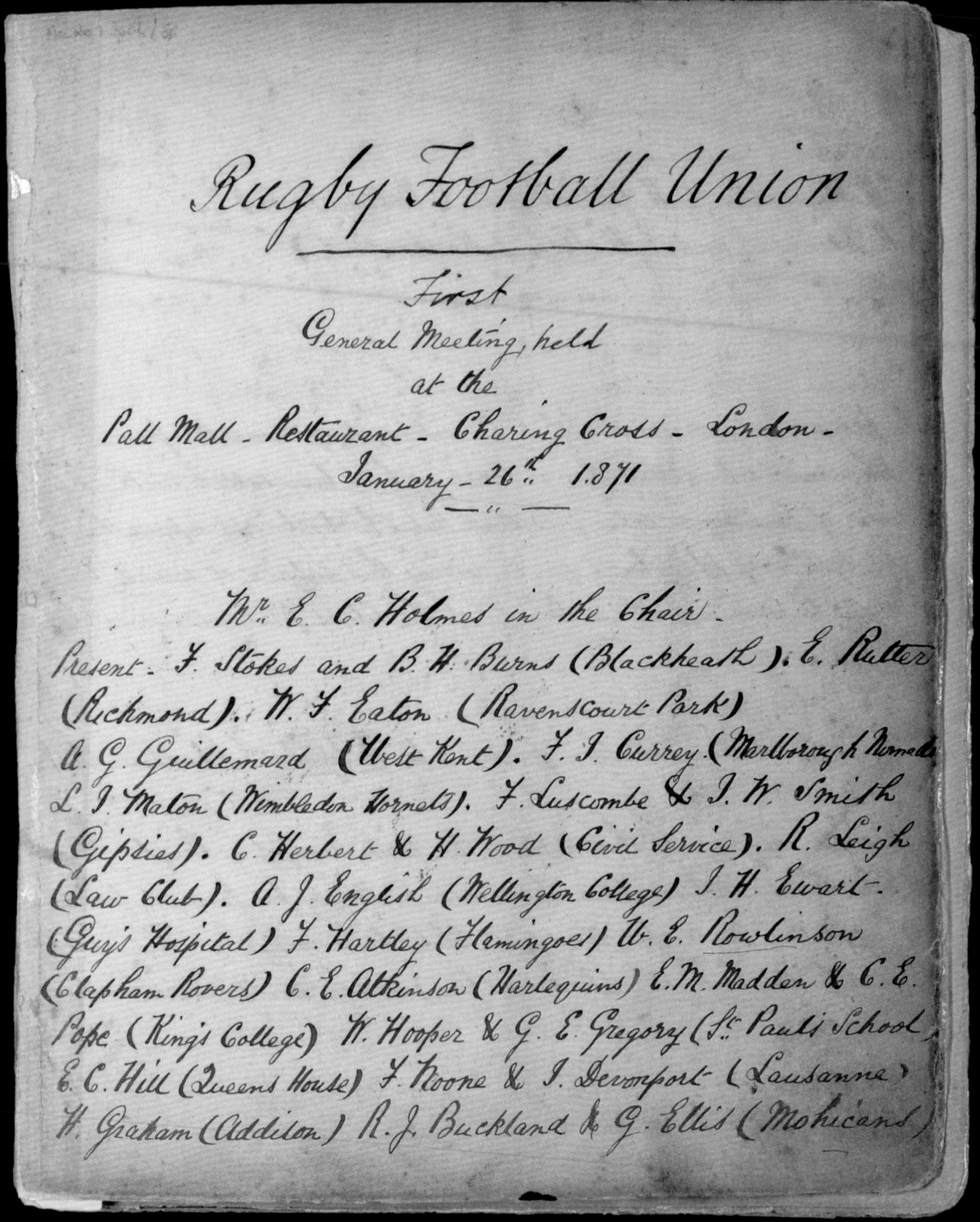

Rugby Football Union

First
General Meeting, held
at the
Pall Mall - Restaurant - Charing Cross - London -
January - 26th 1871

Mr. E. C. Holmes in the Chair -
Present - F. Stokes and B. H. Burns (Blackheath). E. Rutter
(Richmond) . W. F. Eaton (Ravenscourt Park)
A. G. Guillemard (West Kent). F. I. Currey (Marlborough Nomads)
L. I. Maton (Wimbledon Hornets). F. Luscombe & I. W. Smith
(Gipsies). C. Herbert & H. Wood (Civil Service). R. Leigh
(Law Club). A. J. English (Wellington College) I. H. Ewart.
(Guy's Hospital) F. Hartley (Flemingoes) W. E. Rowlinson
(Clapham Rovers) C. E. Atkinson (Harlequins) E. M. Madden & C. E.
Pope (King's College) W. Hooper & G. E. Gregory (St Pauls School
E. C. Hill (Queens House) F. Noone & I. Devonport (Lausanne)
H. Graham (Addison) R. J. Buckland & G. Ellis (Mohicans)

The minutes of the inaugural RFU meeting, held on 26 January 1871 in London

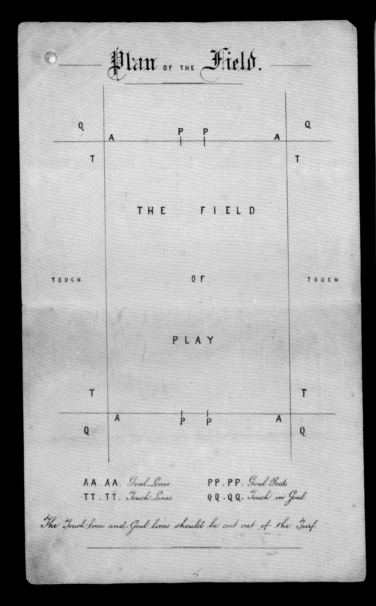

The first Rugby Laws,
dating from 1871

SCOTLAND 1G 2T
ENGLAND 1T

27 March 1871, Raeburn Place, Edinburgh

The world's first representative international football match took place at Raeburn Place, Edinburgh, on 27 March 1871. Played in accordance with Rugby School rules, the contest would be noted for the vigour of the forwards and the gentlemanly conduct of all.

In common with practitioners from Rugby School, England wore white shirts adorned with the red rose that featured prominently in the school's coat of arms. By the end of the contest some reporters thought that Scotland were wearing brown jerseys, but they were in fact blue with a large, prominent white thistle.

It was a fine spring day and 4,000 people had gathered to show their support. A civilised air pervaded but both sets of players were committed to seeing their own side win. Perhaps predictably, a forward battle ensued with neither side gaining an advantage in what became a steady war of attrition that lasted for the entirety of the first half.

In the second half, however, the Scots' superior fitness came to the fore. Angus Buchanan became the game's first international tryscorer, which William Cross converted into a goal.

England redoubled their efforts and shortly afterwards

The International Foot-Ball Match at Edinburgh, a sketch from the Illustrated Newspaper in April 1871

Reginald Birkett became England's first tryscorer. Goals decided games, however, and the failure to convert meant that Scotland retained the lead. In the latter stages Cross demonstrated conclusively which was the better side with a second try for Scotland.

At the final whistle England congratulated their opponents and quietly resolved that next time would be very different.

FOOTBALL MATCH BETWEEN ENGLAND AND SCOTLAND.

On Monday the great football match, "England versus Scotland," was played at Edinburgh in the presence of a large number of spectators. The twenties pitted against each other were the representatives of the best clubs in the two countries. The game was keenly contested, and during the first fifty minutes both sides touched down and were equal. After changing sides, the Scotch twenty invaded the quarters of the English and became entitled to a try. The kick off resulted in a goal being obtained. The English twenty afterwards got a try, but failed to obtain a goal. After a hard struggle the Scotch team again got a touch down in the English ground, but did not succeed in obtaining a goal with their try. Time being then up, the Scotch were declared the winners by a goal and a touch down

Scotland WD Brown, T Chalmers, A Clunies-Ross – TR Marshall, W Cross, JW Arthur – FJ Moncreiff*, A Buchanan, AG Colville, D Drew, JF Finlay, J Forsyth, RW Irvine, WJC Lyall, JLH McFarlane, JAW Mein, R Munro, G Ritchie, AH Robertson, JS Thomson

England AG Guillemard, A Lyon, RR Osborne – W Maclaren – JE Bentley, JF Green, F Tobin – F Stokes*, RH Birkett, BH Burns, JH Clayton, CA Crompton, A Davenport, JM Dugdale, AS Gibson, AStG Hamersley, JH Luscombe, CW Sherrard, DP Turner, HJC Turner

Scoring G = Goal, T = Try, DG = Drop Goal

Relics of the Realm in the World Rugby Museum – the England jersey worn by John Clayton and the England cap worn by Arthur Guillemard, both worn in 1871

FREDERICK STOKES & LENNARD STOKES

Born 12 July 1850 **Died** 7 January 1928
England career 1871-1873, 3 caps **Position** Forward **Club** Blackheath

Born 12 February 1856 **Died** 3 May 1933
England career 1875-1881, 12 caps **Position** Full Back /3Q **Club** Blackheath

The choice of Frederick Stokes (*above*) as England's first captain seems to have been a natural one. The consummate all-rounder, Stokes was described by a contemporary as "one of the very best examples of a heavy forward, always on the ball and first-rate either in the thick of a scrummage or in a loose rally".

He had honed his ability at one of England's great clubs, Blackheath FC, and was selected to captain England at the age of 20. Though Scotland won on that occasion, Stokes retained the captaincy and led England to a first victory the following year at The Oval by two goals to one. To complete the set, Stokes captained his side for a third time in 1873 when England and Scotland drew 0-0.

The following year, at the age of 24, Stokes was made President of the RFU and is to this day the youngest person to have held the office.

As the rugby career of Fred Stokes wound down, his younger brother Lennard (*above right*), born in 1856, was forging a formidable reputation in the Blackheath team as an exceptional three-quarter with exemplary handling skills as well as a renowned place and drop kicker. Standing six foot in height and with an athletic physique, he was described as the very model of an athlete, a faultless catch and field and an extremely difficult player to tackle.

Len won the first of his 12 England caps as one of the two full backs in the first international between England and Ireland in February 1875. By the time of his final match against Scotland in 1881 he had captained England a record five times and was the most capped three-quarter and centre in international rugby. His 17 career conversions would stand as an English record for 100 years. His six conversions in the first international against Wales in 1881 would not be equalled for more than 25 years. He signed off by kicking one of the longest drop goals in international rugby to help England retain the Calcutta Cup, which they had won for the first time a year earlier.

ENGLAND 1G 1DG 1T IRELAND 0

15 February 1875, The Oval, London

The England and Ireland sides that first met in 1875

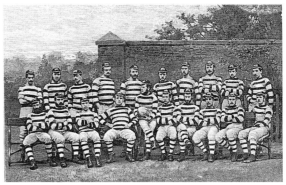

The first four international matches, all between England and Scotland, had already established that the bar for Test matches was considerably higher than club level. It was, therefore, understood that any additions to the international fold would take time to acclimatise. Nonetheless, in 1875, the time was deemed right for Ireland to join the annual list of fixtures. Their first game would be against England at The Oval on 15 February 1875.

While Dublin University contributed almost half of the Irish team, another six were drawn from the North of Ireland. England, led by Richmond's Henry Lawrence and with the great Len Stokes of Blackheath making his debut at full back, took the lead with a try from Arthur Michell after 20 minutes.

Two second-half goals stretched England's lead but brave and sometimes frantic Irish tackling prevented further scores on a pitch that very quickly came to resemble a quagmire. England had won their first encounter with Ireland by two goals and two tries to nil – but the Irish would soon dramatically improve.

England AW Pearson, L Stokes – WH Milton – WE Collins, AT Michell, EH Nash – Hon HA Lawrence*, FR Adams, T Batson, EC Cheston, CW Crosse, EC Fraser, HJ Graham, WHH Hutchinson, F Luscombe, JEH Mackinlay, MW Marshall, ES Perrott, DP Turner, R Walker

Ireland HL Cox, RB Walkington – RJ Bell, AP Cronyn – R Galbraith, J Myles, EN McIlwaine – GH Stack*, WS Allen, G Andrews, WH Ash, M Barlow, BN Casement, A Combe, W Gaffikin, E Galbraith, FT Hewson, JA McDonald, RM Maginiss, HD Walsh

THE CREATION OF THE CALCUTTA CUP

The Calcutta Football Club was founded in 1872 and became affiliated with the RFU two years later. The mainstay of the club was the Buffs (Royal East Kent Regiment) 1st Battalion, who were stationed in Bengal through most of the 1870s. When the Buffs began to move out, the club lost momentum and decided to disband in 1877.

A letter was then sent to the RFU by Mr GA James Rothney, detailing the club's intention of using the remaining funds in the club's bank account to do "some lasting good, for the cause of Rugby Football". Rothney's proposal was that a 'Challenge Cup' be produced and he asked the RFU if they would like it to be produced in India, using Indian silversmiths, or if they would prefer the money so that the trophy could be produced in London.

Out of respect for the silversmiths of Calcutta, the RFU requested the trophy be produced there and informed Rothney that the trophy would be presented to the winners of the annual international contest between England and Scotland.

Having withdrawn the remaining 270 silver rupees from the club's

PRICE THREEPENCE.

Scottish Football Union.

GRAND INTERNATIONAL MATCH,
SCOTLAND *v.* ENGLAND,

TO BE PLAYED AT THE

Academical Cricket Ground, Raeburn Place,

On MONDAY, 10th MARCH 1879.

Play to commence at Three p.m.

STEWARDS—

THE COMMITTEE OF THE SCOTTISH FOOTBALL UNION, AND
THE OFFICERS AND COMMITTEE OF THE RUGBY FOOTBALL UNION.

SCOTLAND.		ENGLAND.	
FORWARDS.		**FORWARDS.**	
R. W. IRVINE, Captain,	*Edinburgh Academicals.*	F. R. ADAMS, Captain,	*Richmond.*
J. H. S. GRAHAM,	*Edinburgh Academicals.*	A. BUDD,	*Blackheath.*
D. R. IRVINE,	*Edinburgh Academicals.*	G. W. BURTON,	*Blackheath.*
E. EWART,	*Glasgow Academicals.*	R. WALKER,	*Manchester.*
J. E. JUNOR,	*Glasgow Academicals.*	F. D. FOWLER,	*Manchester.*
J. B. BROWN,	*Glasgow Academicals.*	C. ROWLEY,	*Manchester.*
A. G. PETRIE,	*Royal High School F. P.*	H. SPRINGMAN,	*Liverpool.*
H. M. NAPIER,	*West of Scotland.*	N. F. M'LEOD,	*Cooper's Hill.*
N. T. BREWIS,	*Institution F. P.*	G. HARRISON,	*Hull.*
R. AINSLIE,	*Institution F. P.*	S. NEAME,	*Old Cheltonians.*
QUARTER-BACKS.		**QUARTER-BACKS.**	
J. NEILSON,	*Glasgow Academicals.*	W. A. D. EVANSON,	*Richmond.*
J. A. CAMPBELL,	*Glasgow Academicals.*	H. H. TAYLOR,	*St. George's Hospital.*
HALF-BACKS.		**HALF-BACK.**	
M. CROSS,	*Glasgow Academicals.*	L. STOKES,	*Blackheath.*
N. J. FINLAY,	*Edinburgh Academicals.*		
BACK.		**BACKS.**	
W. E. MACLAGAN,	*Edinburgh Academicals.*	W. J. PENNY,	*United Hospitals*
		H. HUTH,	*Huddersfield.*

THE SCOTTISH UNIFORM.—White knickerbockers and dark blue stockings, dark blue jerseys, with the Scottish Thistle as a badge ; blue velvet caps, with silver badge and lace.

THE ENGLISH UNIFORM.—White knickerbockers and dark brown stockings, white jerseys, with the English Rose as a badge ; rose velvet caps, with silver badge and lace.

*None but Stewards and Representatives of the Press are allowed within the Ropes.
Spectators are particularly requested not to encroach upon the Field of Play.*

A. R. STEWART, Hon. Sec.

bank account, the coins were then melted down by Cashmere Silverwork and fashioned into a loving cup of pure silver. Rothney reports actual specimens of king cobra snakes being used in the production of the trophies' three handles. The elephant on the lid is described as being of Viceroy stock, in reference to the British Governor-General and the elephant processions that had carried the rulers of India for more than 2,500 years.

The result is one of the most beautiful and unique trophies in world sport. It was contested for the first time in 1879, when the match finished a tie, and in 1880 it was claimed for the first time by England after Len Stokes' side's resounding win at Whalley Range, Manchester.

Although Rothney was clear that "the Cup should remain the absolute property of the RFU", a gentleman's agreement means that the trophy is, to this day, awarded to the most recent winner of the world's oldest international Test match.

The programme from the first Calcutta Cup match, played in 1879

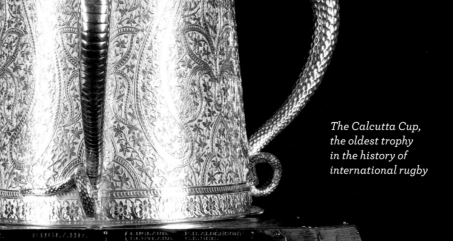

*The Calcutta Cup,
the oldest trophy
in the history of
international rugby*

ENGLAND 7G 1DG 6T WALES 0

19 February 1881, Richardson's Field, Blackheath

Wales had played Gloucestershire and Somerset earlier in the 1880-81 season and the RFU accepted the challenge of the South Wales Football Union to play a full international at Blackheath in January 1881. The original date, 9 January, was not mutually acceptable, and the subsequent date, 22 January, was postponed due to a severe frost. This historic first encounter was eventually played on 19 February and was the first international match to be played in Blackheath before the Blackheath rugby club, which supplied four players to the England side for this match, moved to Rectory Field.

England had won their four previous internationals and had two weeks earlier beaten Ireland at Whalley Range, Manchester, by four tries and two conversions to nil. The referee for the Wales clash would be the President of the Rugby Union and an old English international back, Arthur Guillemard, a veteran of the inaugural international against Scotland in March 1871.

The Wales team in their scarlet jerseys with the Prince of Wales feathers on the front contained only seven players from the southern heartland of Welsh rugby – the Cardiff, Llanelli and Newport clubs – and no players from Swansea. Inevitably, with their limited experience they were unable to cope with the greater skill and drive of the English forwards and the outcome was ruthless and predictable.

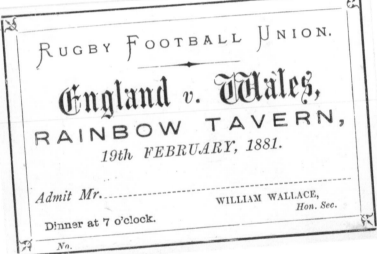

The 1881 Wales team picture and an invitation to the post-match dinner in central London after the match

Their defeat by 13 tries, seven conversions and a drop goal to nil remains the largest defeat suffered by Wales against England. The English forwards, led by the redoubtable Gurdon brothers from Richmond, were dominant throughout, George Burton from Blackheath scored four tries and Harry Vassall from Oxford University, making his international debut, scored three. The captain Len Stokes set a new world record with six conversions.

The sheer scale of the Welsh defeat was such that there were two direct consequences. England wouldn't play an international against Wales the following season and – far more importantly – a meeting at the Castle Hotel in Neath of the major Welsh clubs on 12 March 1881 saw the establishment of the Welsh Football Union and the effective dissolution of the South Wales Football Union, which never met again as an independent organisation.

England TW Fry – L Stokes*, R Hunt – HH Taylor, HT Twynam – A Budd, GW Burton, CWL Fernandes, H Fowler, C Gurdon, ET Gurdon, WW Hewitt, H Vassall, HC Rowley, CP Wilson

Wales CH Newman, RHB Summers – JA Bevan*, E Peake – EJ Lewis, L Watkins – G Darbishire, BE Girling, GF Harding, BB Mann, WD Phillips, FT Purdon, TA Rees, E Treharne, RDG Williams

THE ADVENT OF THE TRIPLE CROWN

After tasting defeat in the inaugural Test match of 1871, England were determined to do better the following year. In July 1871 a challenge was issued to Scotland that they visit London for a return contest. England's first home international match would take place at the Kennington Oval on 5 February 1872. The Oval, then and now home to Surrey County Cricket Club, was one of the pre-eminent sporting surfaces in London and 4,000 people turned out on another fine day to bear witness.

England made 14 changes but retained Fred Stokes as captain together with Arthur Guillemard, John Bentley, Charles Sherrard, Dawson Turner and the remarkable Alfred St George Hamersley of Marlborough Nomads. Into the side came forward Francis Isherwood as well as Harold Freeman for the first of three consecutive caps.

Once again Scotland started the brighter and took the lead with a kick from CW Cathcart. This time the setback seemed to galvanise the English, however, and stout work from Turner allowed Hamersley to drive over for a try, which Isherwood converted.

In the second half, Freeman demonstrated all of his technical skill by landing a dropped goal to put England ahead. Two further English tries followed from forward Frank D'Aguilar and lively half back Stephen Finney. The Scots were well beaten and England had tasted victory for the first time.

The Oval would remain England's home ground for the remainder of the decade and England would win five further internationals there, two against Scotland and three against Ireland, as they confirmed their status as the outstanding side of the decade.

Fred Stokes played his final game for England in the drawn contest with Scotland in 1873. The match was the first of an unbroken 10 caps for outstanding tight scrummager Murray Marshall, an impressively strong player who excelled in the 20-a-side game. Marshall's consecutive appearance record would stand for 26 years.

Hamersley took over as captain in 1874 and another drop goal from Freeman secured victory. Fred Stokes' younger brother Lennard earned the first of his 12 caps in 1875, three days after his 19th birthday.

As rugby football became more popular, Len Stokes was perhaps England's first star player. Switching between full back and three-quarter, he had pace, footwork and a "capital knowledge of the science of the game". His 17 career conversions remained an England record for more than 100 years.

Meanwhile, Oxford and Cambridge Universities had begun experimenting with 15-man rugby in an effort to reduce the attritional nature of the game and the RFU embraced the change permanently in 1877. This shift initially bore mixed fruit for England. After beating Ireland, they lost to Scotland for the first time since 1871 and the following year alterations were made to the English pack. Marshall retained his place and was joined by George Thomson of Halifax, whose roving loose forward style was initially a puzzle for his teammates. Alongside him, Edward Temple Gurdon made his debut. In the backs, Stokes was joined by 30-year-old AN 'Monkey' Hornby of Preston

A drawing depicting England's first home international against Scotland in 1872

THE IDEA OF A TRIPLE CROWN WAS FIRST REFERRED TO BY JOURNALISTS IN THE MID-1890s

capable of beating the other three in a season, was first referred to by journalists in the mid-1890s. After the emergence of Wales in 1881, the notional crown can be backdated to 1883, the first year that a Home Nations Championship can be accounted for.

The 1883 season actually began in 1882, with England opening their campaign in Swansea on 16 December. Making his debut was an Oxford University half back called Alan Rotherham, aged just 20.

Rotherham's contribution, not just to English rugby but to the game generally, would be profound. It was he who first established the practice of the half back linking forward play with back play, an innovation that brought success to England.

Led by their inspirational captain, Temple Gurdon, England were formidable. With his brother Charles to assist in scrummaging and Thomson rampant in the loose, England completed a clean sweep. The Championship was sealed with a try scored by wing Wilfred Bolton in the second half at Raeburn Place.

They repeated the feat in 1884 but a dispute with Scotland over the legality of a try scored by Richard Kindersley meant that the Triple Crown would not be contested the following season. Nonetheless, Gurdon's England continued to dominate, registering four consecutive wins against Ireland and Wales before drawing their captain's final outing against Scotland in 1886.

The dispute with Scotland over the legitimacy of Kindersley's try in 1884 reached its nadir in 1888. Having established the International Board in Manchester in 1886, the Scottish, Irish and Welsh Unions now recognised the International Board as arbiter of the sport. The RFU did not.

As a consequence, in 1888, the Home Nations Championship took place without England. An English XV was selected but didn't play. Two players, Salford's Harry Eagles and Bradford's Percy Robertshaw, were awarded caps but never pulled on an England jersey.

After much deliberation and in time for the 1890 season, the RFU relented and accepted membership of the International Board. In return they received a majority of seats on the board.

Grasshoppers, a consummate sportsman who would go on to captain England at both rugby and cricket.

Performances steadily improved, and the 1880s began with Stokes promoted to captain and a four-game winning streak that saw England back on top of the pile. Indeed, England would lose only two matches across the entire decade.

The glorious run began in earnest in 1880 at Whalley Range, Manchester, where Stokes' side completely dismantled Scotland in a manner that they had not done before. With Temple Gurdon supplemented by his younger brother and fellow Richmond teammate Charles, England ran in five tries to one Scottish try and England became the first side to lift the Calcutta Cup.

In 1881 four unanswered tries at Whalley Range dispatched Ireland, before a record 13 unanswered tries were registered against Wales in the first meeting of the two sides. Stokes stepped down at the end of the season and was succeeded by Hornby, who captained England in 1882.

The idea of a Triple Crown, awarded to any of the Home Nations

Above left: Arthur Guillemard, the pioneering player, referee and RFU President, and (above) George Thomson, the outstanding loose forward of the era

Right: Painting by William Heysman Overend and Lionel Percy Smythe depicting Scotland v England in March 1886. Note the flag that has been inserted on to this print to attract American buyers

TEMPLE GURDON & CHARLES GURDON

Born 25 January 1854 **Died** 12 June 1929
England career 1878-1886, 16 caps
Position Forward
Clubs Old Haileyburians, Richmond

Born 3 December 1855 **Died** 26 June 1931
England career 1880-1886, 14 caps
Position Forward
Club Richmond

Of the many sets of brothers selected for England in the early days, the forwards Temple (*left*) and Charles (*right*) Gurdon were arguably the most influential. Educated at Haileybury College and Cambridge University, they played for Richmond, Middlesex and the South of England for many years.

Temple was born in January 1854 and made his debut for England against Scotland in 1878 after appearing in three Varsity Matches, including two as captain of Cambridge University in 1875 and 1876. He went on to win 16 international caps over eight years, an England record which lasted until 1913. Acknowledged as an outstanding leader, he captained England on nine occasions and was never on the losing side.

He was joined in the England side against Scotland in 1880 by his younger brother Charles who had won his first cap earlier that season against Ireland. Charles was born in December 1855, played in one Varsity Match in 1877 and was President of the Cambridge University rowing club. He played 14 times for England and both brothers made their final international appearances in a drawn match against Scotland at Raeburn Place in March 1886.

In the Reverend Frank Marshall's magisterial *Football – The Rugby Union Game* published in 1892, Arthur Guillemard described Temple as "one of the best forwards that ever represented England". He noted that Charles was the taller of the two brothers and that "he was one of the most massive and muscular forwards that ever stripped". The fearsome combination of the two brothers in the England scrums for almost a decade resulted in England losing only one of the 20 internationals between 1878 and 1886 in which one or both took part.

Temple Gurdon (*left*) became a solicitor during his playing career and served on the International Rugby Football Board from 1890 until 1928. He was elected to serve two terms as President of the Rugby Football Union from 1890 to 1892. He died in June 1929. Charles Gurdon became a leading light in the rowing world and a county court judge who died two years after his brother in June 1931.

FAMOUS GAMES

ENGLAND 1G SCOTLAND 1T

1 March 1884, Rectory Field, Blackheath

The final England match of the 1884 international season against Scotland at Rectory Field, Blackheath, on 1 March proved to be a seminal moment in international rugby due to a disputed incident in the second half. England and Scotland had both already defeated Wales and Ireland in the preceding months so a victory for England would secure a second consecutive Triple Crown and Championship.

The England team was captained by the great Richmond forward Temple Gurdon in his 13th international. A star-studded back line included one of the leading 19th century full backs in HB Tristram, the prolific try-scoring wings Wilfred Bolton and Gregory Wade, and the experience of Alan Rotherham and Henry Twynam at half back. Allied to a cohesive and mobile forward pack including Charles Gurdon, this was a formidable side with 13 of the 15 drawn from just three clubs: Oxford University, Richmond and Blackheath.

The Scotland team was captained by the powerful three-quarter Bill Maclagan who had played for both Edinburgh Academicals and London Scottish. Both teams played as selected and the scene was set for a historic clash in excellent weather conditions in front of an estimated crowd of 7,500-8,000 spectators.

The Scottish forwards started the match well and dominated the early phases of play. Scotland took the lead midway through the half when their West of Scotland forward John Jamieson followed up a kick ahead after a five-yard scrum. The try was scored wide out and was not converted. The match up to half-time

remained evenly poised and Scotland held a narrow one-try lead at the break.

In the second half, England scored their disputed try 15 minutes from the end of the match. Richard Kindersley, an Oxford University forward in his second international, had been involved in a passing move near the centre of the field. The ball went into touch and, after Twynam and one of the Gurdon brothers had handled the ball following the lineout, Kindersley received the ball again and dived to score under the Scottish posts. Before the conversion could take place, the Scottish

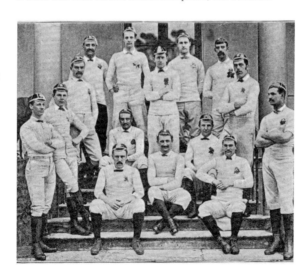

The England side that won the 1884 Championship with a bitterly disputed win over Scotland

captain objected to the try being awarded on the grounds that one of the Scottish players had knocked back the ball in the lead-up to the try.

The match was held up for almost 10 minutes as the Scottish captain's objection was considered. The Irish referee George Scriven decided that, as the English players had not complained about the knock back, there were no grounds not to award the try. Bolton duly kicked the easy conversion to give England the lead which they did not relinquish despite Scotland's increasingly desperate attacks in the 15 minutes remaining.

The dispute was referred to the Rugby Football Union after the match. The RFU insisted that the referee's decision must be upheld so England took the victory, the Triple Crown and the Championship. The Scottish Football Union, dissatisfied with the outcome, cancelled the next year's Calcutta Cup match and the issue was not fully resolved until the International Rugby Football Board was set up six years later.

England HB Tristram – WN Bolton, AM Evanson, CG Wade – A Rotherham, HT Twynam – ET Gurdon*, C Gurdon, RSF Henderson, RS Kindersley, CJB Marriott, EL Strong, WM Tatham, GT Thomson, CS Wooldridge

Scotland JP Veitch – WE Maclagan*, DJ Macfarlan, ET Roland – AGG Asher, AR Don Wauchope – T Ainslie, CW Berry, JB Brown, J Jamieson, D McCowan, WA Peterkin, C Reid, J Tod, WA Walls

THE INTERNATIONAL RUGBY FOOTBALL BOARD

The dispute over the legality of the try scored by England's Richard Kindersley in 1884 against Scotland caused a lasting rift that would have significant repercussions for the RFU and the future administration of the game. Scotland refused to play England the following year, and on 5 December 1887 representatives of the Scottish, Welsh and Irish unions met in Manchester where they penned 'the four principles of the International Rugby Football Board'.

At first, the RFU would not acknowledge the primacy of the new multi-national organisation. As a result, England were barred from entry to the Home Nations Championships of 1888 and 1889.

In 1890 a compromise was found. England were awarded six of 12 seats on the International Board and re-entered the Championship. The International Rugby Football Board, later shortened to the International Rugby Board and now known as World Rugby, has administered the game globally ever since.

South Africa, New Zealand and Australia (SANZAR) were given voting status in 1948 and France in 1978. Today 18 different rugby playing nations are represented, together with a further six regional organisations.

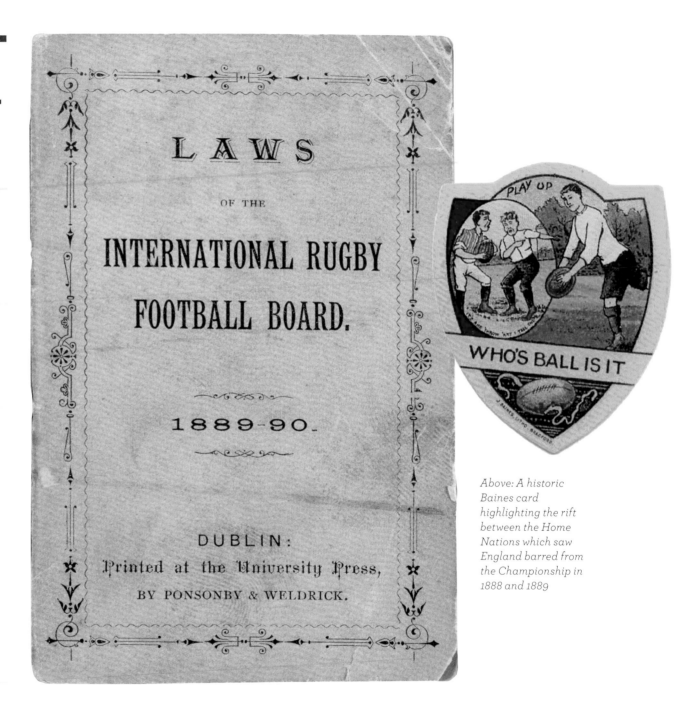

LAWS

OF THE

INTERNATIONAL RUGBY

FOOTBALL BOARD.

1889-90.

DUBLIN:
Printed at the University Press,
BY PONSONBY & WELDRICK.

Above: A historic Baines card highlighting the rift between the Home Nations which saw England barred from the Championship in 1888 and 1889

ENGLAND 1G 4T NEW ZEALAND NATIVES 0

16 February 1889, Rectory Field, Blackheath

England's only fixture of the 1888-89 season was against a visiting side from New Zealand. Originally called the New Zealand Maoris, but later renamed the New Zealand Natives, the side faced England at Rectory Field, Blackheath, on 16 February 1889.

The game generated considerable controversy. England's AE Stoddart, while on the attack, lost a portion of his shorts. As was customary, Stoddart's teammates formed a circle around him to protect his modesty while he collected himself. As this was taking place, England forward Frank Evershed casually claimed a try in the corner. Most expected the try to be ruled out, but the referee, RFU Secretary George Rowland Hill, awarded the score. Incensed, three of the visiting team walked from the field but were finally persuaded to return, while John Willie Sutcliffe converted Evershed's try and his own subsequent try to make the final score 7-0 to England.

The match was watched by 12,000 spectators and marked the first time that the Haka was performed in an international Test match on English soil.

England AV Royle – RE Lockwood, AE Stoddart, JW Sutcliffe – F Bonsor*, WM Scott – C Anderton, H Bedford, JW Cave, F Evershed, D Jowett, FW Lowrie, A Robinson, HJ Wilkinson, W Yiend

NZ Natives W Warbrick – E McCausland*, WT Wynyard, C Madigan – W Elliot, DR Gage, P Keogh – W Anderson, TR Ellison, HH Lee, R Maynard, T Rene, RG Taiaroa, GA Williams, G Wynyard

Left: The New Zealand Natives' 1888-89 tour itinerary

Below: England's AE Stoddart, the player whose loss of dignity pre-empted the scoring of a controversial try that almost ruined the match

2

THE GREAT SCHISM

1889-1905

THE NORTHERN POWERHOUSE

As rugby football grew in popularity and new clubs began to spring up in all corners of England, the social makeup of the national team started to change. Throughout the 1880s the gentlemen old boys of Rugby and Marlborough were joined by a new type of player often drawn from the manufacturing towns of Lancashire, West Yorkshire and elsewhere.

The speed of change intensified with the creation, in 1889, of the County Championship, an annual knock-out competition in which the talent hot-spots of England were clearly identified. The county of Yorkshire won seven of the first eight editions of the competition and their players in particular began to proliferate. Bradford's Rawson Robertshaw, Fred Bonsor and Edgar Wilkinson were all selected for the first time in 1886, while Dewsbury's jack-in-the-box centre Dicky Lockwood made his debut against Wales in 1887.

In 1890 England would play Scotland for the first time since 1887. The season began with defeat to Wales. The following week they lost comprehensively to Yorkshire in a trial match and it was clear that changes were required. Bradford's tireless forward Jack Toothill and Huddersfield wing Jack Dyson came into the side, together with Randolph Aston of Cambridge University and the industrious forward Edgar Holmes of Manningham.

Toothill's impact was immediate as he proved just as useful in attack as he was in defence. It was his quick hands that fed Burton's fleet-footed forward Frank Evershed for England's opening try at Raeburn Place. Evershed was then involved in the second score, breaking the gain line and feeding Dyson for a try, converted by Heckmondwike's Donald Jowett. England held out to win by one goal and one try to nil, or 6-0 under the new scoring method pioneered by the SRU.

The impressive AE 'Drewy' Stoddart of Blackheath was restored to the wing for the final game of the season and was one of three try scorers

Previous pages: The Battle of the Roses, painted by WA Wollen in 1893

Above: The great Frank Evershed and his England cap

Above right: Influential England captain Fred Alderson

against Ireland at Rectory Field. The following season debuts were given to two influential players, forward William Bromet of Tadcaster and centre Fred Alderson of Hartlepool Rovers. Held in the highest regard for his leadership and tactical acumen, Alderson became the first player since Fred Stokes to captain England on his debut. In addition, the mercurial Lockwood returned at three-quarter. Now in the form of his life, he scored three tries and two conversions as England finished second behind Scotland.

By 1892 the England team was transformed. Of the 15 players that took the field against Wales at Blackheath, 11 played for northern clubs. Where once England had consisted of solicitors, doctors and merchants, they were now mixed with woollen printers, iron moulders, publicans and colliers. Prominent among those making their debuts were William 'Pusher' Yiend of Hartlepool Rovers and Blackheath's Alfred Allport.

The side would make history and is now regarded as one of England's finest. In their opening fixture against Wales they simply

WHERE ONCE ENGLAND HAD CONSISTED OF SOLICITORS, DOCTORS AND MERCHANTS, THEY WERE NOW MIXED WITH WOOLLEN PRINTERS, IRON MOULDERS, PUBLICANS AND COLLIERS

ran riot. Lockwood converted two of England's four tries, while their captain Alderson converted a third, and England cruised to an utterly comprehensive 17-0 victory.

In the second match England faced Ireland at Whalley Range. Alderson was missing but Sammy Woods, who played Test cricket for both England and Australia, ably stepped up. Slippery conditions kept Lockwood out of the game and Ireland made most of the running in the first half. In the second half, however, Evershed and Woods combined twice to produce tries, the first converted by Woods as England won 7-0.

The final match of the season took place at Raeburn Place in front of 15,000 spectators, with Alderson restored to the captaincy. Scotland too had won both of their games and so all rested on the outcome of the match. A pensive atmosphere gripped both players and spectators.

Perhaps predictably, the game became a war of tight scrummaging and mauling. Woods went close to touching down before Bromet did, leaving Lockwood to calmly kick the three points. The game ended 5-0 to the visitors. England had secured a first Triple Crown since 1883 and in completing a clean sweep of victories without conceding a single point they achieved a feat that has never been repeated.

Stoddart returned to the captaincy in 1893 and four fellow Blackheathens were given debuts. These included half back Howard Marshall, whose three tries at Cardiff Arms Park under normal circumstances might have been enough to secure victory. A redoubtable Welsh side under the captaincy of Arthur 'Monkey' Gould fought back from nine points down to steal victory 12-11. Billy Bancroft's unorthodox drop-kicking of the first international penalty goal proved the difference. Wales went on to claim their first Triple Crown and, remarkably, Marshall didn't play again for England.

Lockwood was installed as captain in 1894 and the four three-quarter system was introduced. It paid instant dividends and Lockwood converted three of five tries at Birkenhead Park to record a crushing 24-3

Fred Alderson makes some hard yards against Scotland at Raeburn Place, Edinburgh, on 5 March 1892. England were en route to their third Triple Crown

victory against Wales. The tables were turned in the following game as Ireland too adopted the system and beat England 7-5 on the way to their first Triple Crown.

After a decade of incremental increase in the number of northern players in the England team, the situation was dramatically reversed in 1895. The catalyst was a huge 36-0 victory by the South over the North in a trial match in December 1894. Sammy Woods was made captain and responded with the only try of his 13 international caps, one of four English tries in a 14-6 victory over Wales.

A narrow victory over Ireland at Lansdowne Road followed and, with home advantage, England might have expected a Triple Crown in their final fixture against Scotland at Richmond's Athletic Ground. The 20,000 spectators certainly felt confident but it was Scotland that completed the clean sweep through a try and penalty from West of Scotland's GT Neilson.

Despite the relative success of these years, an undercurrent of mistrust had existed within English rugby since the late 1880s. Events would conspire over the summer of 1895 that would profoundly impact the fortunes of the English side and fundamentally alter the character of the sport for decades to come.

ENGLAND *versus* SCOTLAND
THE INTERNATIONAL FOOTBALL MATCH PLAYED AT RAEBURN PLACE, EDINBURGH — ALDERSON RELIEVES THE ENGLISH LINE

History in the making
TRIAL MATCHES

For around 120 years, formal and informal matches have been played to assist selectors in identifying the best players to represent England.

By 1914, four main routes for the aspiring international player had been established, three of which were described in newspapers as 'trials' but were not *officially* given that designation.

The annual Varsity Match between Oxford and Cambridge Universities started in 1872 and proved fertile ground for the selectors over the next hundred years. More than 160 players have been capped for England while at the two universities and countless more after graduation.

The County Championship began in 1888-89, with finals from 1896, while an England v the Champion County match was first staged in 1889.

The North v South fixture was played 44 times between 1874 and 1908. In 1909 England played trial matches against both the North and the South before a Probables v Possibles match at Twickenham to make final adjustments. From 1927 there became established a pattern of England v Possibles, Probables v Possibles and finally England v The Rest trial matches, with players shifting from team to team until the strongest side had been identified.

The appointment of a sole England coach and selector in the 1980s led to the disbandment of a formal trials structure.

INTERNATIONAL MATCH AT KIRKSTALL, LEEDS.

THE ENGLISH TEAM v. THE REST

March 7th, 1903.

G. Tattersall (Yorkshire) D. Dobson (Devon) D. Dibble (Somerset) G. Vickery (Somerset) B. A. Hill (Blackheath) P. Hardwick (Northumberland) V. H. Cartwright (Oxford) F. C. Hulme (Cheshire)
J. T. Taylor (West Hartlepool) B. Oughtred, Captain (Durham) R. Forrest (Somerset) F. M. Stout (Gloucestershire)
A. T. Brettargh (Lancashire) T. Simpson (Northumberland) R. Dudley Wood (Lancashire)
COPYRIGHT.

YORKSHIRE IG 3T REST OF ENGLAND IDG IT

22 February 1890, Park Avenue, Bradford

In 1890 Yorkshire were declared the champion county after finishing their season undefeated. Their reward was a match against a Test-strength 'Rest of England' side. Captained by Francis Fox, the Rest of England included 13 players who had gained or would gain full England caps, including Fred Alderson, Frank Evershed, John Rogers and Sammy Woods. It also included eight of the England side that had lost to Wales the previous weekend.

Yorkshire (*right*) boasted a fearsome pack that included Jack Toothill, Edgar Holmes, Harry Bedford, Donald Jowett and captain Laurie Hickson.

The match was played at Park Avenue, Bradford, in front of a crowd of 10,000. The Rest of England opened the scoring with a try from JH Crompton but Jowett scored at the other end to bring Yorkshire level. Crompton struck again with a drop goal to give the Rest a half-time lead.

In the second half the nine-man Yorkshire pack began to achieve dominance. The lively Huddersfield wing Jack Dyson put Yorkshire in front with a try, before Hickson scored another. Rest of England tried gamely to get back into the match but were deprived of the ball by the excellent Yorkshire forwards. More good running by Dyson confirmed victory with a fourth try.

A week later Jowett, Toothill, Bedford, Holmes and Hickson were all selected for the national side, the latter as captain. Dyson too was called up for his first cap and contributed a try as England won in Scotland for the first time since 1883.

Yorkshire S Mawson – AL Brooke, S Eastwood, JW Dyson – J Naylor, WH Stadden+ – JL Hickson*+, H Bedford+, E Holmes, G Jacketts, JH Jones, D Jowett+, W Nicholl, J Richards, JT Toothill
+ = *International*

Rest of England WG Mitchell+ – FHR Alderson, JH Crompton, PH Morrison+ – FH Fox*+, MT Scott+ – H Eagles+, F Evershed+, PF Hancock+, T Kent, JL Mayger, FE Pease+, A Robinson+, JH Rogers+, SMJ Woods+

PLAY UP

YORKSHIRE

JACK TOOTHILL

Born 15 May 1866 **Died** 29 June 1947
England career 1890-1894, 12 caps
Position Forward **Club** Bradford

John Thomas 'Jack' Toothill was born in 1866 in the village of Thornton, outside Bradford, West Yorkshire. He began playing rugby as a boy in Manningham, before joining Bradford's hugely successful team in 1887. He was selected to play for Yorkshire for the first time in 1888.

Combining strength and speed, he was a lithe, running forward and skilled ball carrier. His breaks helped to create chances and relieve pressure and were a feature of every team he played in. He would play 50 times for a dominant Yorkshire, losing only three matches as they won six County Championships in seven years. He captained the side between 1892 and 1895 and didn't lose a game.

In 1890 he helped Yorkshire to defeat England in a trial game and was selected for England in their next match. He contributed to wins against Scotland and Ireland, helping England to a share of the Championship. He won twice again in 1891 but missed the decisive match against Scotland, which England lost. The following year he played in all three matches and helped England to the most dominant Triple Crown in her history.

He played 12 times for England in total before calling it a day. A proponent of broken-time payments, he was once reprimanded for having missed a match after working a Friday shift in a dye house. He followed his club into the Northern Union in 1895 and helped them reach the final of the Challenge Cup in 1898.

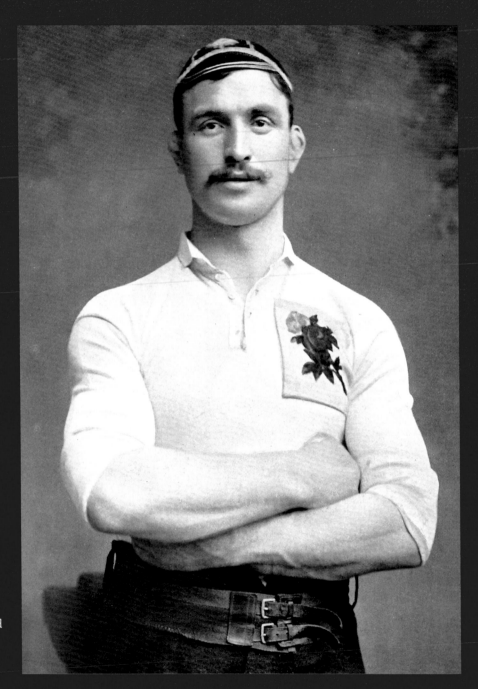

FAMOUS GAMES

ENGLAND 17 WALES 0

2 January 1892, Rectory Field, Blackheath

The England selectors made eight changes for this match at Rectory Field on 2 January. Bradford's Charles Emmott and Arthur 'Spafty' Briggs were selected at half back. Wardlaw Thomson, GC 'Scatter' Hubbard and Alfred Allport all came in from Blackheath, Wigan's Ned Bullough earned his first cap, as did Brighouse Rangers' William Nichol.

Hartlepool's Fred Alderson was selected as captain in the centre alongside Dicky Lockwood. Frank Evershed, Tom Kent, Jack Toothill, Bill Bromet and Pusher Yiend were all present in England's nine-man pack.

Wales, captained by Arthur Gould, had a strong side of their own, with Tom Pearson and Billy Bancroft alongside Gould in the backs. They maintained their four three-quarter system, which gave England an extra man in the scrum.

Neither side dominated the opening exchanges but England took the lead with a try from Nichol after the Welsh half backs had squandered possession. Hubbard added another, converted by Lockwood, to give England a 7-0 half-time lead.

Hubbard left the field to receive treatment early in the second half and was temporarily replaced on the wing by Evershed. Alderson seized the initiative to score a third try which he converted himself to give England a 12-0 advantage.

With nothing to lose Wales struck back with a try, only to have it disallowed by the referee. Evershed then scored England's fourth try, which Lockwood converted, as the home side got their campaign off to the best possible start.

England WB Thomson – RE Lockwood – FHR Alderson*, GC Hubbard – A Briggs, C Emmott – A Allport, WE Bromet, E Bullough, F Evershed, T Kent, W Nichol, J Pyke, JT Toothill, W Yiend

Wales WJ Bancroft – TW Pearson, RM Garrett, AJ Gould*, WM McCutcheon – HP Phillips, GR Rowles – AW Boucher, T Deacon, TC Graham, J Hannan, F Mills, CB Nicholl, RL Thomas, WH Watts

Top: An England try, as depicted in the Illustrated London News, *and the team that lined up against Wales (above)*

THE ALL-ROUNDERS

In the second half of the 19th century, an era when the concept of the all-round sportsman was lauded as perhaps never before, four English rugby captains earned particular admiration from the public by also playing cricket at an international level

Albert Hornby (1847-1925) of Preston Grasshoppers, Manchester and Lancashire played nine times for England between 1877 and 1882 and as captain against Ireland and Scotland in 1882. A formidable tackler and a gifted runner, he was one of England's first solo full backs. As a cricketer, he played three Tests for England and earned sporting immortality when he captained England in the legendary Test against Australia at The Oval in 1882 that gave birth to the Ashes.

Andrew Stoddart (1863-1915) of Blackheath and Middlesex played 10 internationals between 1885 and 1893, captaining England four times. A dashing, speedy centre and wing three-quarter, he was famous for his drop kicks. An outstanding cricketer for Middlesex and England, he played in 16 Tests and captained England eight times. He scored two memorable centuries against Australia, 134 at the Adelaide Oval in March 1892 and 173 at the Melbourne Cricket Ground in 1894-95.

Sammy Woods (1868-1931) was born in Australia but educated in England and won 13 international caps between 1890 and 1895. An exceptionally mobile forward and a ferocious tackler, he captained England five times. As a cricketer, he was famous for his fast bowling which led to his being capped in three Tests for Australia in 1888. A stalwart of Somerset County Cricket Club for many years, he also played three Tests for England against South Africa in 1896.

Frank Mitchell (1872-1935) was born in Yorkshire and rose to prominence as an accomplished forward. By the time he left Cambridge in the summer of 1896, he had won three blues and six international caps, including captaining England against Scotland in 1896. A Yorkshire county cricketer for many years, he played two Tests for England against South Africa in 1899 and then, after going to live there, captained South Africa against Australia and England in the Triangular Tournament of 1912.

The England Greats

DICKY LOCKWOOD

Born 11 November 1867 **Died** 10 November 1915 **England career** 1887-1894, 14 caps
Position Wing/Centre **Clubs** Dewsbury, Heckmondwike

Richard Evison Lockwood, better known as 'Dicky', made his England debut in 1887. He would go on to become the first working-class captain of the national team as the game grew in popularity in the manufacturing towns of Lancashire and West Yorkshire. Born and raised in Crigglestone, outside Wakefield, he spearheaded an influx of talented northern players who would profoundly challenge the culture and ethos of rugby union in the years ahead.

A diminutive 5ft 4½in three-quarter, Lockwood might have been overlooked if not for his impressive attacking play and cat-like runs from inside his own half. His rise through the ranks was rapid, as he made his debut for Dewsbury at just 16, before progressing to Yorkshire, the North and then England at the age of 19.

Rumours of professionalism coincided with a break from the England team at the end of the 1880s, but he was reinstated in 1891 and scored tries against Ireland and Scotland. In 1892 his goals against Wales and Scotland helped England to an unbeaten season and it was his runs from deep that relieved the pressure on his side and delivered victory in the decisive match against Scotland. In 1894 he was made captain and rewarded selectors with a try and hat-trick of conversions in a 24-3 victory against Wales.

The following year Lockwood was one of many gifted players who defected to join the Northern Rugby Football Union. He played on into the early 1900s as a professional with Wakefield Trinity.

> ## "WE DON'T KNOW A MORE POPULAR OR UNASSUMING PLAYER THAN LOCKWOOD, AND IT IS PITY THAT THERE ARE NOT MORE OF HIS CLASS"
>
> *Athletic News Football Annual, 1893*

RULES AS TO PROFESSIONALISM

The Rugby Union Committee deem it advisable, as the game spreads in all parts of the country, to draw the attention of all players to these rules.

THE PRINCIPAL RULES AS AFFECT THE INDIVIDUAL ARE AS FOLLOWS:—

1. Professionalism is illegal.

2. Acts of Professionalism are:—

   Asking, receiving, or relying on a promise, direct or implied, to receive any money consideration whatever, actual or prospective, any employment or advancement, any establishment in business, or any compensation whatever for:—

   (a) Playing football or rendering any service to a football organisation (provided however, that the Secretary and Treasurer of a Club who has definitely ceased playing football may be excepted under special conditions).

   (b) Training, or loss of time connected therewith.

   (c) Time lost in playing football or in travelling in connection with football.

   (d) Expenses in excess of the amount actually disbursed on account of reasonable hotel or travelling expenses.

   Playing for a Club while receiving, or after having received from such Club, any consideration whatever for acting as an official, or for doing or having done any work about the Club's ground or in connection with the Club's affairs, unless such work was done before the receiver became a football player.

   Remaining on tour at his Club's expense longer than is reasonable.

   Giving or receiving any money testimonial. Or, giving or receiving any other testimonial, except under the authority of this Union.

   Playing on any ground where gate money is taken:—

   (a) During the close season (that is between 21st April and 1st September, except when the Tuesday in Easter Week falls later than 21st April, when the close season shall commence from the Wednesday in the Easter Week), except where special permission for the game has been granted by this Committee.

   (b) In any match or contest where it is previously agreed that less than 15 players on each side shall take part (except where, in exceptional cases, this Committee may have granted special permission for less than 15 players aside to take part).

   Knowingly playing with or against any expelled or suspended player or Club, or with or against any professional player or Club.

   Refusing to give evidence or otherwise assist in carrying out these rules when requested by this Union to do so.

   Being registered as, or declared a professional, or suspended by any National Rugby Union or by the Football Association.

   Playing within 8 days of any accident for which he has claimed or received insurance compensation, if insured under these rules.

   Playing in any benefit match connected with football (except where this Committee has given permission for a *bona fide* charity match).

   Knowingly playing or acting as referee or touch judge on the ground of an expelled or suspended club.

   Receiving money or other valuable consideration from any person or persons as an inducement towards playing football.

   Signing any form of the Northern Union (Rugby League).

   Advocating or taking steps to promote Northern Union (Rugby League) or other professional football.

   The penalty for breach of these Rules is suspension or expulsion. (Expulsion carries with it the formal declaration of professionalism).

   This Union shall have power to deal with all acts which it may consider as acts of professionalism and which are not specifically provided for.

   October, 1924.   *BY ORDER OF THE COMMITTEE.*

IGNORANCE OF THE RULES IS NO DEFENCE.

Codes of Conduct such as pictured here were a common feature of rugby clubhouses across England at the beginning of the 20th century

History in the making

DIVIDE AND RULE

In 1889, the RFU launched the County Championship competition that continues to this day. Yorkshire won seven of the first eight championships and Lancashire the other (*in 1891, medal below*) reflecting the growing popularity and strength of rugby football in the urban manufacturing districts of the two counties. Representatives of both Lancashire and Yorkshire began to feature prominently in the national team.

The outstanding 1892 side, which claimed the Home Nations Championship without conceding a point, is evidence of the quality of this generation of rugby players, no fewer than 10 of whom were selected from the two counties. Their selection came at a cost however. Travelling long distances to play for England often necessitated absences from their place of work and, in 1889, Halifax Football Club conceived of the notion of broken-time payments to ensure that the men were not out of pocket.

The proposal was not universally popular. Many administrators, several of whom had played their rugby several years earlier, felt that such payments contravened the amateur ethos of the game. In 1891 club representatives voted on the issue. More than half voted in favour of compensatory payments but the motion did not pass as it had been decided in advance that a two-thirds majority was required.

This created division within the game and two footballing cultures began to emerge. Many players didn't see why they should lose out and northern club owners, often motivated by gate receipts, wished to see the very best players pull on their colours and understood that incentives were required.

Having witnessed how the Football League had quickly transformed association football into a professional sport 10 years earlier, the RFU believed their sport to be different and doubled down on their commitment to the principles of amateurism. Secretary George Rowland Hill (*right*) went so far as to say that he would "rather break the whole edifice of rugby union than give in to professionalism".

Consequently, in August 1895, 21 clubs from Yorkshire, Lancashire and Cheshire convened at the George Hotel in Huddersfield. They formed the Northern Rugby Football Union and rugby's Great Schism had become a reality.

THE AFTERMATH OF THE SPLIT

Although 22 clubs had defected from the RFU to the NRFU in the summer of 1895, six of the seven new caps selected at the start of the 1896 season were from northern clubs, including Castleford, Bramley, Lancaster and Sowerby Bridge. Swinton centre Jim Valentine was recalled six years after earning his first and only other cap to that date. Blackheath's Dick Cattell and Rockcliff's EW 'Little Billy' Taylor were selected at half back, the latter as captain.

Perhaps in defiance, England dismantled a strong Welsh side with seven unanswered tries in a comprehensive 25-0 victory at Rectory Field; but the illusion of all being well was undermined when full back Samuel Houghton left to join NRFU side Runcorn. Houghton had played in the Wales match and been selected to play against Ireland. England lost the remaining two games of the season and clubs and players continued to defect over the summer months.

But rugby union was far from lost to the north. In 1897 RF 'Bob' Oakes of Hartlepool Rovers earned the first of his eight caps. He would dedicate his life to the betterment of the game in County Durham and Yorkshire and as President of the RFU in 1933-1934.

The schism of 1895 was not restricted to England. In 1897 Wales withdrew from the Championship in protest at the treatment of their former captain Arthur Gould. In recognition of an illustrious 12-year career the WRU, with the help of donations from the Welsh public, had bought him a house. The International Rugby Football Board (IRFB) ruled that this amounted to professionalism. This remarkable situation was not fully resolved until 1899.

Despite patchy form, England did record victories against Scotland in 1897 and Wales in 1898, the latter under the captaincy of Moseley full back JF 'Fred' Byrne, earning the last of his 13 caps.

Two significant players would earn their first caps for England at the start of the 1899 season: John 'the Prophet' Daniell, a tenaciously

Above: Fred Byrne, a fine full back and captain of England in the late 1890s

Right: John 'the Prophet' Daniell, a renowned scrummager and England's captain during the post-split era

strong scrummager and HT 'Octopus' Gamlin, a full back who earned his unusual nickname for the manner of his tackling. Neither were able to halt the march of a prodigiously talented Welsh side about to embark on the most successful period in their history. Defeat to Wales was followed by defeats to Ireland and Scotland and, for the first time, England suffered a clean sweep of the negative variety.

In response, the English selectors replaced the entire side except Gamlin at the start of the 1900 season. The only player, apart from Gamlin, not making his debut was Cattell, now captain in his first match for England since 1896. Kingsholm was the venue and the all-new English pack combined well but not well enough to contain a Welsh side who cantered to a 13-3 victory.

Daniell had been unavailable for the second two matches in 1899 and the opening match of 1900 but was restored and made captain for the match against reigning champions Ireland at Richmond. Bolstered by Fin Todd of Blackheath and Harry Alexander of Birkenhead Park, Daniell's pack competed with renewed vigour and kept the Irish at bay until the final quarter of the match. A drop goal put Ireland in front, but England's players looked the fresher. Percy Park's Tot Robinson scored two of England's three late tries to bring his then total to six in five appearances in an intermittent international career. It was England's first victory against Ireland since 1895.

Daniell led his side to a creditable draw against Scotland at Inverleith in the final match of the 1900 season but was unavailable for the entirety of the 1901 season. Ten new caps were selected to face Wales at Cardiff Arms Park but none of them could make an impression as England lost 13-0. Subsequent defeats to Ireland and Scotland ensured England would finish bottom of the table for the second time in three seasons.

Such a return was not acceptable for the world's oldest union. For the third consecutive season more than half the team were replaced with new caps. These included Oxford University's John Raphael, of whom much was hoped, but the constant upheaval hindered the development of combination play. England opened the 1902 season with defeat to Wales through a late penalty at Rectory Field.

Daniell then returned as captain to face Ireland as England played at Welford Road for the first time. An improved showing with tries from leaping wing Sidney Coopper and Devonport Albion's Sam Williams delivered a narrow victory. The side then travelled to Inverleith, Williams opened the scoring and enterprising play by Raphael and JT 'Long John' Taylor of West

England take on Wales at Leicester in 1904 in a match that ended in a hard-fought 14-14 draw

Hartlepool gave England a 6-0 lead at the interval. The second half was perhaps Gamlin's finest. AN Fell pulled a try back and Scotland pressed determinedly for another. Time and again it was the last-ditch tackling of the English full back that prevented a score and England held on for a 6-3 victory and a respectable second place in the Championship.

For the second time in three years, Daniell's return had triggered an improvement in English fortunes. Unfortunately, he would not be available in 1903 and again England suffered a clean sweep of defeats with only the performances of Taylor, Gamlin and new cap Vincent Cartwright offering much cause for optimism.

Daniell earned his final two caps in 1904. The first was an impressive 19-0 victory against Ireland at Rectory Field. In the second he suffered only the second defeat of his career and his first against Scotland who, with JI Gillespie and David Bedell-Sivright, collected a second consecutive Championship.

In 1904 the number of NRFU clubs exceeded the number of RFU affiliated clubs for the first time. Despite this and England's deep malaise on the field, the popularity of rugby union continued to grow. In 1905 England suffered three consecutive defeats to finish bottom of the Championship table before hosting New Zealand at Crystal Palace in front of 45,000 people.

FOR THE THIRD CONSECUTIVE SEASON MORE THAN HALF THE TEAM WERE REPLACED WITH NEW CAPS

HT 'OCTOPUS' GAMLIN

Born 12 February 1878 **Died** 12 July 1937
England career 1899-1904, 15 caps
Position Full Back
Clubs Devonport Albion, Blackheath

Herbert Tremlett Gamlin's career straddled the last decade of the nineteenth century and the first of the twentieth and he is regarded as one of the greatest England full backs.

He played his club rugby for Devonport Albion and Blackheath and appeared for Somerset at the age of 17. He played five times for the South against the North, firstly at Bristol in December 1898. He was first selected for England the following month in a 26-3 defeat against Wales at St Helen's, Swansea. Dropped for the match against Ireland, he was recalled for the final international of the season against Scotland.

Powerfully built and a sure line kicker, his reputation as one of the hardest-tackling full backs seen in rugby to that date earned him the sobriquet 'Octopus' on account of his ability to lure opponents into the tackle and prevent them passing to supporting players.

He was capped 15 times over five years and finished his international career in the Calcutta Cup match against Scotland at Inverleith in March 1904. Although on the winning side in only four of his internationals, his consistently outstanding performances were an essential boost at a difficult time for English rugby following the establishment of the Northern Union.

Captain of the Somerset county rugby side between 1901 and 1904, he also played cricket for Somerset while a schoolboy.

"THE GREATEST BACK I EVER SAW... GAMLIN NOT ONLY TACKLED, HE CRUSHED"

EHD Sewell

ENGLAND 0 NEW ZEALAND 15

2 December 1905, Crystal Palace, London

The arrival in the UK in 1905 of a rugby team from New Zealand remains one of the landmark events in rugby history. The clamour for tickets was so great that the match had to be moved to Crystal Palace from Rectory Field due to the demand. The 15,000 seats were sold a fortnight before the match and the *Times* recorded the eventual crowd as 45,000, a record for an international match in England.

The England selectors had a number of problems. Almost all available players had already experienced defeat at the hands of the travelling All Blacks and there were few tried and tested combinations to fall back on. Nevertheless, it was a considerable surprise when they picked eight new caps and John Raphael, the experienced Old Merchant Taylors' centre, as an extra half back to counter the threat of the formidable roving wing forward and New Zealand captain Dave Gallaher.

England captain Vincent Cartwright (*with the ball at his feet,*

above) was joined in the side by three Leicester players, left wing Alfred Hind, half back John Braithwaite and forward RF 'Tosh' Russell. Durham provided two players, Henry Imrie and George Summerscales, both new caps. Of the debutants, only John Jackett of Falmouth, went on to have a long international career.

The game was played in muddy conditions and was just five minutes old when All Black wing Duncan McGregor scored in the right-hand corner. He scored again 10 minutes later after a searing break by Billy Stead. A third McGregor try was added before half-time after Stead and Fred Roberts had fashioned another opening.

New Zealand retained their 9-0 advantage until the 70th minute. The powerful 6 foot and 15 stone forward Fred Newton then powered over for the fourth try and,

just before the close, McGregor scored New Zealand's fifth try after yet another break by Stead. The match ended 15-0 with the All Blacks convincing victors by five tries to none and their unbeaten team marched on. They would suffer their sole defeat of the tour at the hands of Wales in Cardiff a month later.

England EJ Jackett – HM Imrie, RE Godfray, HE Shewring, AE Hind – JE Raphael, DR Gent, J Braithwaite – VH Cartwright*, CEL Hammond, BA Hill, JL Mathias, EW Roberts, RF Russell, GE Summerscales

New Zealand GA Gillett – D McGregor, RG Deans, WJ Wallace – J Hunter, JW Stead, F Roberts – D Gallaher*, ST Casey, GA Tyler, FT Glasgow, F Newton, JM O'Sullivan, A McDonald, CE Seeling

Top: The respective England and New Zealand (above) teams that met at Crystal Palace during the All Blacks' groundbreaking 1905 tour

History in the making

THE FIRST SCHOOLBOY INTERNATIONALS

The establishment of the England Schools Rugby Union (ESRU) was in large part down to the pioneering efforts of schoolteachers across the country. Chief amongst these was James Cooper, who administered the Medway Street Team in Leicester. In 1894 the Leicester Schools Football League (Rugby Union) became the first schools union in England.

Similar developments were taking place concurrently in Wales and so Cooper applied to the RFU to form a National Schools Union. The request was granted and the ESRU came into being at the YMCA room in Leicester on 26 March 1904, by which time the first schoolboy international match had already taken place.

Wearing rose-embroidered, long-sleeved, woollen white jerseys, England schoolboys took to the field for the first time at Cardiff Arms Park on 12 March 1904. It was not a close match, with Wales eventually winning comfortably 23-5.

Under the guidance of Cooper, Welford Road was in 1905 chosen as host for the first schoolboys

Ramsden

ENGLAND v WALES
AT LEICESTER 1905.

international on English soil (*pictured above*), with Wales once more triumphant, this time 6-0. England avoided defeat for the first time in 1908 and in 1910 they secured their first victory.

Evidencing the usefulness of the schoolboy international side as a development tool, the 1910 side that defeated Wales 4-3 featured future international Tom Voyce of Gloucester as half back, who would go

on to become one of England's most influential players of the 1920s and President of the RFU in 1960-61.

Limited to under 16s, a second schoolboy side of under 18s was introduced in 1949.

*A woollen jersey
from the England
schoolboys
international against
Wales in 1905, the
first on English soil*

Wearing the

No-one knows the emotions that playing for England conjures better than Jason Leonard or Rocky Clark. The all-time record cap winners talk about the joy – and sometimes pain – involved in pulling on the white jersey

By Duncan Bech, PA England rugby correspondent

I t is a quirk of English rugby that the nation's highest-capped male and female players operated in one of the game's most demanding positions. Jason Leonard and Rochelle Clark were remarkably durable loose-head props who wrote their names into Twickenham folklore by becoming both Test centurions and World Cup winners.

Both careers were launched by debuts that were eventful for different reasons. Leonard won the first of his 114 England caps – he accumulated an additional five on British & Irish Lions duty – as a raw 21-year-old. As the youngest prop to represent England, facing Argentina in Buenos Aires was a step into the lion's den.

"I remember it vividly. We were the first English team of any sport to play in Argentina after the Falklands War," says Leonard, who donated the shirt from that 25-12 win to his junior club, Barking. "Emotions were running very high and tempers frayed. I loved it and in a quirky way Argentina has popped up in my career quite a lot. It's a beautiful country and we were really well looked after, but the rugby was brutal.

"Every single time I pulled the jersey on I was

Jason Leonard

white shirt

"We went up the stairs into the stadium and the first thing I saw was a soldier with a machine gun and a guard dog. That gave a feeling for what the atmosphere would be like. It was a football stadium, so there was a wire fence with barbed wire at the top to stop supporters getting on to the field – which I was pleased about!

"The national anthems started and halfway through *God Save the Queen* someone decided that was enough. It was being played on an old gramophone and you could actually hear crackling and a sudden screech where the record had been pulled off.

"They'd throw stuff at you on the field. You'd stand at a lineout and an orange would come flashing past your nose. An empty whisky bottle, a pair of scissors and a bath tap were some of the things hurled at us. I remember that more than what happened on the pitch, because the game goes by in a heartbeat."

Whereas Leonard recalls his debut as a "baptism of fire", the start of Clark's 137-cap odyssey against Canada in 2003 was more of a rude awakening that helped shape a cornerstone of the Red Roses for the next 15 years.

"I wasn't the finished article at that stage at all," says Clark, the sport's most-capped female player and known affectionately as 'Rocky' by most within the sport. "I was overweight and the game was so fast. It was played in 34-degree heat and I was purple at half-time! It was so hot I thought I was going to have a heart attack and I was just trying to keep up with the pace of the game.

"That experience spurred me on to lose a lot of weight because I was very heavy when I was first capped. I was 110kgs and I got down to 85kgs. I worked really, really hard at that.

Jason Leonard (left) on his 86th cap in 2000 and Rocky Clark (right, on shoulders) on her 114th in 2016

thinking, 'Don't let them down, don't let them down'"

"I developed an athlete's mentality, whereas before I was just bobbing along at uni, eating and drinking what I liked, playing rugby for fun. I've always played it for fun, but I took it a lot more seriously after that."

Fires had been lit, but the prospect of amassing a century of caps was not on the radar of either player. A host of Five and Six Nations titles and Grand Slams followed, as did the ultimate prize in the shape of World Cup winners' medals. Milestones of Test appearances came and went. And fuelling both was a recognition that not only were they accountable to themselves, but also to those who had contributed to reaching the pinnacle.

In a sentiment shared by Clark, Leonard says: "Standing there for *God Save the Queen*, you'd feel this immense pride at being given this incredible opportunity, but at the same time humbled that you were representing your family, friends, coaches, school PE teachers, neighbours who would take you to training – all those who had helped you out along the way.

"It gives you a massive sense of responsibility. Every single time I pulled the jersey on I had those thoughts. I was thinking, 'Don't let them

down, don't let them down' and that was exactly the same from the first cap to the 114th."

Apart from the silverware won, the records broken and the sheer joy of playing Test match rugby, success was also measured by personal barometers not visible to the outside world.

"There were quite a few looseheads who came into the team and changed to tighthead," Clark says. "That was quite a compliment – they thought, 'Rocky's there, so we'll give tighthead a go'.

"And losing all that weight was a hugely proud moment for me because it showed how disciplined I could be and how I had changed my mindset from being a chunky monkey to being one of the fittest front rows at the time. I'd also give second rows a run for their money in terms of fitness back in the early days.

"I always took pride in my work rate and ability to get front-foot ball. When games were hard, I knew what to do. And I was able to do that week in, week out."

For Leonard, it was rugby's emerging social mobility that allowed him to extract an extra layer of meaning from a career that to the outside eye is measured only by trophies won, caps gained and opponents overcome.

"Growing up in East London and Essex, I didn't really come from a rugby background or rugby area," says Leonard, who worked as a carpenter during the amateur era.

"I was one of the first true products of the system in terms of if you're good enough, you'll make it because you'll get seen. I didn't go to a posh school, I wasn't Oxford or Cambridge.

"I came from a very unfashionable club at the time, which was Saracens. But in that era scouts started going out to look at players, keeping an eye on them and saying, 'Let's see how he gets on over the next year or so'. I came through that way and that's something to be proud of."

Leonard downplays his durability as mere luck, citing the general absence of injury apart from neck surgery in 1992. But as a scrummaging

Rocky Clark (right) and her England colleagues wave to friends and family during their triumphant 2014 World Cup campaign

"Thousands of hot baths and hours spent with amazing physios kept me patched up for the last eight years of my career" Rocky Clark

The respect between the pair is deep, their shared achievements supplemented by genuine warmth

that the demands placed on his body could no longer be tolerated made bearable by the absence of any regret. Indeed, he had achieved everything he wanted to – and more besides.

It is still raw for Clark, however, even as her club career has been given a new lease of life as player-coach at Saracens. The game's most-capped front row knew the timing was right as England were looking to develop the next generation. And she takes pride in finishing on her terms, signed off by a conclusive victory over Ireland in 2018. But a void remains.

"Everyone jokes: 'How are you finding retirement?' I won't lie, it's been really hard. There's a massive gap in my life because I miss it," she says.

"I have very fond memories and most of my adult life – 15 years – was part of a very special team. I made so many amazing friends along the way, had some brilliant coaches and physios. I travelled the world and it's a life I absolutely loved. It's one I miss now."

technician who could also operate at tighthead, the length of his career is a marvel and reflects a fierce competitiveness belied by the affability that earned him the nickname 'Fun Bus' from teammate Martin Bayfield.

Clark, meanwhile, drew strength in the camaraderie of a rugby squad where she acted as a constant as players and coaches came and went.

"I was driven by the hunger to keep going and keep playing," she says, "and thousands of hot baths and hours spent with amazing physios who kept me patched up for the last eight years of my career.

"I saw so many people come in and out of the squad. Young players would come in and I kept making new friends. The lift the younger teammates would give me kept me young. They'd take the mickey out of me and there would be lots of banter.

"And I was also a highly competitive athlete. I wanted to do my best in every training and I'd give it my all. I wouldn't leave anything on the park and that was probably one of the secrets to my longevity."

The respect between the pair is deep, their shared achievements supplemented by genuine warmth. Leonard is quick to correct people when he is described as England's most capped player: "I say no, that's Rocky." He actually presented her with her 100th cap at Twickenham when the day came, and in Clark he found a grateful recipient. "Jason was my idol growing up so to have my name in the same sentence as him is amazing," Clark explains.

When the end eventually came, they both knew it was time to go. Leonard finished in 2004 and he embraced retirement, the knowledge

Above left: Rocky and Jason share some of their on-pitch experiences

Left: 'Fun Bus' on the victory bus! Jason Leonard (right) with Mike Catt as they celebrate England's 2003 World Cup win

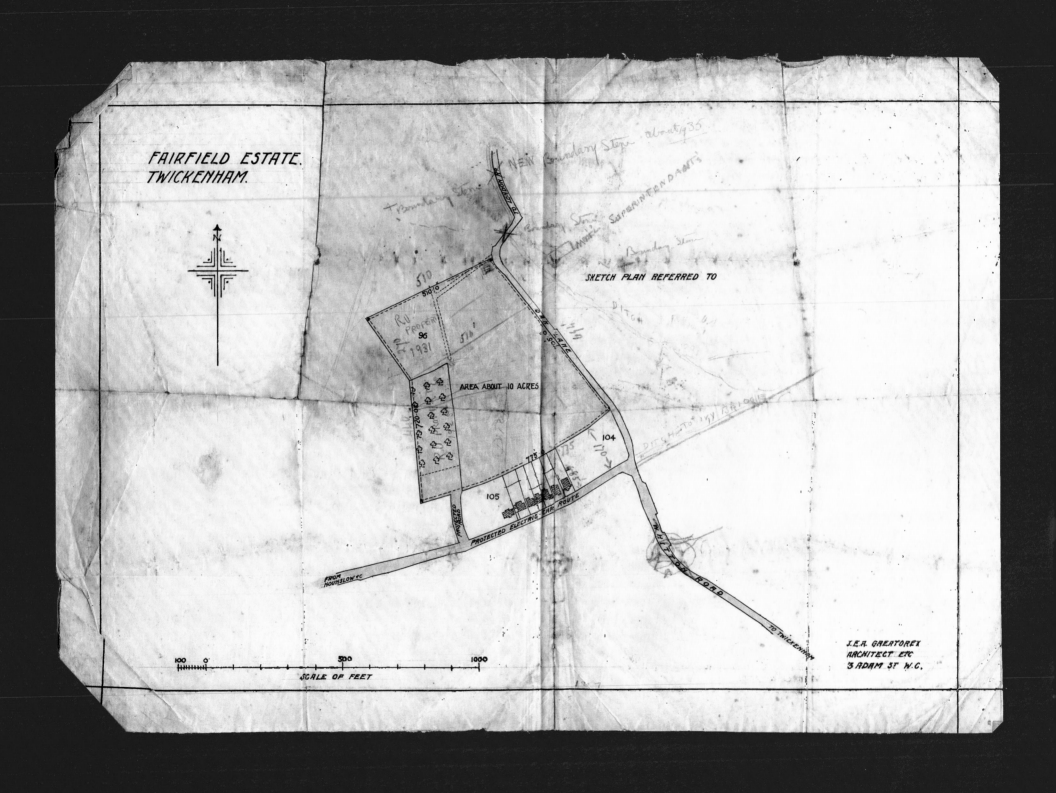

FAIRFIELD ESTATE.
TWICKENHAM.

SKETCH PLAN REFERRED TO

AREA ABOUT 10 ACRES

J.E.A. GREATOREX
ARCHITECT ETC
3 ADAM ST W.C.

SCALE OF FEET

3

BUILDING FOR THE FUTURE

1906-1914

FINDING A PERMANENT HOME

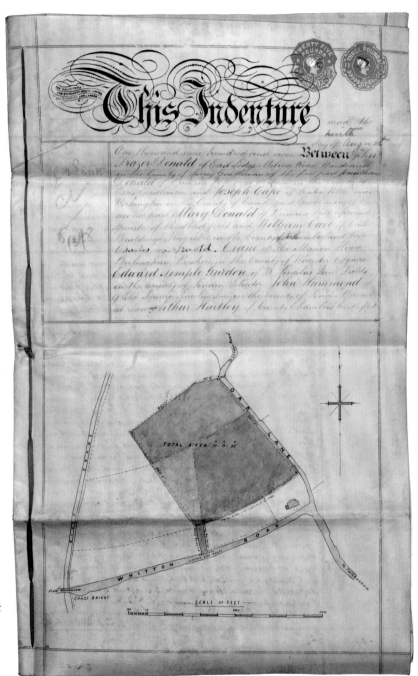

Previous pages:
The Fairfield Estate at Twickenham – the site of rugby's future 'HQ'

In 1906, defeats to Wales and Ireland extended England's run of losses to seven. Questions were asked of the RFU and its management of the English game, but behind the scenes William Cail and Billy Williams were working on a quite unexpected solution. In the meantime, England had the small matter of the Calcutta Cup match in Inverleith, a fixture that England hadn't managed to win since 1902.

Into the team at half back came Jimmy Peters of Plymouth, to play alongside Adrian Stoop of Harlequins. Behind them came another Quin, John Birkett, son of 1871's try-scoring Reginald Birkett. In the forwards, Bridgwater Albion's Robert Dibble would support captain Vincent Cartwright of Nottingham.

The English pack took the initiative in the first half, providing a platform for the quick-passing Stoop and innovative Peters in midfield. In the backs, the physical Birkett and John Raphael of Old Merchant Taylors' combined well. A try apiece saw the scores level at half-time. In the second half, Rockcliff wing Thomas Simpson evaded several tacklers to score a superb individual try before Birkett charged through once more. William Mills touched down a third try and England won 9-3.

A largely unchanged side then ran in nine tries in a 35-8 victory over France at Parc des Princes and later in the year England managed a respectable 3-3 draw against a strong South Africa side at Crystal Palace, the first meeting between the sides.

The idea of a permanent home for England's national rugby team is believed to have occurred

Above: Robert Dibble, England's captain in 1909 and 1912

Left: The deeds to Twickenham, dated 1907

to RFU Treasurer William Cail on 2 December 1905, when England hosted New Zealand at Crystal Palace in front of 45,000 people. Though England lost the match, the gate receipts were very welcome and the financial benefit of hosting Test matches was very apparent to Cail, whose role it was to balance the RFU's books.

It may seem strange that an organisation that had so recently railed against professionalism would now seek the commercial benefit that a permanent home might bring. Nonetheless, the RFU still had bills to pay. On 15 March 1907, Cail's motion to finance and develop a permanent football ground was passed and the search commenced that would lead them to a piece of land, then known as the Fairfield Estate, on the margins of Isleworth, Whitton and Twickenham.

More than 10 miles from central London and a considerable walk from the nearest train station, the location initially raised eyebrows. To make matters worse, the farmed land was a flood plain for a nearby river. Crucially, however, it was within budget, unlike proposed alternative sites at Stamford Bridge and in Wembley.

On the pitch, England's performances remained poor. In 1907 England were beaten by all of Wales, Ireland and Scotland for the sixth time inside nine seasons but convincingly beat France, with Harlequin Daniel Lambert scoring a record five tries on his debut. Matters improved in 1908 as Liverpool's Noel Slocock and Hartlepool Rovers' Harry Havelock shored up the scrum. In the backs, Birkett was in fine form contributing four tries across four matches. Victories against France and Ireland were secured but old problems remained. Havelock signed professional terms with Hull FC at the end of the season.

Ten new caps were selected to face the visiting Australians in January 1909, among them Northampton wing Edgar Mobbs, whose try would not be enough to avoid a 9-3 defeat. After losing in Cardiff, Dibble's side was bolstered by three new caps as they hosted France at Welford Road. In the backs a precocious 19-year-old named Ronald Poulton of Harlequins and Oxford University earned the first of his caps and combined well with Mobbs and Leicester's Frank Tarr. England scored six tries and ran out 22-0 winners against a French side that had yet to play consistently well at Test level.

A victory at Lansdowne Road gained England a foothold in the championship table but was followed by defeat to Scotland at Richmond. To his credit Mobbs had scored four tries across the season and Dibble, Rockcliff's Alf Kewney and HC 'Dreadnought' Harrison of the Royal Marines gave England a solidity in the scrum missing since John Daniell's time.

IN THE WOOD AND STEEL OF TWICKENHAM THERE WAS THE PROMISE OF A BRIGHTER FUTURE

Top: Twickenham's East Stand nears completion in 1909

Above: Daniel Lambert, who scored five tries on debut in 1907

By the autumn of 1909 the Twickenham ground was ready. A year earlier, Adrian Stoop had contacted the RFU to enquire if the new ground might be utilised as the home of the nomadic side Harlequins FC. Understanding that a national rugby ground might otherwise run the risk of being underused, the RFU agreed. And so Harlequins and Richmond contested the first match at Twickenham on 2 October 1909. It was the start of an enduring relationship that lasted until 1990 when the Quins moved into their own home, also in Twickenham and appropriately named the Stoop.

A total of 2,000 people turned out for that first game and twice as many came the following month when Quins played Northampton, while similar numbers attended the England trial fixtures that followed. Clearly there was evident promise in the wood and steel of Twickenham of a brighter future ahead after a decade of poor results, and on the morning of 15 January 1910 a new phase of English rugby was about to begin.

JAMES PETERS

Born 7 August 1879 **Died** 26 March 1954
England career 1906-1908, 5 caps
Position Half Back/Fly Half **Club** Plymouth

Jimmy Peters was a richly talented fly half who became the first black player to play for England when chosen to play outside Adrian Stoop against Scotland at Inverleith in March 1906.

He was born in Salford, Lancashire. His Jamaican father died when he was young and he was brought up in an orphanage in Southwark. An exceptional athlete, he played for Bristol from 1900 to 1902 and then for Plymouth. He first appeared for Devon in 1903 and his performances alongside diminutive Devonport Albion scrum half Raphael Jago brought him to the attention of national selectors in the 1905-06 season.

In 1905 Peters was in the Devon side that lost 55-4 to the visiting All Blacks, but Devon went on to win the County Championship the same season. After defeats to Wales and Ireland, the English selectors made changes and Peters played in the final two matches of the season against Scotland and France, becoming the first black player to represent England in the process. Both matches were victories, with Peters contributing a try in the 35-8 victory over France.

The following season, Peters failed to hold his place in the England side for the matches against South Africa, France and Wales. He was recalled for the match against Ireland, replacing Adrian Stoop at fly half, and was partnered for the only time in an international by Jago. He scored the sole English try in the last international of the season against Scotland.

His final appearance for England took place in the famous fog-bound match against Wales at Ashton

Gate, Bristol, where Wales convincingly beat England by 28-18 in conditions so murky that the spectators missed much of the action. He played on for Plymouth and Devon and then, following a dockyard incident in which he lost three fingers in 1910, went north to play rugby league for Barrow and St Helens before retiring from rugby in 1914.

Much admired as a player and a person, particularly in his adopted county of Devon, Jimmy Peters is remembered as a trailblazer who overcame prejudice to represent his country with distinction.

ENGLAND 3 SOUTH AFRICA 3

8 December 1906, Crystal Palace, London

The fourth international on the first Springboks tour of the United Kingdom was the match against England at Crystal Palace on 8 December 1906.

The South African tourists had created a favourable impression with their open rugby and, although defeated by Scotland in their opening international, they had beaten Ireland and Wales and were clear favourites going into the match against England. They had a settled side but picked one new cap in the forwards, the future captain of the 1912-13 Springbok tour of Europe, Billy Millar.

England were captained for the sixth time by the Nottingham forward Vincent Cartwright. The team contained two new caps, both contentious selections who were never picked for England again. FG 'Freddie' Brooks on the left wing was Rhodesian by birth and, although schooled in England, had narrowly missed selection for the Springbok touring party because he had not fulfilled the necessary five-year residential qualification. The Guy's Hospital forward, Arnold Alcock, had appeared for the victorious Rest of England side in the trial match a week earlier, but is generally

SOUTH AFRICAN TEAM. SEASON 1906-7.

ENGLISH TEAM. SEASON 1906-7.

— THE ENGLISH TEAM AT THE CRYSTAL PALACE —

F.J. DOBBIN.

H.A. de VILLIERS.

J.W.E. RAAFF.

W.A. MILLAR.

H.C. DANEEL.

S. MORKEL.

S. JOUBERT.

A.F. MARSBURG.

D.J. BRINK.

P.A. LE ROUX.

D. MORKEL.

J.A. LOUBSER.

D.C. JACKSON.

S.C. de MELKER.

SPRINGBOKS NEARLY OVER THE LINE: JACKSON CLAIMS A TRY.

AFTER THE HEEL OUT: SCRUM BREAKING UP.

LINING OUT FOR A THROW IN.

JACKETT HURT TRYING TO PREVENT SPRINGBOKS FIRST TRY.

— CARTWRIGHT KICKS OFF —

HEELED OUT: A DASH FOR THE BALL.

P. ROOS.

A THROW IN: MARK YOUR MEN.

believed to have been selected over the Liverpool forward Noel Slocock through a selectorial error.

A large crowd of more than 30,000 saw a close match in persistent rain on a muddy and waterlogged pitch (*pictured left*). Handling skills were in very short supply and both tries in the 3-3 draw came from errors by the defending team. Five minutes before half-time, the experienced English full back John Jackett fumbled a kick ahead and the Springboks forwards drove over the line, with Millar scoring a try which was not converted.

The Springboks maintained their lead until midway through the second half when England scored a remarkably similar try. Following a kick ahead by fly half Adrian Stoop and an English forward rush, the Springbok centre de Melker miskicked the rolling ball behind his try line and Freddie Brooks rushed up to dive on the ball to claim the equalising try. Cartwright missed the conversion and the final quarter of the match was played out with the English forwards in the ascendancy but unable to drive home their advantage.

With Congratulations & Greetings from

1906 Springbok postcard from the Cape of Good Hope

England: EJ Jackett – T Simpson, HE Shewring, JGG Birkett, FG Brooks – AD Stoop, RA Jago – VH Cartwright*, A Alcock, R Dibble, J Green, BA Hill, TS Kelly, WA Mills, CH Shaw

South Africa: SJ Joubert – JA Loubser, SC de Melker, HA de Villiers, AFW Marsberg – FJ Dobbin, DC Jackson – PJ Roos*, DJ Brink, HJ Daneel, PA le Roux, WA Millar, DFT Morkel, WS Morkel, JWE Raaff

History in the making

THE ORIGINAL TWICKENHAM

'One of the greatest and stateliest homes in British sport' – OL Owen, 1955

As today, the original Twickenham Stadium had north and south try lines separated by 100 metres of turf, with 13-metre in-goal areas. A concrete terrace was constructed for spectators to stand at the south end and nothing but a raised grassy bank accommodated spectators in the north. To receive visitors in comfort, the ground boasted relatively luxurious covered and seated grandstands on both the west and east sides. Seats cost four shillings but it was cheaper to stand.

Between 18,000 and 20,000 spectators arrived for the inaugural Test match against Wales in 1910. Facilities, however, remained limited and it might shock today's rugby fans to learn that the original ground had only one bar.

Such matters could not continue indefinitely. By 1913, 30,000 spectators were finding their way to Twickenham. Matters were interrupted by war but shortly after rugby reconvened plans were made for the ground's extension.

Naturally, the north was the first to be developed. Architect Archibald Leitch was appointed to construct a two-tier grandstand, unveiled in time for the first visit of New

Zealand in 1925, by which time capacity had reached 60,000.

The East and West Stands were then doubled in size, becoming two-tier grandstands that opened in 1927 and 1931 respectively. In 1932, the south terrace was extended again and Twickenham could now accommodate upwards of 70,000 people. The ground had entered its 'classic' period and would remain largely unchanged until the 1980s.

Work continued under the stands, particularly in the west, which would boast two dressing rooms, a President's room, committee room and royal retiring room. By the early 1950s, the ground included five tea rooms and 12 bars, one of which was capable of seating up to 400 people.

Around the ground the Rowland Hill Memorial Gates, built to commemorate the administrator who had done most to retain the amateur status of rugby union, was opened to great fanfare in 1929. Behind the south terrace, a clock tower stood until 1950 when it was replaced by Kenneth Dalgleish's iconic weathervane. 'HQ' was well and truly open for business.

Twickenham's North Stand in development in 1924 (above); the East Stand pictured in 1927 (left) and the West Stand in 1931 (below)

Far left: The completed West Stand in all its glory and packed to the rafters on matchday

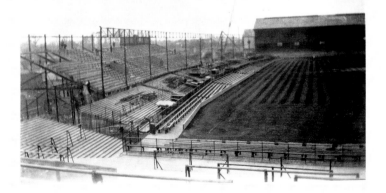

ENGLAND 11 WALES 6

15 January 1910, Twickenham

The gates of England's new rugby ground opened at 12.30pm on 15 January 1910 for the first international to be played at Twickenham with the Prince of Wales as guest of honour (*pictured below*). There was a steady stream of spectators that grew into such a crowd that the scheduled 2.30pm start of the eagerly anticipated match against Wales had to be delayed by 15 minutes. As the post-match report in *The Globe* stated: "Perhaps never before had such a large crowd been seen on a Metropolitan rugby ground as that which gathered around the arena when the game was commenced."

It was England's first international of their season and they had not beaten Wales in 11 matches, a run stretching back to 1898. Following the England team's defeat in the final trial at Twickenham, the selectors picked eight new caps, four of whom had played in the Rest of England side a week earlier. The side was captained by the inspirational Harlequins fly half Adrian Stoop, recalled to the England side after three years in the wilderness. Bill Johnston of Bristol was the new full back and would go on to win 16 caps. The wings allied the pace of Durham's Fred Chapman with the mercurial genius of Ronald Poulton. In the centre, the brilliant Redruth and Cornwall centre Bert Solomon was making his debut, alongside Harlequin John Birkett. The Swansea-born Dai Gent of Gloucester was Stoop's partner at half back.

The match started late but in spectacular fashion. The Welsh forward Ben Gronow kicked off and Stoop caught the ball. Rather than kicking for touch, Stoop ran to his left and linked up with Poulton, who cross-kicked. The Gloucester forward Henry Berry secured the ball from the loose scrum that followed and Gent passed out to Stoop. So disorientated were the Welsh defenders that all that was required was for Stoop to pass to Solomon, who linked with Birkett and gave the final pass to Chapman, who scored on his international debut in the right-hand corner just one minute after kick-off.

Chapman failed to convert his own try but with England on the attack he did kick a penalty goal in the 16th minute to give England a 6-0 lead. Wales replied with a try through Jim Webb shortly afterwards but before half-time Solomon, with a dummy to his wing, carved his way through the centre of the Welsh defence and past Bancroft to score a superb try, which Chapman converted.

It was uncertain whether a half-time lead for England of 11-3 was sufficient to win the game and a try by the Cardiff winger Reg Gibbs after just three minutes immediately cut England's lead to five points. Wales attacked but, inspired by the spoiling work of Cherry Pillman and his fellow forwards, England gradually gained the upper hand. Two chances came the way of the Welsh three-quarters in the final 20 minutes, but a fumble and a forward pass deprived them of both and the English defence, under Stoop's direction, held firm in the dying minutes to record a historic victory.

England WR Johnston – FE Chapman, JGG Birkett, B Solomon, RW Poulton – AD Stoop*, DR Gent – LE Barrington-Ward, H Berry, EL Chambers, L Haigh, WA Johns, HJS Morton, CH Pillman, DF Smith

Wales J Bancroft – RA Gibbs, JP Jones, WJ Trew*, P Hopkins – R Jones, RM Owen – TH Evans, B Gronow, H Jarman, CM Pritchard, J Pugsley, DJ Thomas, J Webb, I Morgan

An embroidered corner flag from the first international match at Twickenham

The Wales jersey worn by Ben Gronow (right), who kicked off the match, and an England jersey that was exchanged with Charlie Pritchard after the final whistle (left)

ADRIAN STOOP

Born 27 March 1883 **Died** 27 November 1957 **England career** 1905-1912, 15 caps
Position Half Back/Fly Half **Clubs** Oxford University, Harlequins

Adrian Dura Stoop was one of the most influential English players of all time. A deep thinker about the game, Stoop devoted much of his life to rugby and advocated individual fitness, training and analysis of the sport. He was first selected for England in 1905 and earned five caps over the following three seasons, racking up three wins and a draw before suffering a crushing 22-0 defeat at Swansea in January 1907.

Over the next two years he developed a style of play at his club Harlequins that involved a clear distinction in the two half back roles which would see the emergence of the fly half and scrum half. His side was so successful that he was able to force his way back into the England set-up in time for the first international Test at the new Twickenham ground in 1910.

Stoop, therefore, captained Harlequins in Twickenham's first-ever match, in 1909, and again the following year in England's first match at HQ. It was an inspired move and Stoop's attacking intent was rewarded within the first minute of the match when he helped set up England's opening try. A first victory against Wales in 12 years was secured, and later that year a first Championship in 18.

He was awarded the MC for distinguished service in the First World War, and was wounded in what is now Iraq. He fashioned Harlequins into *his* club, and in 1963 their new stadium 'The Stoop Memorial Ground' was built in his memory.

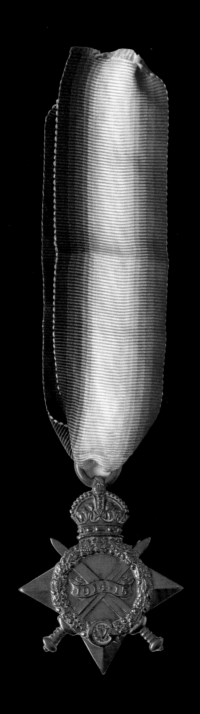
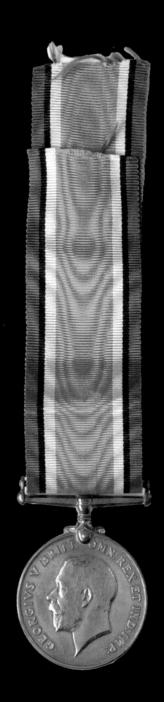
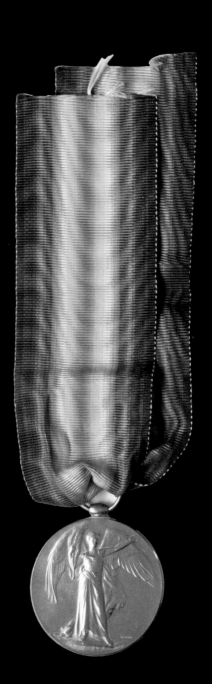

Stoop's 1914-15 Star (left), British War Medal (centre) and Victory Medal, referred to by British soldiers as 'Pip, Squeak and Wilfred'

TWICKENHAM'S FIRST GOLDEN AGE

After beating Wales for the first time in a generation, England went into the remainder of their 1910 fixtures with renewed belief. Edgar Mobbs returned to the side in place of Ronnie Poulton for Twickenham's next match against Ireland, which resulted in a 0-0 draw. Mobbs was promoted to captain the following month in Paris, where England introduced eight new caps including Norman Atherton Wodehouse of United Services and John Ritson of Northern to a pack that had struggled against the Irish.

With victory secured, the side headed to Inverleith for the season decider in front of 30,000 spectators. The influential former captain Bob Dibble returned but Scotland were favourites and opened the scoring with a try from DG Macpherson. John Birkett struck back to level the scores at half-time. In the second half, the English forwards began to provide Adrian Stoop with useful ball. He fed Birkett again for a second score, while Harry Berry and Ritson also touched down to give England a 14-5 victory. England had won the Championship for the first time since 1892.

LG 'Bruno' Brown of Oxford University and Jack King of Headingley made their debuts against Wales in 1911 but couldn't prevent a 15-11 defeat. Danny Lambert returned against France and contributed a world record 22 points in England's 37-0 victory. A narrow defeat to Ireland was then followed by victory over Scotland.

Stoop earned the last of his 15 caps in the penultimate match of the 1912 season, a defeat against Scotland at Inverleith. In the following match against France, Wodehouse assumed the captaincy for the first time. Wodehouse was an assured tactical thinker whose mastery of the scrum had seen him appointed as captain of the United Services, the Royal Navy and now the national side.

The 1913 season began with a visit from the touring Springboks. Poulton, England's exceptional centre, electrified the crowd in the first half with two swerving runs, one resulting in a try. In the second half, the English pack were unable to resist the power of the South Africans and the visitors ran out 9-3 winners.

The game gave debuts to several young players, including WJA 'Dave' Davies and Cyril Lowe, who would go on to become two of the most celebrated players England ever produced. The match would be the only time Davies would experience defeat in an England jersey. Another debutant, wing Vincent Coates, would be one of the stand-out performers in the forthcoming season, contributing a then-record six tries.

The season began for England in Cardiff, where they had never won. Mud and strong winds awaited but the English pack, Charles Henry 'Cherry' Pillman in particular, got the better of the home side. Tries from Coates and Pillman, a conversion by Cambridge University's John Eric 'Jenny' Greenwood and a dropped goal from Poulton allowed England to record a comfortable 12-0 victory over a side they hadn't beaten away since 1895.

England power past France at Twickenham in 1913 on the way to a Grand Slam

ENGLAND REQUIRED A VICTORY OVER SCOTLAND AT TWICKENHAM TO RECORD THEIR FIRST CLEAN SWEEP OF VICTORIES IN THE FIVE NATIONS ERA, AN ACHIEVEMENT NOW KNOWN AS A GRAND SLAM

The same names were on the scoresheet the following week as England powered past the French, who were visiting Twickenham for only the second time, Pillman registered two tries, while Coates scored three. The following month in Dublin, the young fly half Davies began to make his mark, linking up well with Poulton to send Ritson and Coates over in the first half. Coates went over again in the second half, then Pillman, and England won 15-4. They now required a victory over Scotland at Twickenham to record their first clean sweep of victories since 1892 and a first ever in the Five Nations era, an achievement now known as a Grand Slam.

It was far from simple. A closely-fought defensive match was settled by a single try from Australian-born forward Brown. It was enough for England to complete a clean sweep and, but for a late Dicky Lloyd dropped goal in Dublin, they would have emulated the class of 1892 by having done so without conceding a point. Perhaps the most satisfied England player of all was Yorkshireman Jack King, who had been forced from the field against his wishes in Inverleith 12 months earlier after sustaining two broken ribs. In this, his final match for England, he helped put the record straight.

Before the start of the 1914 season, the great Ronnie Poulton let it be known that this year would be his last and so he was duly installed as captain. The season began with a classic encounter in which Wales came within a whisker of beating England at Twickenham for the first time, the boundlessly energetic Pillman denying them with a late try to give England a 10-9 victory.

Lowe contributed the first two of his 18 tries for England the following month as England overcame Ireland. Davies, who together with Francis Oakeley had been left out against Wales, returned and scored one try and helped fashion two more as England won 17-12.

Above: England battle their way to a 10-9 win over Wales in 1914

Below: HC 'Dreadnought' Harrison, who won the DSO in 1916

Another classic followed at Inverleith. Poulton was on form, scoring one try, while Lowe was on fire, contributing three in a 16-15 victory. The only blemish was a broken leg for Cherry Pillman in what would prove to be his final match for England.

England now only needed to defeat the developing French side in Paris to secure back-to-back Grand Slams. They did so in emphatic style, their rampant captain Poulton contributing four individual tries, complemented by a second consecutive hat-trick from Lowe. England eventually won by a massive 39-13 and Poulton's outstanding international career came to an end.

Poulton and all who took to the field for England that day would later enlist with the armed forces and serve during the Great War. He, JHD 'Bungy' Watson, AJ 'Mud' Dingle, Oakeley, Arthur Harrison and Robert Pillman would not return. Neither would Mobbs, Berry, Lambert and King. Wodehouse would serve in both world wars, losing his life in the second, after coming out of retirement to do his duty. Others would return, however, and of the 1914 side, Sid Smart, Lowe, Davies, Greenwood and Brown would all play for England again.

'CHERRY' PILLMAN

Born 8 January 1890 **Died** 13 November 1955
England career 1910-1914, 18 caps
Position Wing Forward **Club** Blackheath

Charles Henry 'Cherry' Pillman (*front row, second from left*) was the most successful English exponent of wing forward play leading up to the First World War. He joined Blackheath after leaving Tonbridge School and was selected to win the first of his 18 caps, aged 20, in the historic opening international at Twickenham against Wales.

He played throughout the 1910 season and was chosen to tour South Africa with the British & Irish Lions where he made a huge impression as a marauding wing forward with rare pace and footballing skills. Unable to play in the first Test through injury, he was surprisingly selected to play fly half in the second Test where he masterminded a series-equalling victory. One of his opponents in that match, the future Springbok captain Billy Millar, wrote: "If ever a man can be said to have won an international match through his own unorthodox and single-handed efforts, it can be said of the inspired, black-haired Pillman I played against on the Crusaders Ground that day – when he played as a fly half, mark you, and not as a forward."

Pillman was restored to wing forward for the deciding third Test, but the Lions were reduced to 14 men after 20 minutes and lost both the Test and the series.

On his return, he played in the England side as a forward until he broke his leg in the Calcutta Cup match in March 1914, thereby missing the final match against France in which his brother Robert – also a Blackheath forward – won his only cap. He played in every other match of England's Grand Slam-winning campaigns of 1913 and 1914 and scored eight tries in his 18 England internationals, a new record for a forward.

He won the Military Cross in 1918 and after the war represented the Mother Country in the King's Cup and resumed playing for Blackheath. He was Kent's first post-war captain but, although he played in a trial match, did not play for England again.

The England Greats

CYRIL LOWE

Born 7 October 1891 **Died** 6 February 1983
England career 1913-1923, 25 caps
Position Wing **Clubs** Cambridge University, Blackheath

Cyril Lowe (*front row, far right*) was educated at Dulwich College where he excelled as an athlete and played for the school first XV alongside Jenny Greenwood. He went on to study at Pembroke College, Cambridge University, where, in addition to winning an athletics blue, he played three times against Oxford University between 1911 and 1913, winning twice and scoring a try in 1913.

He made his first appearance for England against South Africa at Twickenham in January 1913 in a losing cause, but then played the remainder of the season in which England achieved their first Grand Slam. He scored eight tries in the 1914 campaign, including two against Ireland and three each against Scotland and France.

During the war, he served as a pilot with the Royal Flying Corps and is credited with shooting down nine German planes, for which he was awarded the Military Cross and the Distinguished Flying Cross. He remained in the RAF after the war and retired with the rank of Group Captain in 1944.

When rugby resumed in the 1919-20 season, Lowe played his rugby for Blackheath and Surrey and was once again an automatic choice for the England side from January 1920 until the match against France at Stade Colombes at the end of the 1923 Championship. He scored 10 tries for England in the 16 matches during this post-war period and added a drop goal against Ireland in 1921. England won their third and fourth Grand Slams in 1921 and 1923, leaving Lowe's overall record as 21 victories in 25 consecutive appearances, in which he scored 18 tries – a record that stood for more than 60 years.

Dave Davies described Lowe as "the classic wing three-quarter of his day, good enough for any team as might be chosen".

Above: A lineout during France v England in 1914, the last international before the outbreak of hostilities

Right: Five of the French side would not survive the war

Far right: Ronald Poulton, another to be killed in the upcoming conflict, scores one of his four tries

FAMOUS GAMES

FRANCE 13 ENGLAND 39

13 April 1914, Stade Colombes, Paris

The England team that faced France in 1914. This is the photo from which the stunning Forever England painting by Shane Record was created in 2016

The final match of the 1914 Championship was played in front of a staunchly partisan Parisian crowd of 20,000 at Stade Colombes. England arrived in high spirits, having secured narrow victories over Wales and Ireland at Twickenham before a very close victory over Scotland in Edinburgh.

Despite having to make two late changes to the forwards in their side for the encounter against France, England were expected to win their sixth Championship and complete only their second Grand Slam of victories over all four countries in a season. Captained by the mercurial centre three-quarter Ronald Poulton in his 17th international, England possessed a very strong three-quarter line, with Bill Johnston of Bristol at full back, Cyril Lowe of Cambridge University on the wing and the United Services half back pair of Dave Davies and Francis Oakeley.

The English forwards were a strong unit, although they were missing the intuitive pace and positioning of Cherry Pillman of Blackheath, who had broken his leg in the match against Scotland. One of the replacement forwards in Paris was his brother Robert Pillman, who was winning his first and only cap.

France started well and the forward Jean-Louis Capmau of Toulouse scored an early try, converted by the centre Lucien Besset. Lowe replied with an

unconverted try for England but France extended their lead when Georges André crossed for another try. Their lead did not last long as Poulton scored two tries before the interval, both converted by Jenny Greenwood.

With the security of a 13-8 lead at half-time, England powered ahead in the second half and quickly added three more tries, one of which was converted. France did not give up and scored a third try through their forward Marcel-Frédéric Lubin-Lebrere, but the rest of the match was all England. They scored three more tries and reached a winning score of 39-13, with Poulton scoring

four tries and Lowe scoring three. Greenwood kicked six conversions and equalled the record for an individual English player set by Lennard Stokes in 1881.

Tragically, 11 of the 30 who took the field would not survive the war.

France J Caujolle – R Lacoste, L Besset, G Pierrot, G André – M Burgun, L Larribau – F Fauré, E Iguiniz, MF Lubin-Lebrère, P Bascou, M Leuvielle*, J-L Capmau, J-J Conilh de Beyssac, F Forgues

England WR Johnston – CN Lowe, JHD Watson, RW Poulton*, AJ Dingle – WJA Davies, FE Oakeley – LG Brown, JE Greenwood, AL Harrison, HC Harrison, RL Pillman, SEJ Smart, FleS Stone, ARV Sykes

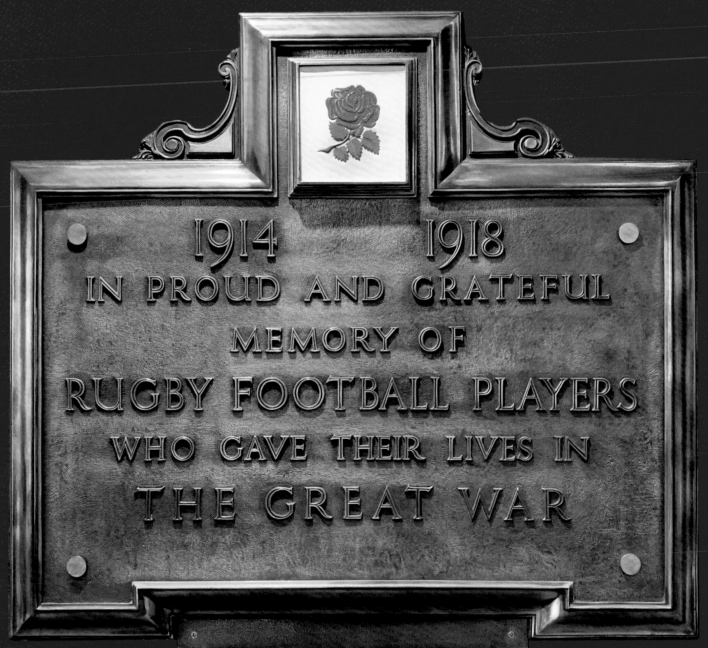

4

THE GREAT WAR

1914-1929

RUGBY AT WAR

O f the 15 players who travelled to Paris to face France in the final match of the 1914 Five Nations, all enlisted and six failed to return from the Great War. They would die in every theatre of war from the Western Front to Gallipoli and beyond. They would fight in the trenches, in submarines, dreadnoughts, aircraft and tanks.

The swiftness with which they answered the call to enlist inspired the War Office to produce a recruitment poster that encouraged sportsmen of every stripe to follow their 'glorious example'. When the Rugby Football Union convened a month after war had been formally declared, they discussed the idea of creating a Rugby Football Corps but concluded it was too late as practically all their members were already in barracks.

When Jack King arrived at the recruitment office he was turned away on account of his height. He stood his ground and three days later was accepted into the Yorkshire Hussars. He was killed on the Somme in 1916 in the act of charging the village of Guillemont alongside fellow international and friend Noel Slocock, who was also killed in the action.

They were replaced in the line by the 24th Division with whom travelled Arthur Wilson and Edgar Mobbs. Mobbs had also been

Above: England internationals Jack King (left) and Arthur Harrison (right) were both lost in combat during the First World War

"This is not the time to play Games" *(Lord Roberts)*

RUGBY·UNION·FOOTBALLERS are DOING·THEIR·DUTY
over 90% have enlisted

"Every player who represented England in Rugby international matches last year has joined the colours."—Extract from *The Times*, November 30, 1914.

BRITISH ATHLETES!
Will you follow this GLORIOUS EXAMPLE ?

ISSUED BY THE PUBLICITY DEPARTMENT, CENTRAL LONDON RECRUITING DEPOT, WHITEHALL, LONDON.   PRINTED BY JOHNSON, RIDDLE & CO., LTD., LONDON. S.E.

initially refused enlistment because of his age as he was 32. Undeterred, he went back to Northampton and raised a corps of 264 men with whom he returned to the recruitment office. He was swiftly welcomed, but was wounded in his charge on Guillemont and killed the following year at the Third Battle of Ypres, better known as Passchendaele.

Of the many tales of gallantry that surround rugby's finest during the Great War, only one resulted in the highest order of merit, the Victoria Cross (VC). Arthur Harrison, a Gunnery Officer aboard HMS *Lion* for most of the war, served in every major naval engagement of the conflict. In 1918 he volunteered to lead the storming party from HMS *Vindictive* during the Zeebrugge Raid. Despite being shot through the jaw, he and his assault team charged a machine gun emplacement while ships were scuttled in the mouth of the Zeebrugge-Bruges Canal. His body was never recovered, and he received his VC posthumously. The raid was declared a success, but German U-boats resumed their use of the canal two days later.

The great wing Cyril Lowe had enlisted as an airman and flew reconnaissance missions over the Western Front until shot through the shoulder mid-air in 1917. Under great pressure, he managed to land his FE2b two-seater aircraft. Undeterred, he retrained as a single-seater fighter pilot. In 1918 he led Squadron 24 on low-flying bombing runs in advance of The Hundred Days Offensive.

On the ground during the same action was Major Laurence Merriam, commander of 'A' Company of the 7th Tank Battalion that would lead the assault on the Hindenburg Line. Merriam would make his England debut in 1920, still sporting his regulation Army moustache. Dave Davies too survived the war, after serving on board the Grand Fleet flagship HMS *Iron Duke* during the Battle of Jutland. His midfield partner Frank Oakeley was less fortunate, his submarine D2 having been lost with all hands in 1914. Davies' next great midfield partner, Cecil Kershaw, was

Top: Laurence Merriam, who would win his first cap in 1920, served in the 7th Tank Battalion

Above: Edgar Mobbs mobilised his own corps after initially being turned down by recruiters

Left: The Army and Navy teams acknowledge the King in 1914

Far left: A poster lauds the courage of rugby's finest

another submariner who kept up the blockade during the war and also made his debut in 1920.

One of the more remarkable experiences was that of Sidney Coopper. Coopper had played on the wing for England seven times between 1900 and 1907. During the Battle of Jutland, he was a Lieutenant Engineer aboard HMS *Sparrowhawk*, part of the destroyer flotilla that took the battle to the German High Seas Fleet during the night. Disabled and later sunk, Coopper managed to keep *Sparrowhawk* operational until sunrise whereupon he and the rest of her survivors were rescued.

Ronnie Poulton, now known as Lieutenant Palmer on account of changing his name as a condition of a will inheritance, played his final game of rugby on 14 April 1915 at the town of Nieppe on the France-Belgian border. The match between 48th Division and 4th Division involved no fewer than nine full internationals, including Palmer, Sid Smart and Ireland's Basil Maclear as referee. Palmer would lose his life to a sniper's bullet exactly three weeks later.

From the earliest stages of the war, rugby was recognised as a means of training and developing soldiers. Edgar Mobbs ensured that it would be counted amongst the secret weapons used to improve the fighting spirit of Kitchener's Army by organising matches between the Barbarians and service teams, raising funds and boosting morale. Indeed, Admiral John Jellicoe, British Commander-in-Chief of the Grand Fleet later wrote: "Rugby Football, to my mind, above all games is the one which develops the qualities which go to make good fighting men."

Such proclamations were not lost on the British public and rugby in England enjoyed a resurgence after 1918 from grassroots level to the national side. Schools across England that had once played association rules football now switched to rugby union, with the understanding that this particular game developed the type of character that they wished to be associated with.

In 1919 rugby returned with a bang as some of the finest players in the world met to contest the King's Cup, a tournament that is often now feted as the first truly global tournament in rugby or any of the other football codes.

The process of demobilisation continued for several years and the Royal Navy in particular was active in repatriating soldiers to all corners of the world. Despite this, rugby clubs hastened to reconvene and some even arranged fixtures as early as 1918. By the summer of 1919 the RFU was ready to resume activity and so the Championship returned in 1920, while in 1921 King George V unveiled a war memorial plaque in Twickenham Stadium's West Stand that remains as a tribute to the fallen to this day.

RONALD POULTON PALMER

Born 12 September 1889 **Died** 5 May 1915
England career 1909-1914, 17 caps
Position Centre/Wing **Clubs** Oxford University,
Harlequins, Liverpool

Ronald William Poulton (later known as Poulton Palmer) was, by general acclaim, the most celebrated rugby player of his day. He was born in Headington, Oxford, one of five children of pro-Darwinian Professor Sir Edward Bagnall Poulton and his wife, Emily.

Often described as having a swerving running style, in his own words, he ran straight and trusted his swinging arms and hips to ensure that opponents would swerve out of his way. Either way, he made waves as a young rugby player and entertained all who saw him play.

He was first selected for England in 1909 at the age of 19. Later that year, he scored a record five tries in the Varsity Match for Oxford University, having already featured for Harlequins in the first game to be played at Twickenham.

A protege of Adrian Stoop, in 1910 he helped his club captain secure England's first outright Championship victory for 18 years. By 1913 he had developed into one of the most dangerous centres

in world rugby and was a standout performer in a campaign that delivered England her first Grand Slam.

However, 1914 was to truly be Poulton's season. Now England's captain, he put in three straight man of the match performances to deliver his side a Triple Crown. In his final game he contributed four of England's nine tries against France to secure a second consecutive Grand Slam.

An Oxford blue and a Harlequin, Poulton was traditional in one sense but a modernist in others. He argued in favour of broken-time payments for rugby players and decried the conditions of the working poor, volunteering much of his free time for lads' clubs in Manchester and Reading.

Later that year, Poulton enlisted with the Royal Berkshire Regiment. He did not hesitate to enlist but privately regretted that civilised nations had embraced the folly of war. In his letters home he expressed his dissatisfaction that peaceful solutions had been neither tested nor embraced.

He was shot and killed by sniper fire in a trench south of Ypres at the age of 25 on 5 May 1915. Purportedly amongst his last words were a lament that he "would never play at Twickenham again".

Remembered and mourned long after his death, in 2018, RFU Editorial Manager Patricia Mowbray arranged for soil from Twickenham to be taken to his grave in Belgium and soil from that grave to be buried beside the Twickenham pitch.

"A BEAUTIFUL PLAYER, A CHARACTER OF THE HIGHEST INTEGRITY, ONE OF THE LOVELIEST AND THE BEST"

AA Thomson, 1957

Above: Mementoes of a life dedicated to rugby and country

ANNIVERSARY TRIBUTE 2018

Above: As part of the RFU's First World War commemorations, former captain Lewis Moody took soil from Poulton Palmer's grave to Twickenham

THE KING'S CUP 1919

As with many communities in all participant nations, the Great War came at a heavy price to English rugby, 27 full internationals losing their lives, together with thousands of others at all levels of the game. Rugby was recognised early in the war as a means of conditioning and developing recruits and the armed forces, including its newest branch, the Royal Air Force, integrated rugby into its training and social provision.

At the end of 1918, British and Dominion forces were dispersed across Western Europe, amongst them the finest rugby players from around the world. Capitalising on this, the War Office organised the Inter-Services and Dominions Rugby Championship, a round-robin tournament that would come to be known as the King's Cup and is now recognised by many as the world's first footballing World Cup.

English players would compete as part of the Mother Country team, which consisted of British players drawn from the Army and Navy. The tournament would also feature the newly formed RAF side that would compete independently against the likes of New Zealand, Australia, South Africa and Canada.

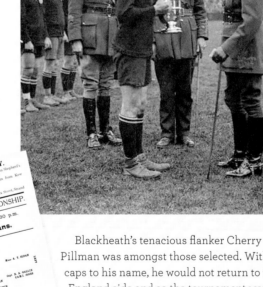

Blackheath's tenacious flanker Cherry Pillman was amongst those selected. With 18 caps to his name, he would not return to the England side and so the tournament would represent his final international honours. He had been injured in the penultimate match of the 1914 season and replaced by selectors with his brother Robert. Sadly, Robert had been killed during a

night raid in 1916 as the Battle of the Somme raged. Alongside Pillman were pre-war England internationals Bruno Brown, John Pym, Joe Brunton and Alex Sykes and a clutch of players who would earn call-ups when rugby resumed, including Harold Day, Reg Pickles and Barry Cumberlege. The RAF side included a young Wavell Wakefield, while the South African side featured Western Province-born Frank Mellish, who would earn six caps for England in 1920-21 and a further six for the Springboks between 1921 and 1924.

The tournament opened in Swansea on 1 March 1919 where New Zealand comfortably defeated the RAF 22-3. Seven days later, at Welford Road, the Mother Country narrowly defeated Australia by 6-3. Perhaps the biggest surprise of the tournament came on 29 March at Kingsholm, when the RAF beat Australia 7-3. The Australians were no pushovers, however, and proved as much by beating New Zealand, 6-5 in Bradford after the Kiwis had defeated the Mother Country in Inverleith 6-3.

With the round-robin complete, the Mother Country and New Zealand were in equal first place in the table having lost a game apiece. A play-off decider was arranged for Twickenham on 16 April. The score finished 9-3 to the New Zealanders, who duly won the competition. No trophy was awarded at this stage, however, but three days later a French side arrived at Twickenham to settle matters. Again New Zealand won, this time by 20-3 and King George V was happy to present the King's Cup to New Zealand captain Jimmy Ryan (*above left*).

Left: Wavell Wakefield's RAF shirt, worn in the King's Cup tournament

Above: Wakefield introduces the King to his team at an RAF match in 1921

ENGLAND ASCENDANT

JE 'Jenny' Greenwood was selected to captain England as Championship rugby resumed in January 1920. Alongside him in the pack were Blackheath's Frank Mellish and Laurence Merriam, as well as Harlequins' young marauding ball-carrier William Wavell Wakefield. In midfield, scrum half Cecil Kershaw of United Services would make his debut 10 years after his partner Harry Coverdale had won his own first cap.

They began their campaign with a 19-5 defeat, inflicted by a strong Welsh pack in Swansea. Two weeks later Dave Davies returned, and the fly half scored the only try in a win against France as he and Kershaw began a run of 14 unbeaten matches as one of England's most celebrated midfield partnerships. Debuts were given during the season to the lively Eddie Myers of Bradford, along with a crop of outstanding running forwards that included Gloucester's Tom Voyce, Northampton's Freddie Blakiston and Geoff Conway of Cambridge University.

England won their final two matches of the season and went into their golden jubilee year with a young side to be feared. The 1921 season began with 12 points in as many minutes against Wales at Twickenham. Old Merchant Taylors' towering second row Ronald Cove-Smith made his debut against Scotland and the Triple Crown was secured in March after two crushing victories against Ireland and Scotland in which England didn't concede a point. Against France, Lowe scored his third try in four matches and contributed two try-saving tackles to keep the score 10-6 in England's favour.

Davies was missing for the opening match in 1922 and so Wales demolished England in Cardiff 28-6. He returned for the following match and shored up the rest of the season in which England finished second in the table.

After narrowly defeating Wales in the 1923 season-opener, England met Ireland at Welford Road in front of a crowd of 25,000. They led 15-0

Above: The triumphant England team who won the Grand Slam in 1924 under the captaincy of Wavell Wakefield (third from right)

Right: Cecil Kershaw, Royal Navy submariner and England scrum half

at half-time and, although Ireland scored a converted try 12 minutes into the second half, comfortably reasserted their authority to record a decisive victory 23-5.

Scotland, captained by the Harlequin AL Gracie and with the future Olympic sprinter Eric Liddell as his wing man, had also defeated both Wales and Ireland. England made three changes for their meeting at Inverleith: the Aspatria full back Tom Holliday, Harold Locke in the centre and Blakiston in the back row. A fiercely competitive match was evenly balanced at half-time, with the score 3-3, a superb try by Smallwood on the left wing being matched by a try from the Scotland centre Teddy McLaren.

Scotland took the lead in the 65th minute but kept it for only five minutes as Locke intercepted a loose ball in his own half, ran for 50 yards before kicking ahead for Voyce to follow up and score. With the score at 6-6, all now hinged on the conversion attempt by Luddington. He was equal to the task and, although Scotland threw absolutely everything at England in the final 10 minutes, the English defence held out to secure their seventh Triple Crown.

For the final match, England travelled to Paris with an unchanged side. It was to be the final match for three of England's greatest backs, Lowe, Kershaw and Davies, the latter playing while actually on honeymoon in France.

The hosts took an early lead but a try by Wakefield after 20 minutes levelled the scores. It took England until the 75th minute to go ahead when Voyce intercepted a pass and sent Conway in for a try, converted by Luddington. In the final act of the match and his own international career, a left-footed drop goal by Davies confirmed victory and his fourth Grand Slam.

With the retirements of such luminaries England might have expected a season of transition in 1924. Instead, under the captaincy of Wakefield they became the first side in history to record a third Grand Slam in four seasons. The versatile Myers replaced Davies at fly half and the scampering Arthur Young made his debut at scrum half, while on the wing Percy Park's Carston Catcheside replaced Lowe.

Wakefield's leadership was inspirational, and the team gelled at once. Catcheside contributed two tries on his debut as England recorded their first win in Wales since 1913. At Ravenhill, Catcheside added a further brace, the second a length of the field score in the final minute to confirm a 14-3 victory.

Myers was in good form at Twickenham for the visit of France. Catcheside hurdled an opponent to score again and his fellow wing HP 'Jake' Jacob scored a hat-trick to help England to a 19-7 victory.

In the deciding fixture against Scotland at Twickenham, Wakefield and his outstanding pack were the difference and the captain himself drove the ball over the line to open the scoring. Myers then took the game away from Scotland with a dropped goal and try after the interval.

Above: Arthur Young, an outstanding scrum half, at 5ft 4in he was known as 'little man'

Below: England and Ireland compete at the lineout at a misty Twickenham in 1927

Not to be outdone, Catcheside then contributed his sixth try in four matches to give England a decisive 19-0 victory.

The midfield partnership of Myers and Young was broken up in 1925 but returned for a successful reprieve in the final game of the season against France. Wakefield played his final matches as captain in the unsuccessful 1926 season but returned in 1927, setting an English record of 31 caps that would stand for more than 40 years.

Cove-Smith took over as captain in 1928 and helped England to an 18-11 victory over the touring New South Wales side. Cambridge University's creative outside centre Carl Aarvold made his debut in the match and Bristol prop Sam Tucker, who had debuted as far back as 1922, scored the last of England's four tries.

Cove-Smith's side went on to carve a last hurrah for the 1920s by etching out another Grand Slam thanks, in part, to the weather in Cardiff and Dublin and to the tenacity of scrum half Young, involved in both English tries in the deciding match against Scotland. Cove-Smith therefore joined Davies and Lowe as one of only four English men's players to have achieved four Grand Slams.

UNDER THE CAPTAINCY OF WAKEFIELD ENGLAND BECAME THE FIRST SIDE IN HISTORY TO RECORD A THIRD GRAND SLAM IN FOUR SEASONS

WJA 'DAVE' DAVIES

Born 21 June 1890 **Died** 26 April 1967 **England career** 1913-1923, 22 caps
Position Fly Half **Clubs** Royal Navy, United Services

William John Abbott Davies, nicknamed 'Dave', was born in Pembroke in 1890. After studying at the Royal Naval Engineering College, Keyham, he progressed to become a Naval Constructor. A regular fly half for the United Services, he also played for Pembroke Dock Harlequins, RNC Greenwich and the Royal Navy.

He made his England debut in 1913, alongside winger Cyril Lowe, against the touring South Africans. Although Davies and England played well, South Africa would win and inflict England's first defeat at Twickenham. Remarkably, in an international career that spanned more than a decade, it would be the only time Davies tasted defeat.

The 1913 side became England's first Grand Slam winning side, under the leadership of Davies' Navy teammate Norman Wodehouse. The following year, Davies shared half back duties with another Navy teammate, Francis Oakeley, and a second Grand Slam was achieved.

During the First World War, Lieutenant Commander Davies served on board HMS *Iron Duke* at the Battle of Jutland, before transferring to the flagship of the Grand Fleet, HMS *Queen Elizabeth*.

When rugby resumed, Davies was initially unavailable for selection but returned during the 1920 season. By now he had matured into the complete footballer. His intelligent defensive kicking time and again relieved pressure on his side and, despite a small frame, he was consistently the most influential player on the field, commanding England's play from fly half. His return to the England side was quietly lamented by the Welsh side, who famously remarked, "when Davies plays, England win".

They were right. Davies was made captain in 1921 and promptly claimed his and England's third Grand Slam. He was absent again for parts of the 1922 season but returned to lead England to an unprecedented fourth Grand Slam in 1923.

The 1923 season would be his last and concluded in Paris. Davies signed off by landing a drop goal with the final kick of the game. A dumbfounded Wavell Wakefield later wrote of his belief that Davies had planned it that way. Unquestionably one of the finest players and fly halves England has ever produced, he probably had.

FAMOUS GAMES

ENGLAND 7
WALES 3

20 January 1923, Twickenham

England approached the opening match of their 1923 Five Nations Championship against Wales at Twickenham with confidence. They had won a third Grand Slam in 1921 and had finished their season strongly in 1922, with two wins and a draw after an early defeat to Wales in Cardiff.

There were two survivors from the pre-war era. On the right wing, Cyril Lowe of Blackheath was winning his 22nd consecutive cap, while captain and fly half, Dave Davies of the Royal Navy was winning his 19th cap alongside his Royal Navy scrum half, Cecil Kershaw. The skilful trio of Eddie Myers, Len Corbett and Alastair Smallwood completed a strong three-quarter line.

A formidable pack of forwards included Ronald Cove-Smith, Wavell Wakefield in his final year at Cambridge University, and Geoff Conway, Tom Voyce and Leo Price in the back row. There were two new caps from Devonport Services and the Royal Navy, full back Fred Gilbert at the advanced age of 39, and Bill Luddington in the front row.

In front of a crowd of 40,000, Wales gave England a hard fight after a sensational opening to the match vividly described by the *Yorkshire Post*: "England scored a try in the first 10 seconds. Wakefield

England captain Dave Davies introduces forward Reg Edwards to King George V prior to the match

kicked off, Price followed up, caught the ball, ran and took a drop at goal. The ball seemed to be going over the bar, but it was held up by the wind and swirled inwards, and as it fell it bounced away from (the Welsh full back) Rees, who perhaps was taken by surprise; at any rate, before he could recover Price had reached the ball again and touched it down by the post for a try."

Wales still had not touched the ball, but Conway missed the simple conversion. Wales

equalised 10 minutes later with a try and the score remained 3-3 in a tight match until the 70th minute when Smallwood, on the left wing, kicked a huge drop goal from near half-way to win the match for England. The route to another Grand Slam lay open.

England F Gilbert – CN Lowe, E Myers, LJ Corbett, AM Smallwood – WJA Davies*, CA Kershaw – ER Gardner, ER Edwards, WGE Luddington, R Cove-Smith, WW Wakefield, HL Price, GS Conway, AT Voyce

Wales J Rees – TAW Johnson, RA Cornish, A Jenkins, R Harding – JMC Lewis*, WJ Delahay – A Baker, DG Davies, G Michael, S Morris, T Parker, T Roberts, SG Thomas, JF Thompson

WAVELL WAKEFIELD

Born 10 March 1898 **Died** 12 August 1983 **England career** 1920-1927, 31 caps
Position Second Row/Back Row **Clubs** Harlequins, RAF, Cambridge University, Leicester

Born in Beckenham in 1898, William Wavell Wakefield grew up on the shores of Lake Windermere in Cumbria before attending Craig School, then Sedbergh.

There he developed as a combative running forward, with a distinctive head down hand-off that sent his opponents flying. Away from rugby, he was an amateur aeronaut. His uncle had built one of the first-ever aircraft capable of taking off and landing on water and the juvenile Wakefield became one of its first pilots.

On leaving school in 1916, Wakefield enlisted with the Royal Naval Air School where his unique skills were, initially, put to use as a flying instructor at Cranwell. Then, as the war entered its most critical phase, he was reassigned for special operations.

In August 1917, Squadron Commander Edward Harris Dunning had become the first man to land an aircraft on a moving ship. Five days later he was killed attempting the same manoeuvre. It was clear that only the most gifted pilots could perform the feat. In 1918, Wakefield arrived at Scapa Flow. Several days later he became only the third man to make a successful landing on a moving vessel. The following year, the newly founded Royal Air Force called on Wakefield to represent them in a tournament now remembered as the King's Cup. With his assistance, the RAF recorded impressive victories against both Canada and Australia.

He was selected for England in January 1920 to play against Wales in England's first competitive match since 1914. A month later, he scored his first international try and helped England finish equal top of the Championship table. The following year, as pack leader, he helped England to a Grand Slam. A second Grand Slam followed in 1923 (*Wakefield is pictured in action against France in that campaign, right*) before Wakefield progressed to captain the following season. The 1924 side that he led was one of the great England sides and, under his captaincy, they won a third Grand Slam in four seasons.

When he retired from international rugby in 1927, he did so with 31 caps, a record that would not be surpassed until the 1960s.

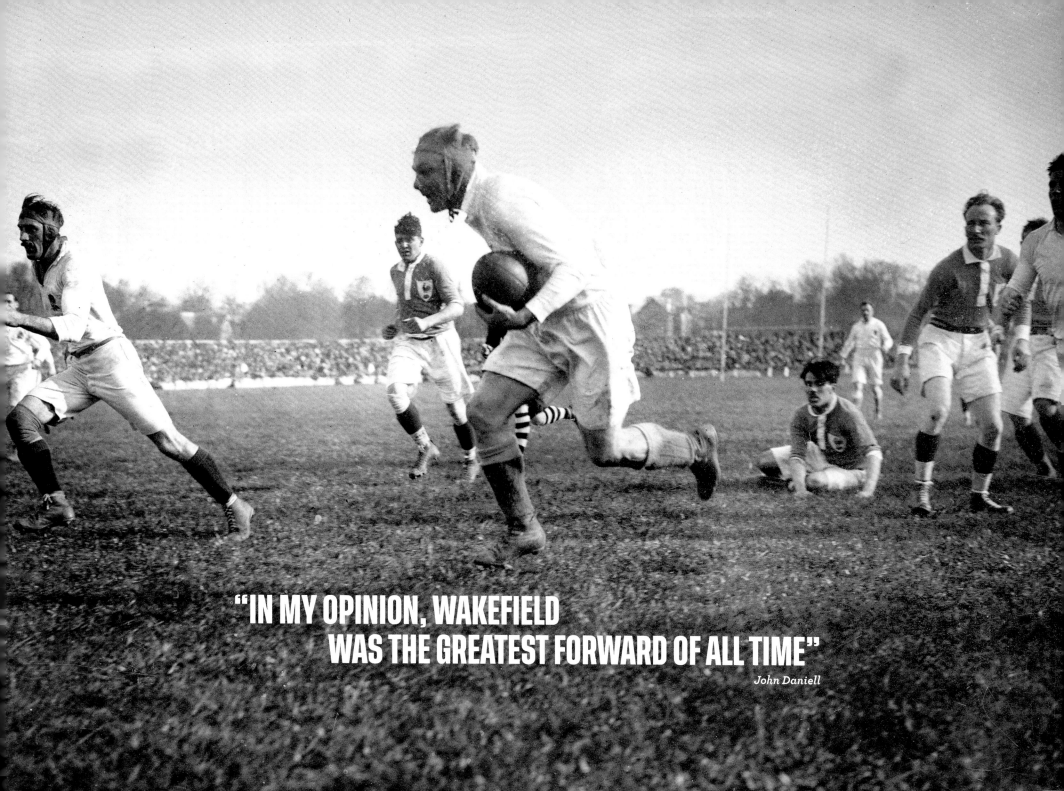

"IN MY OPINION, WAKEFIELD
WAS THE GREATEST FORWARD OF ALL TIME"

John Daniell

ENGLAND 11 NEW ZEALAND 17

3 January 1925, Twickenham

A record crowd, with thousands more locked outside, awaited New Zealand as they prepared to face England at Twickenham on 3 January 1925.

England picked four new caps. Captained by the great Harlequins forward Wavell Wakefield, the strength of the team clearly lay in forwards such as Sam Tucker, Ronald Cove-Smith, and the powerful back row of Freddie Blakiston, Geoff Conway and Tom Voyce, but a young backline that included Arthur Young and Len Corbett contained pace and verve.

A crowd of 60,000, including the Prince of Wales, eagerly awaited the appearance of the two teams and the chance to see such famed All Black three-quarters as the young Maori full back George Nepia, Bert Cooke, fly half Mark Nicholls and the lively Maori scrum half Jimmy Mill. Their pack was no less impressive, with the Brownlie brothers and captain Jock Richardson in the back row.

The match began sensationally. Within minutes, referee Albert Freethy warned both packs of forwards for over-vigorous play and, after issuing two such general warnings, sent off the All Black Cyril Brownlie for deliberately kicking an opponent. The All Blacks now had 70 minutes of the match to play with just 14 men.

Initially, England benefited. Cove-Smith drove over to score an unconverted try after 20 minutes but the All Blacks replied with unconverted tries from their wings Jack Steel and Snowy Svenson. A penalty goal by Nicholls secured their 9-3 half-time lead.

England started the second half strongly but the All Blacks soon found their rhythm. A powerful surge

Above: Two of the four tries scored by New Zealand during a truly incredible match at Twickenham

by Maurice Brownlie produced a third All Black try, converted by Nicholls. Parker then dived over in the corner to give the All Blacks a 14-point lead.

At last the English backs came into the game. Corbett drop kicked a penalty goal with 15 minutes to go, before Richard Hamilton-Wickes broke powerfully down the right wing, drew Nepia and passed to fly half Harold Kittermaster, who ran from half-way to score a thrilling try at the posts. Conway's conversion was the last scoring act of a sensational match as the All Blacks emerged weary but triumphant.

England JW Brough – RH Hamilton-Wickes, VG Davies, LJ Corbett, JC Gibbs – HJ Kittermaster, AT Young – ER Edwards, JS Tucker, RJ Hillard, R Cove-Smith, WW Wakefield*, AF Blakiston, GS Conway, AT Voyce

New Zealand G Nepia – J Steel, AE Cooke, KS Svenson – NP McGregor, MF Nicholls, JJ Mill – JH Parker – WR Irvine, Q Donald, MJ Brownlie, RR Masters, CJ Brownlie, J Richardson*, A White

Corner flags and the match jerseys of Wavell Wakefield and New Zealand's Maurice Brownlie

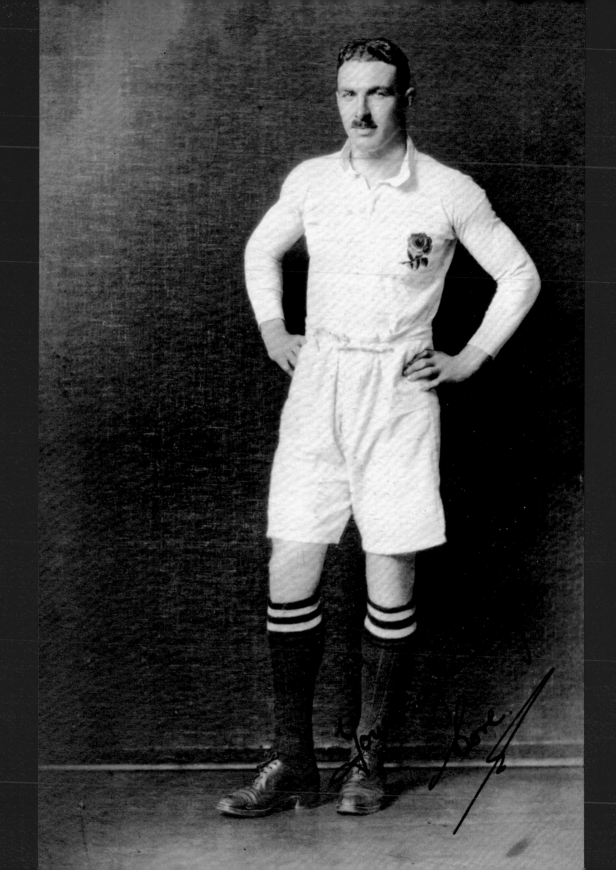

RONALD COVE-SMITH

Born 26 November 1899 **Died** 9 March 1988
England career 1921-1929, 29 caps
Position Front Row/Second Row
Clubs Cambridge University, Old Merchant Taylors',
King's College Hospital

Ronald Cove-Smith was one of the great forwards produced by England in the years following the First World War. He left Old Merchant Taylors' School in 1918 and enlisted in the Grenadier Guards. After his army service, he went up to Cambridge University to study medicine and made an immediate impression as an immensely strong scrummager and highly intelligent forward.

He played in the Varsity Matches for three years, alongside then and future England forwards Jenny Greenwood, Wavell Wakefield and Geoff Conway. He was capped twice by England in the 1921 Five Nations Championship. In the same year, he captained the Cambridge team during the first Varsity Match played at Twickenham.

He was recalled to the England side against Ireland in February 1922 and was first choice for England until the 1926 season. He was captain of England in his final seven matches, which included the 1928 Grand Slam and victory against the touring New South Wales Waratahs. In addition, he led the British & Irish Lions touring party in South Africa in 1924.

His 29 caps included 22 victories. Described as a "rampaging Mephistopheles" by correspondent Denzil Batchelor, he scored his only international try in the sensational match against the All Blacks in January 1925.

Following his retirement from rugby, he held numerous significant appointments in a distinguished medical career.

History in the making

THE HISTORY OF THE ROSE

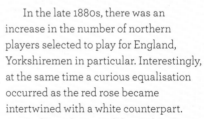

No records have survived documenting why the RFU selected the red rose as the emblem of English rugby, but an association with Rugby School is the likely explanation. The school's founder, Lawrence Sheriff, was grocer to Queen Elizabeth I. In 1559, Elizabeth granted Sheriff a coat of arms that featured the red rose of Lancaster, then and now a royal rose on account of the House of Lancaster's status as victor following the War of the Roses.

The rose naturally found its way into the Rugby School coat of arms (*above*) and

it is likely that the RFU administrators perceived a symbol that could represent the nation, as well as paying homage to the sport's scholarly origins.

In 1871 (*above*) no specifications were given in terms of the shape or size of their roses, and players were charged with sourcing and affixing them to their own jerseys for much of the 19th century. Consequently, we see numerous designs, the style often depending upon which shop, tailor or relative was charged with the duty of supplying the rose to an individual player.

In the late 1880s, there was an increase in the number of northern players selected to play for England, Yorkshiremen in particular. Interestingly, at the same time a curious equalisation occurred as the red rose became intertwined with a white counterpart.

In the early part of the 20th century, the red rose with a four-leafed stem began to achieve dominance (*above*). In 1920, matters were taken in hand and RFU Assistant Secretary Alf Wright was given the task of standardising the rose. Shortly thereafter, Wright

reached an agreement with the royal outfitters, Lillywhites, and from then on rectangular patches adorned with the standard rose were issued to England players on selection.

The RFU's 150 heritage rose (*above*) has an even longer pedigree. Presented in silver on the front of the burgundy velvet caps awarded to England players since 1871, it has remained unchanged throughout the 150 year history of English rugby and so it was to this rose that the RFU looked for inspiration when celebrating their sesquicentenary.

History in the making

THE ROWLAND HILL MEMORIAL GATES

The Rowland Hill Memorial Gates were unveiled in 1929 to commemorate the life of Sir George Rowland Hill, at the time rugby's most famous administrator, who had died the previous year.

Rowland Hill became Secretary of the RFU in 1881 and was at the helm in 1895 during the game's most turbulent period. In August of that year 22 clubs ceded from the RFU to establish a rival professional code in an event that has come to be known as the 'Great Schism'. The Northern Rugby Football Union would later become Rugby League.

Hill's strict adherence to the principles of amateurism ensured rugby union's status as an amateur sport for the next 100 years and, in 1927, he became the first person to be knighted for services to rugby union.

Throughout the 1920s, war memorials had been unveiled across the United Kingdom and Rowland Hill's memorial was unveiled at Twickenham in a similar spirit. Several hundred people turned out to lay wreaths in advance of a specially organised England & Wales v Scotland & Ireland match.

Initially, the gates were located in the south-west corner of the ground, over a track leading on to Whitton Road. The route had served as a farmer's access point to the land before the stadium had been built.

In 1970, a Coade stone lion was donated to the RFU by the Greater London Council. The lion was one of three that stood outside the Lion Brewery in Westminster since 1837. It was placed on top of the Rowland Hill Memorial Gate and in 1991 it was a given a gilded golden coat.

In 1995, the gates were removed and rebuilt in their present location outside the West Stand. Today the players walk through the gates on their way into their dressing rooms. Later in 1995 Gerald Laing's four players were installed on top of the four pillars.

In 2016 the two wooden oak gates either side of the central pillar were replaced by Harry Gray's Rose and Poppy Gates. These specially designed gates pay tribute to rugby players who became victims of war.

Far left: The Rowland Hill Memorial Gates are unveiled in 1929

Above: The English team arrive through the repositioned gates at Twickenham in February 2017

Left: Silhouetted against the sky are the statues added to the gate pillars in 1995

Spiritual home

There's no other stadium quite like it anywhere in the world. Steeped in the game's history and dripping with atmosphere and tradition, a day out at Twickenham – 'Rugby's HQ' – is always something to treasure

By Chris Hewett, rugby writer

Sometimes, when the stars are fully aligned and the sense of anticipation has been sharpening all week, you can smell a great game in the Twickenham air hours before kick-off. The pace quickens as you head down Whitton Road, the low hum of the arriving multitudes intensifying with every step until it achieves a kind of euphony. On matchday, the walk to the stadium – and away from it, if the right side has won – can be as joyous as the rugby itself.

It was once the case that almost all the great rugby cathedrals of the world offered this wrap-around experience, with the before and after contributing just as much as the bit in the middle. But if the home nations have managed to retain much of the seductive spirit of old, while embracing the commercial imperatives of professionalism, can the same be said of major rugby countries further afield?

The French outgrew Parc des Princes, that throbbingly hostile venue on the edge of the Bois de Boulogne, and headed out of arrondissement Paris to Stade de France, a new home with almost twice the capacity. The

Twickenham is one of the
vanishingly few fixed points in
an ever-changing union world

Twickenham as
it was in 1976. It
has undergone a
startling series of
transformations since,
but its inspirational
atmosphere remains
undimmed

Always a discerning audience, the Twickenham faithful

Delirious and never-to-be repeated scenes as Will Carling is chaired from the pitch after England claim the Grand Slam at Twickenham in 1991

is now in the age of pre-match aeronautics, cacophonous fireworks and operatic renditions of unashamedly patriotic songs and arias.

Talking of tickets, it was once just about possible to do without them, if only because the old-style standing areas gave determined interlopers somewhere to hide. Ahead of the Grand Slam match with France in 1991, more than a decade after Bill Beaumont had led a gnarled band of largely northern brethren to a first Championship clean sweep in 23 years (England supporters were closely acquainted with the virtue of patience in those times), your essayist wangled his way into the ground by taking advantage of an elderly turnstile operator who was too engrossed in his bacon sandwich to notice that the 'ticket' produced for the briefest of inspections was in fact a packet of seeds. A variety of garden pea rings a distant bell.

The next stage of the operation, a cloak-and-dagger scuttle onto the terracing near the players' tunnel, was completed with a minimum of fuss and, even though the anthems were still two hours distant, the crush and claustrophobia caused by the arrival of genuine ticket-holders – how dare they barge their way in with such cavalier disregard for the comfort of those who had no right to be there? – had the effect of annihilating time. It is impossible to avoid hearty conversation with people who are standing on your toes.

Many of those in the immediate proximity were French – as naturally as night following day, one of them was armed with a cockerel – and when Philippe Saint-André completed the wondrous 'try from nowhere' after visionary contributions from Pierre Berbizier, Serge Blanco, Jean-Baptiste Lafond, Philippe Sella and Didier Camberabero, they were transported to the highest circle of heaven. Joined, it is important to add, by the England supporters in their immediate vicinity. There are moments in rugby when the breathtaking brilliance of the opposition makes a mockery of mere partisanship. This was one of them.

The third and last of the French tries, scored by Franck Mesnel, was another masterpiece, albeit on a slightly smaller canvas, and in any other set of circumstances the home crowd would have applauded their visitors all the way from field to airport and on to Paris. But on this day of all days, with England surviving the onslaught by hook or by crook, they

Italians likewise. The strolls from Piazza del Popolo to Stadio Flaminio, ended in 2011, replaced by tram or bus journeys to Stadio Olimpico.

Twickenham is one of the vanishingly few fixed points in an ever-changing union world. It hasn't even fiddled around with its name. Rugby Football Union members in charge of such matters have strengthened its position at the heart of the sport and, while BA became the stadium's first principal partner, the name remained as it always has been. Twickers is the Lord's of the union game. Everyone knows the T-word, everyone is conscious of the weight of its history and everyone wants to play there.

Only the lucky few get to do the latter, so the rest of us must find our salvation where we can. Happily, this has rarely been too much of a challenge (assuming you have access to a ticket) for Twickenham has always generated a sense of occasion. This was as true back in the day, when the only 'event manager' who mattered a jot was the referee, as it

had other matters to address, primarily the staging of what would now be described, po-facedly, as a 'pitch invasion' and the hoisting of various white-shirted winners towards the afternoon sky. Will Carling was carried from the field on the shoulders of strangers, as were Rob Andrew and Rory Underwood, while more substantial citizens, like Paul Ackford and Wade Dooley, were left to their own devices. Always a discerning audience, the Twickenham faithful.

Such scenes from the last century, and from a very different sporting epoch, may never be repeated. There are no 'invasions' now – solitary streakers barely get a look-in, let alone celebrating supporters by the thousand – and the idea of sneaking ticketless into an all-seater stadium and staying there is for the birds. Which is as it should be. You cannot congratulate the RFU on taking a bold stand against the scalpers and touters lurking in the surrounding streets and then complain about the relentless efficiency of the Twickenham security operation.

To be sure, there are those who long for the old days of turnstile operators asleep on the job and hamper lunches in the West Car Park, washed down by enough Champers and Chablis to leave entire England packs crying for mercy. But if there is now a different buzz to the pre-and-post-match Twickenham scene – more tented village than luxury car boot sale; more public space than public school – it is in keeping with the spirit of the age. For good or ill, but overwhelmingly for good, professionalism opened up a closed society. Rugby is still a family, which is why affiliated clubs receive tickets for every international. It's just that the family has grown, as families are meant to do.

From memory, that 1991 contest in mid-March unfolded in gloomy, unspring-like weather – the kind of conditions more associated with Tests played in the late autumn window, like the eye-wateringly physical and wholly magnificent match between England and New Zealand in 2005. It is no criticism of the national team's traditionally forward-dominated style that they are so often at their most formidable in the Twickenham murk. It suits their demeanour somehow, just as bristling herds of Springboks seem most intimidating on the unforgiving surfaces of Johannesburg or Pretoria; the Wallabies are most dangerous on the fast going in Brisbane; the Scots appear especially sharp-elbowed and combative when the conditions in Edinburgh are close to freezing; and the All Blacks seem even less beatable than usual when the weather turns grim in Auckland or Christchurch.

When the great outside centre Tana Umaga led the New Zealanders onto the Twickenham pitch in November 2005, just as the afternoon light was failing, there was a feeling amongst the spectators that England, who had been on a hard road since the World Cup triumph two years previously, might be ready to turn a corner. An immediate try from Martin Corry, the England captain, reinforced them in that view and the noise, already unusually loud, grew decibel by decibel into a deep and prolonged roar.

In the event, the All Blacks sneaked home by four points, largely thanks to Umaga's warrior spirit and cold-eyed ferocity in the face of considerable adversity. But the crowd, disappointed but far from distraught, knew they had watched a real Test – the kind of match Twickenham audiences from the dim and distant amateur eras of Wavell Wakefield, Prince Obolensky and Richard Sharp would have understood and enjoyed.

Those who watched England in their Grand Slam campaigns of the 1920s, a golden decade if ever there was one, would routinely have spotted the likes of Wakefield and Cyril Lowe and Ronald Cove-Smith arriving at the stadium on foot, boots in hand. Spool forward to the Stuart Lancaster years between 2011 and 2015 and what do we see? Chris Robshaw, Owen Farrell and company making their way on foot through the West Car Park, cheered every step of the way by the white-shirted masses.

Which just goes to show that the more things change at Twickenham, the more things stay warmly familiar, if not quite the same. The shock of the new is easier to absorb when the old connections survive intact.

The remarkable modern face of Twickenham prior to England taking on Wales in 2019

5

IN SERVICE

1930-1959

The Waterloo wing forward Joe Periton was named as captain ahead of England's first match of the 1930 season, against Wales in Cardiff, while veteran Bristol hooker Sam Tucker was called up as an eleventh-hour replacement. The match was the first for the successful Old Millhillians half back pairing of Roger Spong and Wilf Sobey, who controlled proceedings as two tries from Harlequin Jim Reeve propelled England to an 11-3 victory.

Dropped goals were worth more than tries until 1948 and England lost narrowly in Dublin 4-3 after Ireland's dropped goal outpointed a try from Blackheath wing Tony Novis. Tucker took over the captaincy against France, and Sobey created two tries – the first grounded by Reeve, the second by Periton – to give England an 11-5 victory. The final game of the season was a scoreless draw with Scotland and results elsewhere meant that Tucker and England took the Championship.

Carl Aarvold returned in 1931 and was made captain after a home defeat to Ireland and moved to inside centre. John Tallent came into the side and scored three tries in the final two matches of the season, both of which were lost, and England ended the season without a win for the first time since 1905.

France had beaten England for the first time in 1927 and came within a match of winning the Championship in 1930. Their progress was checked at the end of the 1930-31 season when an old problem reared its head. Charges of professionalism within French rugby led to ties being cut between France and the home unions and for the remainder of the decade the Championship reverted to the Home Nations format of old.

The 1932 season began with a visit from one of the great South African sides. Benny Osler's Springboks defeated England 7-0 at Twickenham after an enormous drop goal from full back Gerry Brand. England then lost their opening game to Wales, while Leicester's

Previous pages: England captain Eric Evans is chaired off by his teammates after their 16-3 win over Scotland in 1957

Above: The Radio Times prior to England v Wales, 1933

Right: Joe Kendrew, who captained England in 1935, and wing Hal Sever, who debuted in 1936 (far right)

powerful scrum half Bernard Gadney made his debut against Ireland. Northampton prop Ray Longland came in against Scotland and England recovered strongly to earn a share of the Championship with Ireland and Wales.

In the opening match of the 1933 season, Wales finally did what they had not managed to do since 1910 and beat England at Twickenham, with a promising side that included a young Vivian Jenkins at full back. Novis came in as captain to help defeat Ireland but England lost to Scotland in Murrayfield.

After just four caps, Gadney became captain in 1934 and seven players were handed their debuts in the opening match at Cardiff Arms Park. Among them were two Oxford University backs in the shape of creative centre Peter Cranmer and South African international cricketer and trainee medical practitioner HG 'Tuppy' Owen-Smith at full back. On the wing, Waterloo's Graham Meikle started his international career with a bang by scoring two tries to help England to a 9-0 win.

Ireland took an early lead in England's next match but clever play by Cranmer allowed Liverpool's Henry Fry to bring the scores level. A surging run from deep by Owen-Smith then culminated in a second try for Fry before Meikle added a third, both converted by Bristol's Gordon Gregory. England were one step away from a Triple Crown.

THE RETURN OF THE HOME NATIONS

CHARGES OF PROFESSIONALISM WITHIN FRENCH RUGBY LED TO TIES BEING CUT BETWEEN FRANCE AND THE HOME UNIONS AND THE CHAMPIONSHIP REVERTED TO THE HOME NATIONS FORMAT OF OLD

Joe Kendrew was recalled to shore up the English pack against Scotland and a tight game was settled with a late try from Lewis Booth. Scotland had taken the lead in the first half before Meikle had finished off a move by Fry and Bath's RA 'Gerry' Gerrard. England had claimed their first Triple Crown since 1928.

Kendrew captained England twice in 1935, before Gadney was reinstated for the Scotland match and the return of the All Blacks after 11 years. The match, in which England ran out comfortable 13-0 winners, saw the try-scoring debuts of wings Alexander Obolensky from Oxford University, and Hal Sever of Sale.

Mixed fortunes attended Gadney's side for the remainder of the season. Influential Waterloo hooker Harry Toft made his debut in the final match against Scotland in which a slightly superior English scrum allowed them to avoid finishing bottom of the table.

Owen-Smith became captain in 1937 with a back division that included Sever, Cranmer and Peter Candler of St Bart's Hospital. Another medical practitioner, Tommy Kemp, would pull the strings from fly half while Robin Prescott of Harlequins joined Toft and Longland in the front row.

An intensely physical match against Wales at Twickenham was won by an opportunist dropped goal from Sever, which outpointed Wales' solitary try as England won 4-3.

The following match against Ireland involved another narrow margin but in entirely different circumstances. Harlequin Arthur Butler scored first but Ireland replied with two tries from FG Moran to lead 8-3. A penalty from Cranmer followed and with only six minutes remaining the brilliant Sever evaded the Irish defence to score in the corner and give England a 9-8 win.

Above: Sealing the Triple Crown against Scotland in 1934

Below: Stylish centre Peter Cranmer, who captained England in 1938

The Triple Crown would be decided at Murrayfield, a ground on which England had yet to win since the opening game in 1925. Good work from Candler and Sever fed Jimmy Unwin of Rosslyn Park who scored on his debut. In the second half Sever again stretched England's lead to 6-0. Scotland could only manage a penalty and for the second time in five seasons England were Triple Crown champions.

Cranmer became captain in 1938 as Owen-Smith was replaced by another South African Harlequin in HD 'Trilby' Freakes. Sever got on the scoresheet for the fourth successive match but England lost in Cardiff. A remarkable seven tries in Dublin saw off Ireland 36-14 to give an outside chance of retaining the Championship against Scotland at Twickenham.

The match was to be a historic occasion, the very first Test match to be broadcast live on television. In a high-scoring encounter, England were swept away by a rampant Scotland – under the inspired leadership of Robert Wilson Shaw – 21-16.

Toft became captain in 1939 and more than half the starting XV were replaced. England won two from three and shared the final Championship before the Second World War with Ireland and Wales.

THE OFFICIAL LINE

The Rugby Football Union has chosen more than 90 referees to officiate at major internationals since 1871. Initially, there were two umpires, one from each country, but a single official was chosen to referee the encounter between England and Ireland at The Oval in February 1875. He was former international **Arthur Guillemard** (*above*) who was refereeing the first of his six matches.

In the early years, referees had close connections to the RFU. **Algernon Rutter**, the first RFU President in 1871, was the second English referee in 1876 and **George Rowland Hill**, long-serving Secretary and future President, took charge of 11 matches in a 10-year period from 1883. **William 'Billy' Williams**, a future Vice-President, who played a decisive role in the purchase of Twickenham, refereed 12 internationals between 1904 and 1913.

Frank Potter-Irwin controlled eight matches either side of the First World War and refereed the Olympic Final between Cornwall and Australia at the White City in 1908. **James 'Bim' Baxter** played three times for England in 1900 and refereed nine internationals between 1913 and 1925. Elected President of the RFU in 1926-27, he was Manager of the British & Irish Lions tour of Australasia in 1930.

Between the wars, **Barry Cumberlege** (*right*) refereed a record 16 internationals after winning eight caps as England's full back in 1920-21. **Cyril Gadney**, brother of scrum half Bernard Gadney, refereed 15 internationals and six Varsity Matches between 1935 and 1948. He too was President of the

RFU in 1962-63 and a member of the International Board from 1965 to 1971.

From 1947 onwards, there have been numerous distinguished English international referees. **Tom Pearce** refereed 11 internationals between 1948 and 1952 and was an England selector for many years. **Dr Norman Parkes** refereed 10 internationals between 1958 and 1962, including four matches in his first season.

In the 1970s, **Roger Quittenton** and **Air Commodore GC 'Larry' Lamb** became controversial figures as their decisions when refereeing 18 and 11 internationals respectively became subject to increasing TV analysis. **RF 'Johnny' Johnson** replaced injured

French referee **Robert Calmet** in the 1970 Wales match at Twickenham and refereed 12 matches.

In the 1980s, **Fred Howard**, a schoolmaster by profession, refereed 20 internationals between 1984 and 1992, including the 1987 and 1991 Rugby World Cups. **Tony Spreadbury** was one of the first full-time professional rugby referees and officiated at the 2003 and 2007 Rugby World Cups. **Ed Morrison** officiated in 30 major internationals between 1991 and 2000, including three Rugby World Cups. He refereed the 1995 Rugby World Cup Final and became England's first professional referee in 1998.

Chris White, a Gloucester Society referee, took charge of more than 40 major internationals between 1998 and 2009 and his experience included 10 matches at three Rugby World Cups and three European Cup Finals.

The doyen of contemporary referees has been **Wayne Barnes**, a serving barrister. He has taken charge of more than 80 internationals, including 21 Rugby World Cup matches, and has also refereed a record number of English Premiership rugby matches.

FAMOUS GAMES

ENGLAND 13 NEW ZEALAND 0

4 January 1936, Twickenham

The New Zealand touring party, under the captaincy of Jack Manchester, arrived in the United Kingdom in the autumn of 1935.

The selected England side was based on a strong and powerful pack, with some exciting runners in the backline. The South African-born full back 'Tuppy' Owen-Smith was a superb sportsman who subsequently played cricket for South Africa. On the wings were Sale's Hal Sever and the flamboyant Russian Prince Alexander Obolensky from Oxford University. The experienced centres RA 'Gerry' Gerrard and Peter Cranmer provided the core of the back line. The side was captained by the Leicester scrum half Bernard Gadney in his ninth international. The English pack was anchored by a formidable front row of prop Douglas Kendrew and hooker Edward Nicholson of Leicester, with Ray Longland of Northampton on the other side of the scrum. Charles 'Marine' Webb from the Royal Navy in the second row and Bill Weston from Northampton at wing forward brought additional strength.

The match began evenly, in front of a crowd of 70,000 spectators, and the All Blacks came close to opening

England clear their lines after another All Black attack

the scoring. It soon became clear that England were the better side and after 20 minutes Obolensky, with a scorching run down the right wing, scored his first try, which went unconverted. Nearly 20 minutes later, just before half-time, Obolensky scored his historic second try, a superb cross-field run of around 40 yards that completely wrong-footed the All Black defence and ended with the Prince crossing the line untouched on the left-hand-side of the field. Gerrard missed the conversion, but England reached half-time with a 6-0 lead.

In the second half, England managed to halt several All Black attacks before extending their lead to 10-0 through a drop goal by Cranmer. With about 20 minutes to go the match was decided by a third English try,

scored by the left wing Sever, who ran 35 yards after being put through a gap by Cranmer. The conversion was missed but England's lead was now 13-0 and the hosts saw out the rest of the match to earn a memorable win.

England HG Owen-Smith – A Obolensky, P Cranmer, RA Gerrard, HS Sever – PL Candler, BC Gadney* – RJ Longland, ES Nicholson, DA Kendrew – AJ Clarke, CSH Webb – EA Hamilton-Hill, PE Dunkley, WH Weston

New Zealand GDM Gilbert – NA Mitchell, CJ Oliver, THC Caughey, N Ball – EWT Tindill, MMN Corner – J Hore, WE Hadley, A Lambourn – ST Reid, RR King – JE Manchester*, A Mahoney, HF McLean

The England Greats

ALEXANDER OBOLENSKY

Born 17 February 1916 **Died** 29 March 1940 **England career** 1936, 4 caps
Position Wing **Club** Oxford University

Born of Russian nobility, Prince Alexander Obolensky and his family fled Russia to escape persecution at the hands of the Bolsheviks in the aftermath of the Russian Revolution. After growing up in north London, he attended Oxford University and gained a blue in 1935.

An instinctive runner and finisher, he had a pair of lightweight boots made that enhanced his speed from the wing. In 1936, aged 19, he was controversially selected for England. On taking the field he was questioned on his eligibility by none other than the Prince of Wales himself. He answered with his performance.

The visitors that day for only the second time at Twickenham were New Zealand. On 20 minutes Obolensky ran 40 yards on the outside to score in the north-east corner. Nearly twenty minutes later Peter Cranmer fed him the ball on the inside and Obolensky ran diagonally to the opposite corner, wrong-footing three defenders for one of Twickenham's most memorable scores. England, who had never beaten the All Blacks, eventually won 13-0 and Obolensky's sensational performance was reported on newsreels around the world.

Later that year, he toured South America with a British Isles team. He played only four times for England before war was declared. Answering the call of his adopted nation, he enlisted with the Royal Air Force Auxiliary and tragically became the first English international to lose his life to the conflict while landing a Hawker Hurricane Mark I during a training accident in Suffolk in 1940. He was just 24.

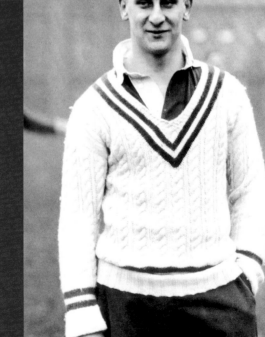

"HIS PLAY, HIS WORK, HIS DEATH WERE ON THE WING" *Ivor Brown*

THE SECOND WORLD WAR

After war was declared in 1939, English rugby and the English rugby community mobilised in support of the war effort. As in 1914, international players enlisted and some, such as Norman Wodehouse and Wavell Wakefield, would serve in both conflicts.

Prince Alexander Obolensky became the first English international player to lose his life while serving with the Royal Air Force Auxiliary in 1940. He would be joined by 13 others before the war ended, Wodehouse amongst them. Bill Luddington, a member of Wakefield's indomitable pack, was killed on board HMS *Illustrious*. Hubert Freakes and Derek Teden were both killed in the service of the RAF, while Henry Rew and Ronald Gerrard lost their lives while serving with the land forces in North Africa.

CC 'Kit' Tanner, who had made his debut as a wing in 1930, served aboard HMS *Fiji* as chaplain. When his ship was hit and eventually sunk by Stukas in 1941, he spent more than four hours rescuing an estimated 30 people from the water. He collapsed and died from his exertions shortly after and was awarded the Albert Cross posthumously.

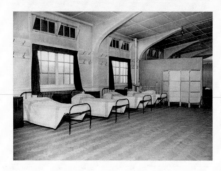

At home, Twickenham Stadium was requisitioned by the War Office and put into service as a civil defence depot. The National Fire Service stored vehicles that would combat the blitz underneath the South Terrace. The West Stand was converted into a decontamination centre (*below left*) to be used in the event of a chemical attack on London. Bags of swarf (*left*) were stored on the terraces of the North Stand to be used in the construction of ships, planes and bombs. All available storage space was used, even under the Rowland Hill Memorial gates, then in the south-west corner (*below right*).

While many of England's players went overseas to serve, another served at home. RFU Secretary Sidney Coopper had survived shipwreck in 1916 and now kept the home fires burning at HQ until the war was over.

In 1944, a German V-1 bomb detonated a stone's throw from the ground, the blast scorching the side of the West Stand. At the end of the conflict the stadium lay in disrepair, the roofs of the stands leaking through dozens of holes created by the 3.7in shells used to defend London during the Blitz.

Repaired flak holes are clearly visible in the roofs of the stands at Twickenham after the war. The face of the main West Stand entrance was also scorched by a bomb blast

NORMAN WODEHOUSE

Born 18 May 1887 **Died** 4 July 1941
England career 1910-1913, 14 caps
Position Forward
Clubs Royal Navy, United Services

Norman Wodehouse was a career naval officer who played in the forwards for the United Services, the Royal Navy, Hampshire and England in the years leading up to the First World War.

He appeared for the Royal Navy against the Army from 1907 to 1914 and captained the Navy in 1912 and 1913. He played in the 1909-10 international trial matches and made his England debut later that season against France at the Parc des Princes.

He played in 13 consecutive international matches over the next three seasons, scoring tries against France and Scotland in 1911. He captained England against France in 1912 and throughout the 1913 season, in which England won their first ever Grand Slam, but lost narrowly to the redoubtable South African touring team.

Wodehouse's leadership was highly rated, and he was described by WJA 'Dave' Davies as "another captain from the scrum who always impressed me. His influence was only equalled by a first-rate knowledge of the game".

His subsequent naval career was distinguished. He fought and was decorated at the Battle of Jutland in 1916. He was appointed aide-de-camp to King George VI, then Commander of the Royal Naval College from 1931 to 1934, and Rear Admiral, Gibraltar, in 1939.

He retired from the service in May 1940 but was recalled as a Convoy Commodore with the rank of Vice Admiral in June 1941. He was drowned when one of the ships in his convoy was sunk off the Canary Islands by a German U-boat on 4 July 1941.

THE VICTORY INTERNATIONALS

With flak holes in the roofs of the stands and an unsafe Upper West Stand, Twickenham found itself in an understandable state of disrepair when the war ended in 1945. Nonetheless, the rugby and wider community were eager to return to the way of life that they had fought to defend and so the Victory Internationals began with the visit of the New Zealand Army Touring Side (*below*) on 24 November 1945, in front of a reduced crowd of 27,300 spectators.

With so many players unavailable, caps were not awarded but the England XV included former internationals Jack Heaton and Harold Wheatley, as well as future internationals such as Harlequins fly half Nim Hall. The Kiwis, captained by Charlie Saxton, were formidable and took the first match 18-3.

The following January, the England XV travelled to Cardiff to play a Wales XV. Full international

England face Scotland for the first time after the war

wing Dickie Guest came into the side and Micky Steele-Bodger was added to the back row, alongside his Cambridge University teammate Eric Bole. In an occasionally dazzling performance, that included two tries from Guest, England ran out 25-13 winners.

Back row forward Joe Mycock was selected to face Ireland in Dublin and England recorded a 14-6 victory over a youthful Irish side. As more men returned from service, each team steadily improved. In February, a Wales side that included such talents as Bleddyn Williams and Haydn Tanner defeated the England XV 3-0 at Twickenham.

With the consent of the War Damage Commission, essential works to make good the damaged Upper West Stand at Twickenham were begun and more than 50,000 turned out to greet the Scotland XV in March (*above*). Having already lost twice at home, things did not look promising at half-time, with Scotland leading 8-0. In the second half, England roared back with a try from Old Cranleighan wing Bob Carr and smart kicking from Heaton

to take the game 12-8. Scotland won the return leg convincingly at Murrayfield in April and, having beaten the New Zealand Army Touring Side already, finished top of the Victory International table. The following year, for the first time since 1931, the Five Nations Championship would reconvene.

THE POST-WAR YEARS

Service personnel in the crowd at Twickenham for the England v New Zealand Expeditionary Forces match in November 1945

In early 1945, a French Services XV played a match against British Empire Forces in Richmond. It was the first time a representative French team had played in Great Britain since 1931 and foreshadowed the re-admittance of France into the Championship, which resumed in 1947.

Fourteen players would make their debuts in England's opening match against Wales. These included fly half Nim Hall, captain Joe Mycock and Micky Steele-Bodger, all having cut their teeth in the Victory Internationals. Northampton's Don White and Coventry's Harry Walker came into the pack. The only cap to have played before the war was nimble Waterloo wing Dickie Guest. White scored England's only try of the match and the scores were level until Hall's dropped goal settled matters 9-6 in England's favour.

Jack Heaton returned against Ireland, but England were crushed 22-0. A frozen Twickenham pitch caused four players to leave the field injured against Scotland, but England won and a narrow victory over France in the final game gave them a share of the Championship with Wales.

Tommy Kemp returned in 1948 and Mycock's Sale teammate Eric Evans was given his debut against the visiting Wallabies, who defeated England 11-0 thanks to an inspired Col Windon. Both Sale men were left out for the rest of the season and England didn't win a single Championship match.

The poor run stretched into 1949 but England rallied to record home wins against France and Scotland under the leadership of Coventry's Ivor Preece. England's only win in 1950 was a significant one against an Irish side that were back-to-back champions and included Karl Mullen and Jackie Kyle.

England lost their next five matches, the last of which represented France's first win at Twickenham. A narrow win against Scotland in 1951 was not enough to avoid finishing bottom of the table for the second consecutive year.

In 1952, England recalled several players including White, whose physicality was not to everyone's taste but whose effectiveness was not in question, and Hall who returned as captain. Evans had returned to the side the previous year alongside Wasp Bob Stirling and versatile forward John Kendall-Carpenter of Penzance & Newlyn. Wasps' powerful wing Ted Woodward would also make his debut.

Improved showings resulted in narrow defeats to both South Africa and Cliff Morgan's Wales, before a resounding four-try victory over Scotland. The death of King George VI delayed the match against Ireland, but England won narrowly at Twickenham and again in Paris to finish second in the table.

Hall moved to full back in 1953 to accommodate Liverpool's Martin Regan at fly half but it was England's settled and industrious pack that was to be their chief asset. A brilliant performance in Cardiff and a try by Lew Cannell delivered an 8-3 victory, their first in Wales since 1947. An end-to-end match in Dublin finished 9-9 after a try by Evans and two penalties from Hall.

Northampton's Jeff Butterfield made a try-scoring debut against France and additional tries from Evans and Woodward gave England an 11-0 victory. England made certain of a first outright Championship since 1937 with a resounding 26-8 win against underperforming Scotland.

Reg Higgins and DL 'Sandy' Sanders came into the pack in 1954 and England maintained their strong form by beating Wales 9-6 before facing the visiting All-Blacks. With painful memories of 1936 still fresh, New Zealand executed a cautious game plan that delivered them victory by a single goal.

First-half tries from Butterfield and Regan helped England to a 14-3 victory against Ireland and a first Triple Crown since 1937 was secured with a second consecutive win at Murrayfield. A clean sweep was denied by Jean Prat's brilliant side, who beat the visitors 11-3, at Stade Colombes as England made do with a shared Championship with France and Wales.

George Hastings made his debut in 1955 but a disappointing campaign followed. With some blaming England's inconsistency on a lack of leadership, Evans returned to the side as captain in 1956 at the age of 34.

Alongside Evans was Northampton's Ron Jacobs. Second rows David Marques and John Currie arrived in the vanguard of a group of international-class Oxford and Cambridge students that included Peter Robbins and later Phil Horrocks-Taylor.

Also making their debuts were fast-passing scrum half Dickie Jeeps, who had shone over the summer with the British & Irish Lions, and Coventry's elusive wing Peter Jackson who, along with Butterfield, gave the side significant attacking potency.

The new-look side fell to an 8-3 home defeat to Wales in their opening match but clicked against Ireland, with Butterfield, Jackson and captain Evans all scoring tries in an impressive 20-0 victory. Sound kicking by Currie helped England to an 11-6 victory against Scotland, before France recorded their third consecutive win against the visitors 14-9.

Above: Wing Peter Jackson, nicknamed 'Nijinsky' for his agile footwork

Below: The English forwards hold back France en route to the Grand Slam in 1957

Only one change was made at the start of the 1957 season, with Harlequin Ricky Bartlett starting at fly half. Wales remained the team to beat and a narrow 3-0 victory in Cardiff, thanks to a Fenwick Allison penalty, confirmed England as contenders.

The English pack came out on top in Dublin, despite England not having won there since 1938. Marques was dominant in the lineout and England won 6-0 with a try from Jackson. Two more tries for Jackson against France and a third for Evans meant England won 9-5 to set up a deciding match with Scotland. Much improved on recent years, the Scots were no match for England who won 16-3 and recorded their first Grand Slam since 1928.

Australia were the visitors in February 1958 and England won a close, physical contest 9-6 in muddy conditions, after an astonishing try in the corner by Jackson. Victories against Ireland and France followed an earlier draw with Wales to keep England in the hunt for the Championship. A late penalty from Hastings in a draw against Scotland was enough to win it outright after France beat Wales.

Butterfield became captain in 1959 after Evans' glittering career came to an end with 30 caps, but it was France who saw out the decade as champions for the first time.

ENGLAND MADE CERTAIN OF A FIRST OUTRIGHT CHAMPIONSHIP SINCE 1937 WITH A RESOUNDING 26-8 WIN AGAINST UNDERPERFORMING SCOTLAND

The England Greats
ERIC EVANS

Born 1 February 1921 **Died** 12 January 1991 **England career** 1948-1958, 30 caps
Position Prop/Hooker **Club** Sale

Schoolteacher Eric Evans was a very mobile hooker and an inspirational England captain who won 30 caps and scored five tries in the years following the Second World War.

Educated at Audenshaw Grammar School and Loughborough College, he won his first cap for England as a prop at Twickenham against the touring Wallabies in 1948. He shifted position and won his second cap at hooker against Wales in 1950. He became England's regular hooker from the 1951 Championship until his retirement from international rugby, aged 37, at the end of the 1958 season. He set a new record of 29 caps as England hooker, surpassing the previous tally of 27 caps set by Sam Tucker in the 1920s.

Appointed England captain in 1956, he equalled the national record of 13 matches as captain set by Wavell Wakefield and NM 'Nim' Hall. He led England to a Grand Slam in 1957, a last-minute victory over the touring 1957-58 Wallabies a decade after his first cap, and the Championship in 1958. Only two matches were lost during his tenure as England captain.

He played for Sale throughout his career, captained the club during the 1951-52 season and played 85 matches for Lancashire. He played for Lancashire & Cheshire against the 1947-48 Wallabies, and for North-Western Counties against the 1951-52 Springboks and the 1953-54 All Blacks. He played on five Easter tours of South Wales and toured Canada in 1957 with the Barbarians. A statue in his honour stands in Audenshaw, Manchester.

FAMOUS GAMES
ENGLAND 26 SCOTLAND 8

21 March 1953, Twickenham

By the time Scotland arrived at Twickenham in 1953, a settled and experienced England had already won 8-3 at Cardiff Arms Park against Wales, 11-0 against France at Twickenham and survived a punishing, hard-fought 9-9 draw against Ireland in Dublin. An added incentive for the players was that victory over Scotland on 21 March would deliver England its first Championship since 1937.

The foundation of England's success lay in a strong and mobile forward unit, while Martin Regan of Liverpool and Lancashire served with flair and timing the fledgling centre pairing of Jeff Butterfield and Phil Davies in their first season of international rugby. Harlequin Nim Hall captained the side from full back.

Scotland began the match well but, after missing two penalties and speculative drops at goal, the relentless pressure of the England pack gradually shifted them onto the back foot. A well-crafted try by Reg Bazley on the left wing, after a decisive break by Don White of Northampton, gave England the lead and, although Grant Weatherstone on the right wing replied with a try for

Above: England's defence fans out as Scotland attack
Top right: Scotland's Ian Thomson converts a try
Right: England's first post-war Championship winners

Scotland, further tries by Bazley and powerful Coventry second-row forward Stan Adkins gave England an 11-3 half-time lead.

The second half belonged to England and the match was over as a competitive fixture after England scored converted tries from the prop and future England captain Bob Stirling and Jeff Butterfield to lead 21-3, by the 50th minute of the match. The Scottish defence proved to be very porous and White, in the English back row, and the English backs were far too strong in the face of weak tackling and a disorganised Scottish defence. Ian Thomson converted a consolation Scottish try from the South African born flanker Chick Henderson, before the England right wing, Ted Woodward of Wasps, scored a remarkable try from midfield after receiving the ball while standing still. Hall kicked his fourth conversion to leave England the winners by an emphatic scoreline, 26-8. It was England's first Championship of the post-war period and a fitting reward for Hall and White, who had represented England since 1947.

England NM Hall* - JE Woodward, J Butterfield, WPC Davies, RC Bazley – M Regan, DW Shuttleworth – RV Stirling, E Evans, WA Holmes – DT Wilkins, SJ Adkins – AO Lewis, JMK Kendall-Carpenter, DF White

Scotland IHM Thomson – TG Weatherstone, A Cameron*, D Cameron, JS Swan – L Bruce-Lockhart, AF Dorward – JC Dawson, JHF King, RL Wilson – W Kerr, JJ Hegarty – JH Henderson, KHD McMillan, WLK Cowie

ENGLAND 16 SCOTLAND 3

16 March 1957, Twickenham

England went into the final match of the 1957 season already assured of at least a share of the Championship, although Scotland could catch them by beating them. In the build-up to the match, journalists coined a new term to describe the feat of winning all four matches, something that England hadn't managed since 1928, and the notion of a Grand Slam came into being.

Under Eric Evans' leadership, England possessed the most feared pack of the period, with the Oxford and Cambridge trio of Marques and Currie in the second row and Peter Robbins at wing forward, alongside Liverpool's Reg Higgins.

Alongside Evans were Ron 'the Badger' Jacobs of Northampton and Gloucester's George Hastings. At the base of the scrum, Dickie Jeeps fed dangerous runners such as Coventry's Peter Jackson and Northampton's Jeff Butterfield, supported by Bristolian full back Robert Challis.

Despite such attacking riches, England left nothing to chance. In a tight first half at Twickenham, they ground Scotland down, Butterfield's feint and Phil Davies' try giving them a narrow 3-0 lead at half-time.

A penalty apiece made the score 6-3 early in the second half, before a powerful drive from Higgins led to a try for Headingley's Peter Thompson. The try was converted by Challis and stretched England's lead

to 11-3. The irrepressible Higgins then added a third, also converted by Challis, and England won 16-3. The Calcutta Cup, Triple Crown, Championship and a new-fangled accolade called a Grand Slam all secured on a single afternoon.

England R Challis – PB Jackson, J Butterfield, WPC Davies, PH Thompson – RM Bartlett, REG Jeeps – CR Jacobs, E Evans*, GW Hastings – RWD Marques, JD Currie – PGD Robbins, A Ashcroft, R Higgins

Scotland KJF Scotland – AR Smith, T McClung, KR Macdonald, JLF Allan – GH Waddell, AF Dorward – HF McLeod, RKG MacEwen, T Elliot – EJS Michie, JWY Kemp – GK Smith, JT Greenwood*, A Robson

Above: Peter Thompson touches down a try for England
Below: The Grand Slam-winning ball

The England Greats

JEFF BUTTERFIELD

Born 9 August 1929 **Died** 30 April 2004
England career 1953-1959, 28 caps
Position Centre
Club Northampton

One of the finest all-round centres in English rugby history, Jeffrey Butterfield was born in Cleckheaton and educated locally before studying at Loughborough University. He played more than 220 matches for Northampton, from 1951 to 1963, and represented Yorkshire more than 50 times. He won the first of his 28 consecutive caps for England against France in 1953, scoring a try on his debut. He scored four more tries during his England career and was a key player in the 1957 Grand Slam-winning side. He played in three outright Championship-winning sides and captained England in the four matches of the Five Nations Championship in his final season in 1959.

He toured with the British & Irish Lions to South Africa in 1955 and was regarded as one of the finest three-quarters to visit that country. He played in all four Tests and formed a notable centre partnership with his fellow Englishman Phil Davies. He scored three tries and a drop goal in the drawn series. He toured a second time with the Lions to Australia and New Zealand in 1959. He was unlucky with injuries and did not appear in any of the Test matches, having withdrawn from the first Test team against Australia after selection.

At the end of his rugby career, he opened and then managed The Rugby Club of London for 25 years, served as an England selector and was closely involved in the development of Golden Oldies rugby festivals in Europe.

UNLIKELY ALLIANCES

A match between a combined team of English and Welsh players opposing a combined team of Scottish and Irish players was a regular highlight when individual unions came to celebrate important milestones in their history.

The first took place on The Close at Rugby School on 1 November 1923, to celebrate the centenary of William Webb Ellis 'picking up the ball' in 1823. England's WJA 'Dave' Davies was captain and outstanding forwards Wakefield, Voyce and Conway were also selected. The combined England & Wales team carried the day, beating the combined Ireland & Scotland side 21-16.

On 5 October 1929, a second match took place at Twickenham to celebrate the

unveiling of the Sir George Rowland Hill Memorial Gates. The England & Wales side was captained by hooker Sam Tucker, but the match was won 20-13 by their opponents.

The third match took place in Dublin on 31 December 1955 to celebrate the opening of the West Upper Stand at Lansdowne Road. England supplied six players to a side captained by Welsh fly half Cliff Morgan. A close match saw the combined England & Wales side win a narrow victory 18-15.

In 1959, the England scrum half Dicky Jeeps, supported by seven English players, led his Anglo-Welsh team to a 26-17 victory to celebrate the Twickenham Jubilee.

In 1970, Bob Taylor captained a combined side to a 14-14 draw and an all-English three-quarter line, outside the illustrious Welsh duo of Barry John and Gareth Edwards, helped celebrate 100 years of international rugby.

Scotland celebrated their own centenary in October 1972, at Murrayfield. A combined Scotland & Ireland side beating England & Wales 30-21, before Tony Neary captained England-Wales to defeat, 17-10, in Ireland's centenary season in April 1975.

Bill Beaumont scored his only international try in a highly entertaining 37-33 Anglo-Welsh victory in the Welsh centenary season in November 1980.

The combined England & Wales team in 1923, wearing white jerseys with a double crest

Above: The joint team badge worn in the Rowland Hill Memorial Match, 1929

Below: England & Wales, in white shirts with hoops, v Scotland & Ireland in 1929

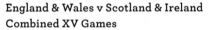

England & Wales v Scotland & Ireland Combined XV Games

Centenary Match at Rugby School
1 November 1923
Rowland Hill Memorial Match
5 October 1929
Opening of West Upper Stand at Lansdowne Road *31 December 1955*
Twickenham Jubilee Match *17 October 1959*
RFU Twickenham Centenary Match
3 October 1970
SRU Centenary Match *14 October 1972*
IRFU Centenary *19 April 1975*
WRU Centenary *29 November 1980*

Far left: England & Wales compete with Scotland & Ireland in the 1959 Twickenham Jubilee Match, and the match programme from the day

Above: The England & Wales side that played in the Twickenham Centenary Match in 1970

Left: Wing Gerald Davies evades a Scottish & Irish tackle in the same game

6

REACHING
A CENTURY

1960-1980

SIXTIES SET-BACKS

After starring in the British & Irish Lions tour of Australia and New Zealand, it was expected that the English midfield duo of Bev Risman and new captain Dickie Jeeps would lead England into the 1960 season. Injury intervened and instead of Risman the lesser-known Cornishman Richard Sharp started at fly half against Wales. Richmond's Mike Weston would partner Fylde's Malcolm Phillips at centre, with Sale's John Roberts on the wing and Percy Park's Don Rutherford at full back. In a fizzing first half, Roberts scored two tries which, along with eight points from Rutherford's boot, were enough to secure a 14-0 half-time lead. Wales came back in the second half, but England held out to win 14-6.

The same XV were selected to face Ireland at Twickenham and a narrow game was settled with a late try from veteran David Marques, as England won 8-5. The subsequent crunching encounter in Paris ended 3-3, before England sealed a Triple Crown and share of the Championship in Edinburgh. It was the first time that England had played the same 15 players across a full Championship season.

Risman returned in 1961 and Marques and John Currie would play the last of a remarkable 22 consecutive matches together in a close defeat to South Africa. A mixed season followed, notable as the first for Bedford flanker Budge Rogers. The social makeup of the England team began to change as grammar schools began to supply players regularly to the national team for the first time. Meanwhile, Risman and St Helens' Ray French were among the players to leave rugby union to pursue professional rugby league careers.

Sharp returned in 1962 and the season began with a goalless draw against Wales. The fly half was in excellent form against Ireland, scoring a try, penalty and two conversions as England won 16-0. Defeat in Paris was followed by a draw in Edinburgh, which denied Scotland a Triple Crown.

Above: The action spills over onto the sidelines during England's narrow 6-5 win over France in 1963

Previous pages: The England pack in the Beaumont era take on Ireland in 1977

A completely new front five was selected in 1963 to face Wales, one that included Cambridge University's Nick Drake-Lee, Torquay Athletic's Mike Davis and Coventry's John Owen. Peter Jackson and Phillips returned after a season-long absence and the latter contributed a try in England's 13-6 victory in Cardiff. A scoreless draw against Ireland meant that no side would collect the Triple Crown, but two penalties from full back John Willcox were enough to see off France narrowly at Twickenham.

Scotland had enjoyed a fine year too, and thus the winner of the Calcutta Cup would also win the Championship. Sharp's sublime skill settled the contest 10-8 in England's favour to confirm the title for the first time since 1958.

In May, England became the first home nation side to tour New Zealand and led the All Blacks at Eden Park into the final quarter before

Wilson Whineray's side pulled away to win 21-11. The All Blacks saw out the series with a late Don Clarke kick to win 9-6 at Lancaster Park.

England stopped off in Sydney on their way home and Owen was joined in the English pack by three Coventry teammates, Phil Judd, Bert Godwin and Brian 'Yeti' Wightman. Unfortunately, three late tries were not enough to prevent an 18-9 defeat.

Veteran Ron Jacobs replaced Harlequin John Willcox as captain midway through the 1964 season, but England's form remained inconsistent. In 1965, Rutherford returned after a four-year absence but Andy Hancock's 90-yard try to equalise against Scotland was a rare bright spot in a disappointing season.

Budge Rodgers assumed the captaincy at the start of the 1966 season and he and his Bedford teammate David Perry were joined in the back row by Northampton's Bob Taylor, and Taylor's clubmate David Powell debuted in the front row alongside Bristol hooker John Pullin.

Sharp bowed out against Australia in 1967 as Northampton's Peter Larter made his debut. Moseley centre Colin McFadyean's try against Ireland and two more against Scotland helped England to two wins in a year that ended with an autumn defeat to Brian Lochore's New Zealand.

Harlequin Bob Hiller came into the side at full back in 1968 and a more resilient England took an 11-3 second-half lead against Wales before a converted try and Barry John's late dropped goal ensured the spoils were shared 11-11. The opposite occurred against Ireland as Hiller's late penalty squared things at 9-9 for another draw. France beat England in Paris on their way to their first Grand Slam, but England saw the season out with victory at Murrayfield.

Coventry's David Duckham and Cambridge University's John Spencer formed an exciting new centre partnership against Ireland in 1969. Duckham scored a try but it wasn't enough to avoid a 17-15 defeat. The captaincy was restored to Rogers against France as he overtook Wavell Wakefield's 42-year appearance record. Tries from Moseley's Keith Fielding, Bristol's Dave Rollitt and Coventry's Rodney Webb delivered

Above: Ray French, a tenacious second-row forward who later switched to Rugby League

Below: Bob Hiller, full back, captain and England's record points scorer when he retired in 1972

a crushing 22-8 victory over the misfiring champions. A win against Scotland was followed by a comprehensive 30-9 defeat against Gareth Edwards' Wales before South Africa arrived at Twickenham under a storm of anti-apartheid protest.

To arrest the malaise within the national side the RFU looked to modernise their coaching practices. Don Rutherford was appointed Technical Director and Don White returned as coach. For the first time a 30-man squad was selected. Brian 'Stack' Stevens of Penzance & Newlyn would debut along with Harlequin's scrum half Nigel Starmer-Smith. Hiller would be captain.

England had yet to beat South Africa and things didn't look promising when Piet Greyling opened the scoring for the visitors with a try after six minutes. England closed the gap through good work by Starmer-Smith, resulting in a try for Larter. In the second half, a penalty from Hiller and a try from Pullin put England ahead. Hiller kicked the conversion to stretch England's lead to 11-8, before becoming the first England player to be substituted as Carlisle's Chris Wardlow took the field in his place.

Minutes later, England had recorded their first win over South Africa, a full 63 years after the sides had first met.

TO ARREST THE MALAISE WITHIN THE NATIONAL SIDE THE RFU LOOKED TO MODERNISE THEIR COACHING PRACTICES

Dickie Jeeps feeds
the ball to his backs
against South Africa
in 1961

DICKIE JEEPS

Born 25 November 1931 **Died** 8 October 2016
England career 1956-1962, 24 caps
Position Scrum Half **Club** Northampton

Richard 'Dickie' Jeeps was a tough, wiry and competitive scrum half who had an exceptional career with England and the British & Irish Lions in the 1950s and early 1960s. Educated at Bedford Modern School, he played for Cambridge City before moving to Northampton where he played until his retirement in 1965. He was picked as an uncapped player for the Lions tour of South Africa in 1955 and played in all four Tests of the drawn series. On his return, he made his England debut against Wales in 1956 and, although dropped after that match, he was selected throughout England's 1957 Five Nations Grand Slam campaign.

He toured Australia and New Zealand with the Lions in 1959 and played in five of the six Tests. On his return from that tour, he was appointed England captain, a role he fulfilled in 13 consecutive internationals until his final appearance against Scotland at Murrayfield in 1962. His international career finished with the Lions tour of South Africa in the summer of 1962 in which he played in all four Tests and captained the Lions in the final Test in Bloemfontein.

He retired as the most capped English scrum half, with 24 caps, and he remains the most capped Lions scrum half of all time with 13 Test caps. He became an England selector and was President of the Rugby Football Union in 1976-77. A sports administrator and Chairman of the Sports Council for seven years, he was appointed CBE in 1977.

ENGLAND 10 SCOTLAND 8

16 March 1963, Twickenham

Scotland came to Twickenham in 1963 with a chance of winning the Championship for the first time since 1938. England too were unbeaten, having defeated Wales in Cardiff, drawn 0-0 against Ireland in Dublin and beaten France narrowly 6-5 at Twickenham. The winner of the contest would win the tournament outright.

England had an experienced back line, led by their willowy fly half Richard Sharp of Wasps and Cornwall, who was winning his 13th cap. Their forwards were relatively untested and faced a combative pack of hardened Scottish forwards, which included David Rollo at prop and Mike Campbell-Lamerton in the second row.

Scotland started quickly and were 8-0 up within 15 minutes. A converted try by the England prop Nick Drake-Lee in

Richard Sharp is applauded off the pitch by the Scots

the 28th minute reduced the deficit and the scene was set for an exciting second half.

Five minutes after the break, Sharp scored the try for which he is remembered. Receiving the ball 40 yards from the tryline, he shaped to pass but held on to the ball, thereby wrong-footing the Scottish defence. With two further dummies, the final one completely outwitting the Scottish full back Colin Blaikie, he ran on to score his famous try to the left of the goal posts.

Full back John Willcox converted, and England led 10-8. A desperate Scottish fightback followed but

England held on to win the Championship. *Sharp's Match* was over but would live long in the memories of all who witnessed it.

England JG Willcox – PB Jackson, MS Phillips, MP Weston, J Roberts – RAW Sharp*, SJS Clarke – PE Judd, HO Godwin, NJ Drake-Lee – AM Davis, JE Owen – DP Rogers, DG Perry, DC Manley

Scotland CF Blaikie – C Elliot, BC Henderson, DM White, RH Thomson – KJF Scotland*, S Coughtrie – JB Neill, NS Bruce, DMD Rollo – FH ten Bos, MJ Campbell-Lamerton – RJC Glasgow, JP Fisher, KI Ross

BUDGE ROGERS

Born 20 June 1939 **England career** 1961-1969, 34 caps
Position Wing Forward **Club** Bedford

One of the leading wing forwards of the 1960s and the most capped English player with 34 caps on his retirement, Derek 'Budge' Rogers OBE was in every sense a local man. Born in Bedford, he went to Bedford School and became one of the greatest one-club men with Bedford Rugby Club, making 485 first-team appearances between 1957 and 1976.

His outstanding play for Midland Counties in their drawn match against the touring Springboks in November 1960 led to his international selection against Ireland in Dublin in February 1961. Although England lost 11-8 in a closely fought match, he launched his illustrious international career with a charge down try midway through the second half.

Rodgers retained his England place for the rest of the season and played the opening three matches of the 1962 Championship. He played in the first and fourth Tests of the 1962 British & Irish Lions tour of South Africa and was ever-present in England's Championship-winning side of 1963.

He played 21 consecutive matches and captained England throughout the 1966 season. Although omitted in 1968, he was recalled in 1969 and played four matches, captaining England a further three times and surpassing Wavell Wakefield's record of 31 caps. His final appearance was against Wales in Cardiff in April 1969.

Following his retirement, he remained involved in the game as Chairman of the England selectors in 1979-80, Manager of the 1979 England tour to the South Pacific and President of the Rugby Football Union in 2000-01.

LEAN YEARS

E ngland captain Bob Hiller entered the 1970s having scored in nine consecutive matches from his debut in 1968. He stretched his record to 10 with two dropped goals that, together with a try from Harrogate's Ian Shackleton, meant that England opened their 1970 campaign with a 9-3 home win against Ireland.

Tries from David Duckham and John Novak gave England a 13-3 half-time lead against Wales, before the visitors struck back, inspired by substitute Chico Hopkins, to win 17-13. England ended their campaign with defeats in Edinburgh and Paris.

1971 was the centenary year for the RFU and the international game, but it was the Welsh who were playing champagne rugby. England were crushed 22-6 in Cardiff as Broughton Park's flanker Tony Neary made his debut.

After a two-match absence, Hiller returned in Dublin, his three penalties outpointing Ireland's two tries as England won 9-6. Against France at Twickenham, he was England's points man again, a try, conversion and three first-half penalties gave England a 14-6 half-time lead before France struck back to tie the game 14-14.

England ended the Championship by losing to Scotland at Twickenham for the first time since 1938 and lost again at Murrayfield the following Saturday in a specially arranged match to celebrate the events of 1871. In addition, John Spencer captained England in a match against a star-studded President's XV invitational side that boasted some of the finest players in the world. With Colin Meads, Bryan Williams, Jo Maso and Frik du Preez in their ranks, the invitational side won 28-11.

Alan Old of Middlesbrough, Andy Ripley of Rosslyn Park and Gloucester's Mike Burton were among the new faces in a 1972 season that is remembered for matters off the field. Escalating civil and military unrest in Northern Ireland caused both Wales and Scotland to cancel their fixtures in Dublin and the season was not completed for the first time since the end of the Second World War.

Hiller earned the last of his 19 caps for England against Ireland, kicking two penalties and a conversion. He had scored in every match he played for England and gave way with a record tally of 138 Test points. Having lost all their Five Nations matches England confounded

England forwards Roger Uttley, Bill Beaumont, Fran Cotton, Peter Wheeler and Robin Cowling face up to defeat at Cardiff Arms Park in 1977

expectations by recording an unbeaten seven-match tour of South Africa, culminating in an 18-9 Test victory over the Springboks at Ellis Park.

The political instability in Ireland continued into 1973 but, to the surprise of some, Pullin and his teammates chose to answer the call of their British & Irish Lions colleague Willie John McBride by travelling to Lansdowne Road in February. The match, which England lost, facilitated a public expression of friendship between the English and Irish rugby communities. In his post-match after-dinner speech Pullin quipped to considerable applause: "We might not be much good but at least we turned up." Despite Pullin's good-natured comment, with Fran Cotton in the front row and Gosforth duo Roger Uttley and Peter Dixon in the pack, England were developing a resilient spine, one that was expertly marshalled by scrum half Steve Smith of Sale. Flanked by Coventry teammates Geoff Evans and Peter Preece, Duckham ran in two tries and England recorded their first win in the Championship for two seasons by despatching France 14-6 at Twickenham, with Peter Squires winning the first of his 29 caps on the wing.

Left: England lock Chris Ralston out-jumps Samuel Strahan in the lineout at Eden Park in 1973. England's 16-10 win was the first time England had defeated the All Blacks in New Zealand

Below: Mike Slemen scores at Murrayfield in 1980 as England win the Grand Slam for first time in 23 years

The English pack was to the fore against Scotland too with Ripley and Uttley particularly influential at the lineout. A late Evans try stretched England's lead to 20-13 and for the first and only time in Five Nations history all five teams shared the Championship with two home wins apiece.

An autumn tour of New Zealand followed and, after losing three provincial matches, England overturned the form book by defeating the All Blacks 16-10 at Eden Park. Trailing 10-6 at half-time, controlled 10-man rugby, orchestrated by Old and Moseley scrum half Jan Webster, overturned the margin and second-half tries by Stevens and Neary sealed the game for England.

Back at Twickenham, England hosted and comfortably defeated Australia 20-3 with tries from Neary, Ripley and Old. Remarkably, in an otherwise undistinguished decade, Pullin's England had recorded victories over all three southern-hemisphere heavyweights in a little under 18 months.

Nottingham full back Dusty Hare made his debut in 1974, while Leicester hooker Peter Wheeler and Fylde lock Bill Beaumont were selected in 1975, but England were unable to record more than a solitary win in either season. They finished winless and bottom of the Championship table in 1976 but began stronger in 1977, with a resounding 26-6 win against Scotland and narrow win in Dublin. They lost their final two matches, with only Bristol full back Alastair Hignell contributing points.

Beaumont assumed the captaincy in 1978 and Paul Dodge came in at centre. Again, they defeated Scotland and Ireland but lost to France and Wales, both of whom were enjoying golden periods. Arguably the most significant result of 1979 was the Northern Division's defeat of New Zealand 21-9 at Cross Green, Otley. England was unable to repeat the result at Twickenham, but a Lancashire-infused side managed a creditable 10-9 defeat.

In 1980 tries from Smith, Mike Slemen and John Scott helped England to a 24-9 opening day victory over Ireland. Tony Bond went off with a broken leg and was replaced by a young Clive Woodward at centre. Impressively, England followed up the win with a first victory in Paris since 1964. Beaumont, alongside Maurice Colclough, with the trio of Wheeler, Cotton and Phil Blakeway, controlled the field for a tenacious 17-13 victory.

Dusty Hare's boot delivered the tightest of victories in a fractious encounter against Wales to set up a Grand Slam decider at Murrayfield. Again, the English pack exerted maximum pressure in the scrum. Woodward's creative running caused problems and by half-time England led 19-3 through tries from Slemen and two more from Orrell's John Carleton. A sublime passage of play culminated in a try for Smith, before Carleton completed the first English hat-trick since 1924 as the visitors won 30-18. It was England's first Grand Slam since 1957 and arguably the hardest-earned to date.

The England Greats

DAVID DUCKHAM

Born 28 June 1946
England career 1969-1976, 36 caps
Position Centre/Wing
Club Coventry

The rugby world sat up and took notice as the long-striding centre David Duckham looped round his opponent and accelerated 40 yards across the Dublin turf to the Irish line for a try in his first international appearance. By the end of the 1969 season he had scored two further tries in an 8-3 victory over Scotland at Twickenham and it was clear that England had unearthed a gem.

Born and educated in Coventry, he played for Coventry Rugby Club and Warwickshire. After playing in the victorious England side against the Springboks in December, he ran in one of the great Barbarians tries from 60 yards in the final match of the Springbok tour in January 1970.

He remained in the centre for England during the 1970 season but was moved to the left wing for the opening match of the 1971 campaign. For most of his continuing England career he played on the wing and was an automatic choice for the next five years (*pictured against Scotland in 1973, right*).

He was chosen to tour Australia and New Zealand with the British & Irish Lions in 1971. He returned to the wing for the Barbarians in 1973, with a sensational performance in their victory over the All Blacks.

His England career ended in February 1976 when he won his 36th cap, a record for an England back, against Scotland at Murrayfield. Strong, fast and exceptionally elusive, he had scored 10 tries and been on the winning side for England 11 times.

"A DASHING SIDE-STEPPER WITH AN EYE FOR THE GAP AND THE SHEER SPEED TO UTILISE IT"

Barry Bowker, 'England Rugby'

1971 CENTENARY CELEBRATIONS

In 1971, the Rugby Football Union celebrated its 100th year. Victorian in spirit, it had retained much of the imperial splendour that typified that earlier age. This was reflected in the elaborate and often lavish programme of events that accompanied the marking of its centenary.

A Centenary Congress took place at Corpus Christi College, Cambridge, followed by a cocktail party to which 3,000 people from all corners of the globe were invited. A government reception at Westminster Banqueting Hall followed, with former players, 14 union Presidents, the Prince of Wales and Prime Minister Edward Heath all in attendance. A combined England & Wales had taken on a combined Scotland & Ireland in October 1970. A second international fixture against Scotland took place in March 1971 at Murrayfield. Finally, in April, an all-star squad, featuring the very best players from around the world, played three matches against the English divisions, before finishing their tour with an international against the full England side at Twickenham.

Captained by the All Black forward Brian Lochore (*No 8, right*), the RFU President's Overseas XV contained some of the greatest rugby players of their era. The Springbok captain and scrum half Dawie de Villiers, was the fulcrum of a multi-talented backline. Two outstandingly gifted French runners in Pierre Villepreux at full back and Jo Maso in the centre played alongside the crash-tackling Springbok centre Joggie Jansen and

the prodigiously gifted young Samoan All Black flyer Bryan Williams on the wing. As for the forwards, any pack that contained the Australian hooker Peter Johnson, the All Black Colin Meads and the Springbok Frik du Preez in the second row, and Brian Lochore in the back row, supported by the Australian captain Greg Davis and the future All Black captain Ian Kirkpatrick on the flanks, was genuinely formidable. The strength of the Overseas XV meant there were genuine fears that England would not be able to live with the power and skill of their opponents. England were captained by John Spencer, with David Duckham alongside him in the centre and Bob Hiller at full back. In the pack there were two new caps at wing forward, Peter Dixon of Harlequins and Roger Creed of Coventry, alongside the experience provided by John Pullin the Bristol hooker, Stack Stevens, the Cornish prop, and Peter Larter from the RAF and Northampton in the second row.

What followed was a highly entertaining match in front of a crowd of around 50,000 spectators. Bob Hiller scored his third try of the season, an England record for a full back at the time, while the Overseas XV ran in six tries to record a convincing 28-11 victory.

Six of the selected English players went on the Lions tour of New Zealand in the summer and played significant roles in that historic series-winning tour: Bob Hiller, John Spencer, David Duckham, John Pullin, Stack Stevens and Peter Dixon. The RFU looked to its next half-century with optimism.

A match programme
and a President's
Overseas XV shirt
from the 1971
centenary game

The statue presented
to the RFU from
its member clubs
to mark 100 years
of English rugby

JOHN PULLIN

Born 1 November 1941
England career 1966-1976, 42 caps
Position Hooker
Club Bristol

John Pullin was a Bristol and Gloucestershire stalwart who occupied the hooker position in the England side with distinction on 42 occasions over 10 years, following his international debut against Wales in January 1966. A farmer, educated at Thornbury Grammar School and Cirencester Agricultural College, he became the most-capped Englishman when passing DP 'Budge' Rogers' total of 34 caps against France in 1974 and set an English record of 36 consecutive international appearances between 1968 and 1975.

Appointed captain for the short tour of South Africa in 1972, he went on to captain England on 13 occasions. During this period, he became the first person to have captained England to victories over South Africa, New Zealand and Australia. He was the captain when England played Ireland in Dublin at the height of the troubles in 1972 and famously remarked at the after-match dinner that although England were not much good, they had at least turned up.

His career with the British & Irish Lions was no less distinguished. He toured South Africa in 1968 and played in three Tests. He was then involved in all four Tests during the victorious 1971 series in New Zealand.

He also played many matches for the Barbarians, including their historic victory over the All Blacks at Cardiff in 1973, where he gave the pass to John Dawes in the lead-up to Gareth Edwards' famous try at the beginning of the match.

"EVERY SECOND IS SEARED IN MY MIND FOREVER"

John Pullin on THAT Barbarians try

The England Greats

JOHN SPENCER

Born 19 August 1947
England career 1969-1971, 14 caps
Position Centre
Clubs Cambridge University, Headingley

The England centre John Southern Spencer was another product of that famous rugby nursery, Sedbergh School. He went on to Queens' College, Cambridge University, in 1967 to study law. He played in three Varsity Matches against Oxford University, scoring a try from the left wing in his first match, and captaining Cambridge from the centre in a defeat in his final match in 1969.

A powerful centre with soft hands, he won his first cap against Ireland in Dublin in 1969 and quickly established an exciting and much-heralded centre partnership with another new cap, David Duckham. Spencer played in 14 internationals and scored two tries, the first a remarkable long-range effort against Scotland at Murrayfield in 1970.

He captained England in four matches, including the centenary internationals against Scotland at Murrayfield, and a formidable RFU President's XV at Twickenham in March and April 1971. He toured with the British & Irish Lions to Australia and New Zealand in 1971, where he played in ten matches but did not play in any of the Tests. He played in three matches on England's tour of South Africa in the summer of 1972.

A player for Headingley and Wharfedale, he also represented Yorkshire and the Barbarians on many occasions. He returned to New Zealand with the Lions in 2017 as Tour Manager and succeeded the late Micky Steele-Bodger in 2019 as only the sixth President of the Barbarians Rugby Club. He was President of the Rugby Football Union in 2018-19.

"TO PLAY FOR AND CAPTAIN ENGLAND IS SOMETHING YOU CHERISH"

ENGLAND 9 WALES 8

16 February 1980, Twickenham

The build-up to the third match of the 1980 Championship, against Wales at Twickenham on 16 February was intense, with both sides in contention. England had beaten Ireland at Twickenham and France in Paris and both teams were unbeaten, but the record of Welsh teams at Twickenham in preceding years had been impressive.

The England selectors had called-up six players from the Northern Division and four from Leicester, with second-row forward Bill Beaumont as captain in a formidable pack. They included the calm marksmanship of full back Dusty Hare; the balanced centre pairing of Paul Dodge and Clive Woodward; the game management of John Horton at fly half alongside Steve Smith; and the power of Phil Blakeway at prop alongside Peter Wheeler and Fran Cotton. They had also restored Roger Uttley to the back row alongside John Scott and Tony Neary.

The experience of this team, containing eight current or future England captains, was to prove crucial for England in the swirling cauldron. The referee gave a warning about foul play to the two captains very early in the match and Paul Ringer, the Welsh wing forward, was sent off in the 15th minute for a late tackle on Horton. Dusty Hare kicked the resultant penalty, but Wales soon went ahead with a try when England lost control of the ball at the back of the scrum.

Wales held their 4-3 lead until the 68th minute of this bad-tempered match, when Dusty Hare kicked his second penalty goal. Amazingly, Wales came back

Above: Wales lock Geoff Wheel and England captain Bill Beaumont square up during a tense encounter
Right: Wales' Jeff Squire and Clive Williams shield the ball despite the best efforts of No 8 John Scott

with a try by their right wing Elgan Rees to take an 8-6 lead with three minutes of the match remaining. Fatefully, Gareth Davies missed the conversion and this extraordinary match climaxed with a remarkable penalty goal, kicked from near the touchline, by a seemingly nerveless Dusty Hare in injury time to give England a 9-8 victory over 14-man Wales.

This was only England's second win over Wales in 17 years and set up a historic final match for the Grand Slam in front of a packed house at Murrayfield four weeks later, a match which saw England claim the spoils.

England WH Hare – J Carleton, CR Woodward, PW Dodge, MAC Slemen – JP Horton, SJ Smith – FE Cotton, PJ Wheeler, PJ Blakeway – WB Beaumont*, MJ Colclough – RM Uttley (M Rafter), JP Scott, A Neary

Wales WR Blyth – HE Rees, DS Richards, SP Fenwick, L Keen – WG Davies, TD Holmes – C Williams, AJ Phillips, G Price – AJ Martin, GAD Wheel – P Ringer, ET Butler, J Squire*

The England Greats

BILL BEAUMONT

Born 9 March 1952 **England career** 1975-1982, 34 caps
Position Second Row **Club** Fylde

Sir William Blackledge 'Bill' Beaumont has been one of the most influential figures in rugby for more than 40 years. He led England to a first Grand Slam for 23 years in 1980, amassed 34 caps as a powerful second-row forward and captained England 21 times.

Beaumont was born in March 1952 and joined Fylde Rugby Club in 1969 after leaving Ellesmere College. His Lancashire debut came in 1972, while his England bow came in January 1975 against Ireland in Dublin as a late replacement for Roger Uttley. He subsequently went on tour to Australia that summer and started a run of 33 consecutive caps, which only ended when he suffered a head injury captaining Lancashire in the County Championship Final two weeks after playing against Scotland at Murrayfield. The injury was sufficiently serious to lead to his immediate retirement from the game on medical advice.

His leadership is rightly celebrated, with a golden period coming between 1980 and his final international in 1982 when he led England to 11 victories, two draws

and just two defeats. He also captained a Northern Division side to a historic 21-9 victory over the All Blacks at Otley in November 1979.

Following England's Grand Slam success in 1980 (*left*), he was chosen as the first Englishman to captain the Lions since FD 'Doug' Prentice in 1930, and played in 10 matches in South Africa, including all four Tests.

Much in demand to play in invitational matches, he appeared for the combined England & Wales team against Scotland & Ireland, in which he scored his only international try, and captained the WRU President's XV against Wales later in the Welsh Rugby Union centenary season in 1980-81. He also captained the Barbarians five times in 15 appearances for the club.

England's representative on the International Rugby Board from 1999, IRB Vice-Chairman from 2007 to 2012 and Chairman of the Rugby Football Union from 2012 to 2016, Beaumont was elected Chairman of World Rugby in 2016 and again in 2020. Fittingly, he was also awarded a knighthood for services to rugby in December 2018.

"THANKS FOR ALL YOU HAVE DONE FOR US, FOR FYLDE, LANCASHIRE, THE NORTH, ENGLAND, BRITISH LIONS, AND MOST OF ALL FOR RUGBY"

England scrum half Steve Smith

Success is demanded, sometimes even assumed. And the stakes are always sky-high

Life at the top

International sport is a high-pressure environment, and nowhere is that pressure felt more clearly than at the very top – the coaches who are expected to inspire their sides to take on and beat the very best

By Chris Foy, *Daily Mail* rugby correspondent

W hat does it mean to coach England? Taking charge of the national team means occupying a place on a pedestal within the sport in this country – and accepting the status of a global rugby figurehead.

It is a job which the holder must fulfil under the constant glare of scrutiny from public and pundits. There are no hiding places. Many covet the role but few have the chance to claim it. Success is demanded, sometimes even assumed. And the stakes are always sky-high.

It takes a certain type of character, someone with supreme knowledge of the game, experience and technical expertise but also armed with sufficient belief and conviction to trust their instincts amid an endless clamour of competing opinions and occasional criticism. Coaching England means embracing all aspects of the position – good and bad.

For the incumbents in 2020, Eddie Jones and Simon Middleton, there are similarities when it comes to the meaning of the job but variations as well. As the title-winning head coaches of the men's and women's teams, they have their own personal take on three crucial elements of what they have been chosen to do – the honour; the pressure of expectations; and the sense of responsibility.

Jones was approached by the RFU in late 2015 to succeed Stuart Lancaster after England's pool-stage exit from their home World Cup.

"To be given the chance to coach my country is everything for me"

Simon Middleton

*Right: Eddie Jones
congratulates
Joe Marler after
England's 30-6 victory
against Australia at
Twickenham in 2017*

*Below: Simon
Middleton leads the
post-match huddle
after England's 25-23
win against France in
November 2020*

"I thought, 'If he's that serious about winning, I'd like to help England win'" Eddie Jones

For the Australian the honour lay in the professional recognition, having masterminded Japan's shock victory over South Africa and enjoyed plenty of past success with the Springboks and Wallabies.

His was a gold-plated CV, and the fact that the English union targeted him as the first foreigner to oversee the national team was an endorsement of his hard-earned credentials. It meant a great deal to him.

"I'm very humbled to have been offered the opportunity to coach England," said Jones following his appointment. "It's not really a job I ever thought about. I remember getting a phone call from the RFU saying Ian Ritchie wanted to meet me and I couldn't really work out why. But he was so serious about winning and I thought, 'If he's that serious about winning, I'd like to help England win'. So I accepted the job but I really didn't know what I was getting myself into.

"To be in charge of one of the major teams in the world with such a fan following is a great honour. But being the first foreigner to coach England is a difficult thing, because England want an English coach. So I think it is my job to make sure that when I hand it back, it is in a better place than it was so there is an opportunity for an English coach to be successful."

For Middleton, the honour angle is different. Being offered the chance to coach England was more than just a professional endorsement, it was a chance to serve his country, which generated a profound feeling of pride – and still does to this day.

"It's the ultimate," he said. "It's the pinnacle of anyone's playing or coaching career. It means so much to me. I am patriotic. I love my country, so to be given the chance to coach my country is everything for me. To see the impact that me getting the job had on my family,

especially my parents, gave me a huge sense of satisfaction. It is a fantastic honour; doing the job and everything that goes with it.

"When I first got asked by Gary Street to come and do a guest spot with the girls, I was with Leeds at the time and I think it was a big thing for him to be able to get someone in from the Premiership. But it was even bigger for me. He asked me and I was there in a shot. To end up getting the head coach job was incredible and beyond my wildest dreams."

For both men, the pressure and expectation of their role is linked to England's perennial status as a powerhouse rugby country blessed with vast resources; from a huge depth of playing talent to high-class facilities to a financial clout that is unsurpassed. A minimum requirement for England teams is to compete with the best around, while the bar is often set higher than that. Success in Europe and globally is perceived as a reasonable demand.

Jones conveys the image of a man impervious to pressure and expectation but he is not. "Sometimes it hurts when you are criticised," he said. "We are all human. I'm not trying to hang on to the job and that helps me – I am doing the job because I want to do it and I want to make the players better. But there is a lot of external pressure.

"The England national team is the country's leading rugby team and raises the most resources. If the national team does well, sponsors come in and fans want to be part of it. That funds the rest of English rugby to a large extent – so you are aware of the importance of the team." »

History in the making

ENGLAND HEAD COACHES

England rugby teams were picked by a panel of selectors for almost 100 years. The first person to be appointed to coach England was **Don White**, the highly respected ex-England flanker. He introduced a squad system and coached England to a historic first victory over South Africa at Twickenham in 1969. **John Elders** became coach in 1972 and England beat the three southern hemisphere countries during his term as coach over the next two years.

John Burgess took over and then **Peter Colston**. England's fortunes noticeably improved with the appointment of **Mike Davis** who oversaw the 1980 Grand Slam. **Dick Greenwood** coached the side for three years, before **Martin Green** took the England team to the first World Cup

in 1987. **Geoff Cooke** (*below*) took over as manager of the England team in October 1987.

Cooke brought consistency of selection and a dependable pragmatism to England's match play. His successful term lasted until 1994, during which time England won Grand Slams in 1991 and 1992 and reached the 1991 Rugby World Cup Final. He was succeeded by **Jack Rowell**, the long-serving coach of Bath. Rowell began with a tied Test series in South Africa in the summer of 1994 and a convincing Grand Slam in 1995. After 10 consecutive victories, which equalled the England record, a World Cup full of promise was derailed by New Zealand in the semi-final.

Clive Woodward (*right*) had already earned a reputation for innovation when appointed in 1997. His first World Cup campaign in 1999 ended at the quarter-final stage against a powerful Springbok side, but signs of progress emerged over successive Six Nations campaigns, culminating in 2003 in a Grand Slam and victories over New Zealand and Australia in their own countries.

England's successful 2003 autumn World Cup campaign represented the

summit for English rugby and Woodward was the architect of that great victory. He was subsequently knighted. **Andy Robinson**, Woodward's assistant coach, took over in 2004 but was succeeded two years later by **Brian Ashton**, who took England to a World Cup Final in 2007. **Martin Johnson**, England's 2003 captain, became team manager in 2008, leading England to the 2011 Six Nations Championship and the quarter-final of that year's Rugby World Cup.

Stuart Lancaster, coach of England Saxons, stepped up in 2012 and selected young players with a focus on character. After a disappointing 2015 World Cup, Lancaster resigned and was succeeded by the charismatic **Eddie Jones**. The Australian had coached his home country to the World Cup Final

in 2003 and helped South Africa win the tournament in 2007.

Jones made an immediate impact and England won 24 of their next 25 internationals, including a Grand Slam in 2016 and an unprecedented three-Test series whitewash of Australia. During the 2019 Rugby World Cup, England beat Argentina and Australia en route to the semi-final where they authoritatively disposed of the reigning champions New Zealand. After defeat to South Africa in the final, Jones set out his stall to go one better in 2023.

England coaches
Don White 1969-1971
John Elders 1972-1974
John Burgess 1974-1975
Peter Colston 1975-1979
Mike Davis 1979-1983
Dick Greenwood 1983-1985
Martin Green 1985-1987
Geoff Cooke 1987-1994
Jack Rowell 1995-1997
Sir Clive Woodward 1997-2004
Andy Robinson 2004-2006
Brian Ashton 2006-2008
Martin Johnson 2008-2011
Stuart Lancaster 2012-2015
Eddie Jones 2015-

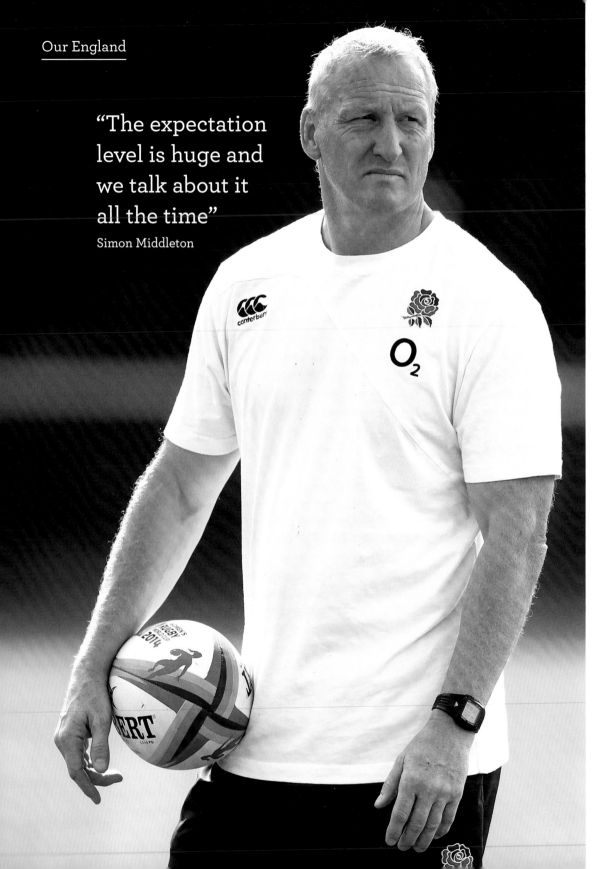

"The expectation level is huge and we talk about it all the time"

Simon Middleton

>> There is also external pressure of a different kind from beyond the borders. Most other countries see England as a prized scalp for myriad reasons linked to historical tension and rivalry, but also because relative prosperity makes them a favourite target.

"Everyone sees England as the golden child because they have this magnificent stadium and always get 80,000 fans in it,' said Jones. "There is a lot of talk about how much money they make from the games – and that does put pressure on. Everyone is envious of that and they want to beat you." That money is also invested in the game in England at every level, strengthening rugby nationwide.

For several years, England's women have been standard-bearers in Europe and vying with New Zealand to be the world's pre-eminent force. So Middleton is exposed to a similar type of pressure to that exerted on Jones and his side, albeit with subtle distinctions.

"The expectation level is huge and we talk about it all the time," Middleton said. "That comes with being an England player or part of the England staff. It is something you come to live with; that every game, you are expected to win. Every tournament, you are expected to win. You can't always, but you are expected to – so we have to manage that so it is not unbearable."

For Middleton, coaching England also means coping with the expectation that goes with receiving the sort of union commitment and funding which many rivals are denied. "There has been fantastic support from the RFU for the women's game, particularly when other nations haven't been able to provide that same support, or haven't chosen to go about things that way," he said. "For me, the pressure and expectation to deliver on that support is a really key bit of the job.

"People on the outside will always say, 'England get everything and other countries don't'. It's not quite as simple as that but I understand where that point of view comes from. That is probably one of the biggest pressures – justifying that support we get. We have to maximise everything we've got, which is a pressure in itself."

There is a divergence when it comes to the responsibility of the role, a different outlook between the male and female branches of the game. Jones sees it as a duty to the men he is in charge of.

"My responsibility is always to the players," he said. "I am the leading servant to the players. The biggest part of that is selection, which is one of the most difficult things in England. Because of the club structure, you have a lot of players here who are around the same level. The ability to pick out players who have the potential to be world-class is sometimes difficult. That's what we try to do. I pay massive attention to the club

Eddie Jones is all smiles after beating Wales in 2016

game, but I'm trying to pick out players who might be world-class. It is a huge responsibility which weighs on me the most."

Middleton's remit is broader in this sense. He is trying to mould a winning team within a broader duty to the women's game at large. What the job means to him is accepting the need to grasp a historic opportunity.

"There is a spotlight on women's sport in general and we want to start pulling in big crowds, to make the women's game sustainable," he said. "We want to be contributors; we don't want to be taking money out of the RFU. It just feels like we are starting to pull our weight in that way.

"We talk about legacy. We want to look back and say, 'What did we bring, when we had our time?' The growth of the game will certainly be part of that. I want to know that we seized the momentum in women's sport. Trying to raise the whole level of women's rugby in England is a huge part of what we do. We are the main growth machine for women's rugby in this country."

Speaking to those who occupy the hottest seats in English rugby, what becomes apparent is that coaching the national teams means a lot of different things. There are grand aspects and small-detail ones. They have to consider so many moving parts within the job, while respecting the past, taking care of the present and planning for the future.

Jones and Middleton have their own interpretation of life on their sporting pedestals. The same would have been true of their predecessors, Lancaster and Street, and so many others who have controlled England's rugby fortunes. But in summary, the job is founded on certain core factors. Honour. Pressure. Expectation. Responsibility. They wouldn't have it any other way.

History in the making

RED ROSES HEAD COACHES

In 1968, former Scotland captain and 1955 Lions tourist **Jim Greenwood** arrived at Loughborough University to teach English. In the evenings he taught rugby and, by the end of the 1970s, the university had developed a reputation as a finishing school for talented rugby players.

In the early 1980s, the university produced more than a dozen young women who numbered amongst the first generation of international women's rugby players. In 1986, Greenwood was asked to coach Great Britain, the first national team to originate on British soil. The following year, he was given the honour of coaching the very first Red Roses as England played their first-ever match against Wales in Pontypool.

"Jim was a brilliant coach… He set the ball rolling in the early days. Women's rugby owes him a lot," explained Karen Almond.

By 1991 **Steve Dowling** was at the helm and helped the Red Roses to the final of the inaugural Women's Rugby World Cup. Three years later he became the first English coach to oversee a fifteen-a-side World Cup victory.

Steve Jew, **Steve Peters**, **Eric Field** and **Pete Kennedy** took turns in charge, before **Geoff Richards** was appointed in 2000. Favouring more attacking back play, the former Australian international full back helped England to victory over New Zealand in 2001 and consecutive World Cup Finals,

before passing the reins to **Gary Street** (*above, right*) in 2007.

Street brought through a generation of exciting young players who would provide the backbone to English success for more than a decade. In his seven-year spell in charge, the Red Roses recorded five Championships and four Grand Slams. They reached the 2010 Rugby World Cup Final before winning the 2014 Rugby World Cup.

In 2014 Street was replaced by **Simon Middleton**, who recorded Grand Slams in 2017, 2019 and 2020 and helped England reach the final of the 2017 Rugby World Cup.

England women's coaches*
Jim Greenwood 1987
Steve Dowling 1990
Steve Jew 1994
Steve Peters & Eric Field 1997
Pete Kennedy 1999
Geoff Richards 2000
Gary Street 2007
Simon Middleton 2014-
* *By year of appointment*

Assistant coaches 1987-2020
Simon Crabb, Mark Francis, Steve Redfern, Rob Drinkwater, Graham Smith, Giselle Mather and Scott Bernard

7

THE NEW PIONEERS

1981-1989

THE DAWNING OF A NEW ERA

ngland kicked off their 1981 Five Nations campaign in Cardiff. Having been edged out in 1980, Wales were determined to prevail in the WRU's centenary year. Dusty Hare was England's most productive outlet, contributing all of England's 19 points through a try and five penalties, but Gareth Davies' dropped goal was the difference between the sides as Wales won 21-19. Wins against Scotland and Ireland kept Bill Beaumont's side in contention, before they were derailed by Jean-Pierre Rives' France on the way to another Grand Slam for 'Les Bleus'.

The season rounded off with a two-Test tour of Argentina. England XVs had played matches against Argentina and Japan during the 1970s. A new ruling from the International Board meant that the series would be capped and Hugo Porta's Argentina justified the ruling by holding the tourists to a 19-19 draw before England took the second Test 12-6.

Australia were the first visitors to Twickenham in 1982 and a good victory against a strong Wallabies side is often overshadowed in the history books by the half-time intervention of streaker Erica Roe. Headingley flanker Peter Winterbottom made his debut during the match and Nick Jeavons' try helped England to a 15-11 victory.

Serious injury ensured that Scotland would be the last of Beaumont's 34 caps. The game finished 9-9 and was followed by defeat to Ireland. A length of the field dribble and try, concocted by Mike Slemen and Clive Woodward, helped England to a second consecutive win in Paris and England finished the season strongly by beating Wales at Twickenham.

Dick Greenwood, capped five times in the late 1960s, became England coach in 1983. A disappointing Five Nations campaign was followed by the arrival of New Zealand in the autumn. Having beaten the tourists with the Midlands, 34-year-old Peter Wheeler was installed as captain. A physical contest was settled when Maurice Colclough touched down a rolling maul and England won 15-9. It was their first home win against New Zealand since 1936.

Previous pages: England and Wales meet in the inaugural women's rugby union international in 1987

Above: Maurice Colclough (hidden) crosses the New Zealand line to score at Twickenham in 1983, securing England's first home win against the All Blacks for 47 years

England recorded one win in 1984, over Ireland, as Rory Underwood made his first appearance. He would score his first international try the following month in Paris. Over the summer, England controversially toured South Africa, losing both Tests to the Springboks. In November, Wasps' Nigel Melville earned the rare distinction of captaining England on his debut against Australia at Twickenham. Stuart Barnes and Gareth Chilcott were others to be given debuts, but England lost 19-3 to a Wallaby side that included Nick Farr-Jones, Mark Ella and David Campese.

The 1985 season opened with Romania at Twickenham for the first time. England, under the captaincy of Paul Dodge, gave debuts to fly half Rob Andrew and Preston Grasshoppers' lock Wade Dooley and returned to winning ways after five straight defeats. A creditable draw against France was followed by a win against champions Scotland but the campaign fizzled out with defeats to Wales and Ireland. A two-Test series was lost in New Zealand but England continued to strengthen, with Wakefield's Mike Harrison and Gloucester's Mike Teague coming into the side.

Melville returned as captain in 1986 as Simon Halliday replaced Dodge at centre. Andrew's boot helped England to a tense 21-18 win against Wales, before an impressive Scotland brushed England aside at Murrayfield. England struck back at Twickenham with a 25-20 win against Ireland –

Dean Richards contributing two tries on his debut – but succumbed to defeat in Paris as France and Scotland shared the Championship.

The 1987 season began with three straight defeats and England struggling to score tries. A face-saving victory against Scotland completed the season as hooker Brian Moore made his debut in the English front row. The groundbreaking 1987 Rugby World Cup saw England exit at the quarter-final stage, and led to Geoff Cooke replacing Martin Green as coach. Meanwhile, the Red Roses' story began in Pontypool on 5 April as Carol Isherwood's England Women's side recorded a comfortable 22-4 victory against Wales.

Will Carling made his Test debut in 1988 but another try drought saw England lose their first two matches against France and Wales. There were no tries either in Murrayfield but a dropped goal from Andrew and two penalties from full back Jon Webb gave England a 9-6 victory.

England went into half-time at Twickenham against Ireland 3-0 down and having lost their captain to a fractured leg. Melville promptly instructed his teammates to show their concern "with tries". This they did, debut wing Chris Oti contributing three of England's six second-half tries as England turned the tables for a record 35-3 victory as *Swing Low, Sweet Chariot* rang out around the stadium.

England beat Ireland again in April before losing twice in Australia and then beating Fiji in Suva over the summer. In the autumn, Cooke created headlines by appointing the 23-year-old Carling as captain.

THE RED ROSES STORY BEGAN IN PONTYPOOL ON 5 APRIL 1987

Having previously only scored twice across four Five Nations campaigns since 1984 – to go with two tries against Japan in the 1987 Rugby World Cup – Underwood's England career was ignited following his try-scoring performances in the victories against Ireland. By the time England welcomed Australia to Twickenham in the autumn of 1988, the wing had scored seven tries in five matches. Scrum half Dewi Morris and lock Paul Ackford made their debuts and a brilliant England performance followed in which Underwood claimed another two tries on the way to a 28-19 victory.

In 1988, the Red Roses dispatched Wales again 36-6 at Newport. Emma Mitchell came into the side at scrum half, while Waterloo's Gill Burns made her debut later in the year in a 40-0 win against Sweden.

England's men started their 1989 campaign with a draw against Scotland before beating Ireland in Dublin. Carling strode to his first international try on the way to beating France 11-0, before his side lost in Cardiff – a result that allowed France to take the Championship.

A settled England side were now making good progress. Bath's rangy centre Jeremy Guscott made his debut against Romania and scored three tries. Oti, not to be outdone, scored four and England won 58-3.

In the autumn, Underwood returned once again to scoring form and equalled Danny Lambert's 82-year record by scoring five tries in a single match as England ran amok against Fiji. At the same time, he equalled Cyril Lowe's 66-year record 18 tries for his country during the 58-23 victory, in which two Fijian players saw red cards.

Top right: The Red Roses front row prepare for a scrum against Wales in 1987

Left: Will Carling, on debut, closes down France's Serge Blanco in Paris in 1988

PETER WHEELER

Born 26 November 1948
England career 1975-1984, 41 caps
Position Hooker **Club** Leicester

The Leicester hooker Peter Wheeler followed in the footsteps of John Pullin to become one of England's most capped hookers and a leading figure in the development of English rugby for over 40 years.

Wheeler won his first cap against France in 1975 and retired nine years later with 41 caps, having captained England five times in his final season, including a notable victory against the All Blacks at Twickenham in November 1983.

A strong all-round forward with outstanding handling skills and a key figure in the front row of England's Grand Slam team in 1980, he won 22 consecutive caps between 1977 and 1981, and also represented the British & Irish Lions on two tours to New Zealand in 1977 and South Africa in 1980, playing in seven Tests. He also made many appearances for the Barbarians, including matches against Australia in 1976 and New Zealand in 1978, and was in the winning Barbarians Seven at the Hong Kong Sevens tournament in 1981.

Wheeler began his playing career at Old Brockleians and played for Kent, before moving to Leicester for work in 1969 where he remained, playing 349 matches for the Tigers before retiring in 1985. Captain of three successive John Player cup-winning sides in 1979-81, he coached the club when Leicester won the inaugural Courage League title in 1987-88. He was the club's President in 1995-97, Chief Executive from 1996 to 2010 and Director of Rugby from 2010 to 2014. He became President of the Rugby Football Union in 2019.

History in the making

FOUNDATION OF THE WOMEN'S RUGBY FOOTBALL UNION

On 4 February 1984 a group of women met at University College London to discuss the formation of a Women's Rugby Union Association. They represented 12 clubs and universities who had been actively developing women's rugby in England since the late 1970s. At the conclusion of their meeting, the Women's Rugby Football Union (WRFU) was born.

A second meeting was held on 4 May following a meeting between Acting Secretary Sheila Welsh and the RFU Secretary Bob Weighill to discuss their proposal. Weighill informed Welsh that the RFU had no objections and a respectful, mutually supportive relationship was initiated.

At their third meeting, Carol Isherwood was elected Secretary and Debbie Griffin was elected Treasurer, a constitution was devised and a committee established.

The WRFU didn't just represent English rugby but also Welsh and Irish. So it was that in 1986, international women's rugby took root for the first time on British soil with a match at Richmond between Great Britain and France. The following year, England's Red Roses were ready to bloom, taking on and defeating Wales at Pontypool Park.

With the help of those early administrators, women's rugby quickly became one of the fastest-growing sports in England. The National Cup began in 1987 and, by 1994, there were 180 active clubs.

In 1994, WRFU AGM members decided that England, Ireland and Wales should operate independently and so the WRFU disbanded. In its place came the Rugby Football Union for Women (RFUW) which would administer the game in England. The RFUW was granted associate status by the RFU, who signalled its support for the women's game by paying down the financial loss incurred by the inaugural 1991 Rugby World Cup.

"We still have autonomy but we are now joined to the RFU," explained Rosie Golby, the then RFUW President, in 1994.

In 1996, the RFUW was granted funding by the Sports Council. By this time there were as many as 250 clubs in the country.

In 2010, the RFUW became a fully integrated constituent body within the RFU. The RFU funded professional contracts for the first time in 2014 and by 2020 there were more than 500 clubs in England.

Karen Almond of Great Britain on the attack against France in 1986

WALES 4 ENGLAND 22

5 April 1987, Pontypool Park

The first women's international Test match on British soil took place at the Athletic Ground, Richmond, in 1986, when Great Britain took on France. The Red Roses came into being the following year and so began one of the most stirring success stories in the history of English rugby.

Carol Isherwood led her side out at Pontypool Park on a fine and dry spring afternoon in front of just under 2,000 people. Wasps midfield duo of Suzy Hill and Karen Almond had started for Great Britain the previous year, as had wing Debbie MacLaren of Richmond. Seven Loughborough University students were in the squad, including Nicky Ponsford at hooker. Three more were on the opposing side, including Wales captain Liza Burgess.

England started brightly. Almond capitalised on a Welsh error to send Pippa Atkinson over for England's first try. In the 26th minute Almond's perfectly timed looping run delivered her first try and England's second. Hill then fed Atkinson again and England were three tries to the good by half-time.

Wales started the second half with renewed vigour and drove into the English half. In an instant,

Team captains Carol Isherwood and Liza Burgess embrace at the final whistle after a hard-fought match

Almond turned defence into attack and Atkinson was across the tryline again. Such was the quality of the English fly half's play that a partisan Welsh crowd took to applauding her every contribution as the second half wore on.

The captains Isherwood and Burgess rounded off the scoring with a fifth try for England and a deserved consolation try for Wales to deliver England a 22–4 victory. The Red Roses were underway.

England C Willietts – P Atkinson, S Robson, C Gurney, D MacLaren – K Almond, S Hill – J Pauley, N Ponsford, J Watts – E Whalley, T King – S Cockerill, S Treadwell, C Isherwood* (Replacement: D Mills)

Wales R Morgan – R Wyatt, E Davies, S Lovell, GF Paw – A Bennett, S Williams – E Skiffington, M-A Harvey, B Davies – M Farr, F Margerison – H Carey, L Burgess*, J Rosser

NB: Teams selected to start on the day of the match

Left (top to bottom):
Carol Isherwood gives
her pre-match team-
talk; Karen Almond
stretches the Welsh
defence; Sally Cockerill
lines up a pass

Above: Jane Pauley
tackles Wales' Frances
Margerison

Right: Isherwood with
the match-winners
plaque, and Nicky
Ponsford enjoys the
victory at Pontypool
Park (far right)

The England Greats

CAROL ISHERWOOD

Born 27 July 1961 **England career** 1987-1992, 7 caps
Position Back Row **Clubs** Leeds University, Richmond

Leigh-born Carol Isherwood started playing rugby in 1982, at the age of 20. She set up her own side at Leeds University later the same year. In 1984, she helped to found the Women's Rugby Football Union before being elected as its first Secretary.

As a player Isherwood was fast and strong. She began as a prop but it was quickly discovered that she read the game better than almost anyone and she was encouraged to move into the back row. She accepted the challenge, initially as a No 8 and then as a flanker, where her excellent carrying and tackling skills came to the fore.

It was this, allied to her natural game management, that made Isherwood the obvious choice for captain when Great Britain contested the first international match on British soil in 1986. She played well and the following year was asked to captain the Red Roses in their first fixture, against Wales in Pontypool (*pictured far right*). She therefore holds the the unique distinction of being the only person to have captained both England and Great Britain in their inaugural matches.

Between 1986 and 1992, Isherwood played eight times for Great Britain and seven times for England, a run which included the first Women's Rugby World Cup Final of 1991. After hanging up her boots, she remained in camp as a coach and travelled with the England side to Scotland for the 1994 World Cup.

After England had won their semi-final, Isherwood introduced the squad to an unusual game called 'Killing as an Organised Sport' (KAOS), in which players sent each

other inventive death threats. It was intended as a means of distraction to settle the nerves and it worked: England went on to become world champions for the first time.

She has since remained in women's rugby as an administrator and was awarded the OBE in 2003. Described by Sue Day as a "brilliant woman who got women's rugby professionalised", she has done as much as any person to bring the game to where it is today. Asked in her youth "Why rugby?" she simply replied because she loved it.

Carol Isherwood with the IRB Women's Personality of the Year award in 2008

"A PIONEER OF THE DEVELOPMENT OF THE WOMEN'S GAME IN ENGLAND"

The World Rugby statement on Isherwood's appointment to their Hall of Fame in 2014

UNDONE DOWN UNDER

ENGLAND WORLD CUP SQUAD
MAY/JUNE 1987

The first Rugby World Cup took place in Australia and New Zealand in May and June 1987. Sixteen countries took part – although there was no place for South Africa, living under apartheid and banned from official international competition under the terms of the Gleneagles Agreement. Many of the matches were highly competitive with the All Blacks the outstanding team and worthy winners.

England had experienced a poor Five Nations that year. Defeated 17-0 in Dublin by Ireland, they then lost 19-15 to France at Twickenham and 19-12 to Wales in a bad-tempered match in Cardiff. Four English players were suspended by that point, and Wakefield wing Mike Harrison was handed the captaincy. Harrison's penalty try then salvaged something from the season by helping to beat Scotland 21-12 at home.

England were drawn in Pool 1 with Australia, Japan and the USA. They lost 19-6 to Australia in their opening match at the Concord Oval in Sydney. A much closer match than the score suggests, it was notable for a disputed try awarded to David Campese and the debut of Jonathan Webb at full back as substitute for the injured Marcus Rose after 10 minutes. England won their other two pool matches convincingly. They beat Japan at the

Concord Oval by 60-7, with captain Mike Harrison scoring three tries and Webb kicking 20 points, and the USA at Ballymore, Brisbane, by 34-6, with two tries from Peter Winterbottom and 18 points from the boot of Webb. These victories gave England second place in their pool and a place in the quarter finals against Wales in Brisbane.

Wales had won all three of their pool matches and England had impressed in their three matches, but the weather was appalling and the resultant play was little better on a treacherous surface at Ballymore. Wales led by a converted try at half-time and their scrum and lineout were strong throughout. In the second half, they scored two further tries, one a dramatic kick and chase try by their scrum half Robert Jones, and pulled away to win 16-3 and progress to the semi-finals. England's first World Cup campaign was over.

Left: Mike Harrison on the charge against Japan

Above: England take on co-hosts Australia

Right: A scrum during the quarter-final against Wales

Far right: Dean Richards feels the strain

23 May 1987
Australia 19 England 6
Concord Oval, Sydney
Attendance: 17,896

30 May 1987
England 60 Japan 7
Concord Oval, Sydney
Attendance: 4,893

3 June 1987
England 34 USA 6
Concord Oval, Sydney
Attendance: 8,785

POOL 1	P	W	D	L	F	A	Pts
Australia	3	3	0	0	108	41	6
England	**3**	**2**	**0**	**1**	**100**	**32**	**4**
USA	3	1	0	2	39	99	2
Japan	3	0	0	3	48	123	0

Quarter-final
8 June 1987
Wales 16 England 3
Ballymore, Brisbane
Attendance: 15,000

Final
20 June 1987
New Zealand 29 France 9
Eden Park, Auckland
Attendance: 46,000

OFFICIAL MATCH BALL
RUGBY WORLD CUP 1987

5

RORY UNDERWOOD

Born 19 June 1963
England career 1984-1996, 85 caps
Position Wing **Clubs** RAF, Leicester

One of the most exciting and elusive try-scoring wingers in rugby history made his debut for England against Ireland in February 1984. Rory Underwood did not score on his debut, but he did score a magical try on his second appearance against France in Paris and he went on to set an England men's record of 49 tries in his 85 internationals over the next 12 years.

Underwood joined the Royal Air Force after leaving school and played for Leicester and the RAF throughout his international career. He scored nine tries in six consecutive matches in 1988 and a crucial try on the left wing against France at Twickenham in the final match of England's successful 1991 Grand Slam campaign (*right*). He also played in two further Grand Slam sides in 1992 and 1995. In his three World Cup tournaments between 1987 and 1995, including the 1991 World Cup final against Australia, he scored a record 11 tries in his 15 matches.

Underwood toured twice with the British & Irish Lions to Australia in 1989 and New Zealand in 1993, while his final appearance for England came against Ireland at the end of the Five Nations Championship in 1996.

From the autumn of 1992, he was joined on the international stage by his younger brother and fellow back Tony, who played for England until 1998 and scored 13 tries in his 27 internationals. They played in 19 internationals together, including England's 1995 World Cup campaign in South Africa, and their mother became a much-loved presence at Twickenham internationals through the mid-1990s.

History in the making

KEEPING IT IN THE FAMILY

In the 19th century **Reginald Birkett** from Clapham Rovers scored a try in the first English international in 1871. His brother **Louis** played alongside him in 1875-77 and his son **John** played for Harlequins and became the most capped England centre before the First World War.

England's 1871 captain **Fred Stokes** and his brother **Lennard** from Blackheath were followed by **Temple** and **Charles Gurdon** from Richmond in the 1880s. Further notable pairs of brothers in the years before 1914 were **Fred** and **Francis Byrne** from Moseley; **Frank** and **Percy Stout** from Gloucester (*above*); Adrian and Tim Stoop from Harlequins; and Cherry and Robert Pillman from Blackheath.

Stephen and **Graham Meikle** from

Waterloo and **Harold** and **Arthur Wheatley** from Coventry represented England between the wars. **Peter Preece** followed his father **Ivor** into the Coventry and England side in the 1970s. In 1992, the **Underwood** brothers (*below*) made their first appearance together in the England backline against South Africa.

Dick Greenwood played five times and captained England in the 1960s. His son **Will** played 55 Tests and scored 31 tries from 1997 to 2004.

Maxine Edwards captained the Red Roses for the first time at Twickenham in 2003, but it was her sister **Jacquie** whose try in the final helped England to become world champions in 1994.

Andy Farrell played eight times for England in 2007. His son **Owen** made

his debut in 2012. Captain of England at the 2019 Rugby World Cup, he has won more than 80 caps and scored more than 900 points. **Nick Youngs** was a scrum half who played for Leicester and England in the 1980s. Of his sons, **Ben** is the most capped scrum half in English rugby history and his older brother **Tom** won 28 caps as a hooker.

The Vunipola brothers came from a Tongan family that settled in Wales

Coach Andy Farrell pictured with his son Owen and the Calcutta Cup in 2012

then England. **Mako Vunipola** made his England debut against Fiji in 2012. **Billy Vunipola**, the younger brother, made his England debut on tour to Argentina in 2013. Both brothers had won more than 50 caps by the time they appeared in the 2019 World Cup Final against South Africa.

SWING LOW, SWEET CHARIOT

Swing Low, Sweet Chariot is an old Afro-American spiritual song sometimes credited to freed slave Wallis Willis. It is thought to have been inspired by the Red River in Oklahoma and it has been surmised that the chariot refers to the Underground Railway, a secret network of safe houses that helped slaves escape north to the Free States and Canada.

The song had been sung in English rugby clubhouses since the 1960s but was first heard at Twickenham during the Middlesex Sevens, an end-of-season invitational seven-a-side tournament hosted by Twickenham from 1926 to 2011.

On a balmy summer afternoon in 1987, a classic edition of the tournament played out in which Harlequins and Rosslyn Park II progressed to the final. In the Rosslyn Park side was 20-year-old Martin Offiah. Known to his teammates as 'Chariots', Offiah's prolific try-scoring throughout the tournament and earlier in the year at the Hong Kong Sevens inspired the watching faithful to song.

The 'Voice of Rugby' commentator Bill McLaren described the "great waves of song" from the terrace as *Swing Low, Sweet Chariot* rang out at Twickenham for the first time.

It might have proved a one-off but for England's astonishing second-half performance the following year against Ireland at Twickenham. Six second-half tries, including two for Rory Underwood and three for Chris Oti (*right*) on his debut, had fans on their feet and *Swing Low* rang out once more. Since then, *Swing Low* has been an enduring anthem of English rugby and it has a long-held place in the history of the game.

As part of its commitment to improving diversity and inclusion, the RFU continues to use social media and other means to proactively educate fans on the history and provenance of the song.

ENGLAND 28 AUSTRALIA 19

5 November 1988, Twickenham

England's convincing victory in the autumn international against Australia at Twickenham in November 1988 is widely regarded as having been the start of a new era. Geoff Cooke had been the England coach since January 1988 and, after a summer tour of mixed success in Australia and Fiji, he decided that a fresh start was needed.

His most notable decision was the appointment of 22-year-old centre Will Carling, still only in his eighth international, as long-term captain. The backline included Jonathan Webb at full back, Rory Underwood and Simon Halliday in the three-quarters and Rob Andrew at fly half. Props Paul Rendall and Jeff Probyn, hooker Brian Moore, second row Wade Dooley and number eight Dean Richards formed the backbone of the pack. The three new caps were Dewi Morris at scrum half, Paul Ackford in the second row and Andrew Harriman, the Harlequins speedster and sevens specialist, earning his only cap.

The Wallabies, under the captaincy of scrum half Nick Farr-Jones, contained some great players, including Michael Lynagh and David Campese. With England trailing before half-time, Morris touched down after a charge-down to level the scores at 9-9. Australian wing David Campese was always dangerous and a 60-

Will Carling breaks through the Australian defence in his first game as England captain

yard interception try after a loose pass gave Australia the lead. Undeterred, England struck back with two magnificent tries by left wing Rory Underwood, after Australia's midfield defence had twice been exposed. Webb converted the second and kicked a penalty to put England into the lead 22-13. The England back row, with Bath's Andy Robinson in superb form, dominated the close-quarter exchanges but Australia scored a

converted try to bring the score to 22-19 with three minutes to go.

With 80 minutes gone, Carling made a superb break from inside the England half and Halliday sealed victory with a try. Webb's conversion brought the final score to 28-19. Carling was hurt in the lead-up to the try and had to be replaced for the final minutes but, what became known as the Carling era had well and truly begun.

England JM Webb – AT Harriman, WDC Carling* (JRD Buckton), SJ Halliday, R Underwood – CR Andrew, CD Morris – PAG Rendall, BC Moore, JA Probyn – PJ Ackford, WA Dooley – RA Robinson, D Richards, DW Egerton

Australia AJ Leeds – JC Grant, B Girvan, MT Cook, DI Campese – MP Lynagh, NC Farr-Jones* – MN Hartill, TA Lawton, AJ McIntyre – SAG Cutler, WA Campbell – JS Miller, SN Tuynman, JM Gardner

WILL CARLING

Born 12 December 1965 **England career** 1988-1997, 72 caps
Position Centre **Clubs** Durham University, Harlequins

Will Carling is one of the most successful captains in the history of English rugby. A gifted centre and accomplished leader, he was a key personality as rugby transitioned from an amateur to a professional sport.

Carling played his first match for England in January 1988 in Paris and went on to win 72 caps and captain his country a record 59 times – a run which included a record three Grand Slams and two World Cup tournaments.

Educated at Sedbergh School, Carling joined the British Army after attending Durham University – playing for the Army against the Royal Navy in 1987 – but resigned his commission in 1988 and joining Harlequins that summer; he remained at the club until his retirement in January 1998.

England coach Geoff Cooke chose the 22-year-old Carling as his captain for the autumn international against Australia in November 1988, the youngest appointment since Peter Howard in 1931. England won a thrilling match with a late try after one of Carling's trademark busting breaks through the midfield.

His pace and power were combined with outstanding handling skills, and his centre partnership with Bath's Jeremy Guscott is regarded as one of England's greatest. Carling and Guscott played together a world record 44 times between 1989 and 1996, with one additional Test for the Lions in 1993. Carling scored 12 tries in internationals and led England to 44 victories during his eight-year captaincy. He toured with the Lions to New Zealand in 1993 and played in seven matches, including the first of the three Tests.

England's success during Carling's tenure as captain led to a notable increase in media attention, with Carling often at the eye of the storm. His controversial remark about the influence of "57 old farts" on RFU decision-making led to him being briefly stripped of the captaincy. He was reinstated with the support of his teammates in time for the 1995 Rugby World Cup following a public apology.

A gifted public speaker, Carling returned to the England set-up as an advisor to Eddie Jones' team on the eve of the 2019 Rugby World Cup.

"HE WASN'T GIVEN ENOUGH CREDIT FOR HOW GOOD HE WAS. HE WAS ARGUABLY THE BEST INSIDE CENTRE IN THE WORLD"

Jeremy Guscott

The shirt Leonard wore for England's 19-0 victory over Argentina in 2000, when he surpassed Rory Underwood as England men's record cap holder

"TECHNICALLY HE WAS SUPERB AND TEMPERAMENTALLY HE WAS SOUND, A HUGE CHARACTER ON AND OFF THE PITCH"

Sir Ian McGeechan

FIRST TIME OF ASKING

The first Women's Rugby World Cup hosted by Wales bore testimony to the determination and pioneering spirit of a small group of individuals, led by Chairwoman of the Organising Committee Deborah Griffin and including Alice Cooper, Sue Dorrington and Mary Forsyth.

The event would generate £19,117 in income but would cost £83,521, in part because the Russian team arrived without money. It was hoped that the difference might be made up through sponsorship but, while the media turned out in numbers, financial backers proved elusive.

Invitations to play were sent out by fax and 12 countries from around the world arrived in Cardiff to play. England, captained by Karen Almond and with Gill Burns, Emma Mitchell and Cheryl Stennett in the XV, were drawn in the group stages against Spain and Italy, both of whom they defeated.

Getting into their groove, the Red Roses brushed aside a strong French side 13-0 in the semi-finals. On the other side of the draw, the USA defeated New Zealand to take their place in the final.

From the outset Karen Almond had been unsure if England could compete with the athleticism of the American team and surmised that their best chance lay in their scrum. Her analysis proved correct. England started the game well, enjoying pack dominance, but for the most part failed to capitalise on possession. Against the run of play the USA landed a penalty but a penalty try, converted by Burns, gave England a 6-3 half-time lead.

In the second half, and despite England's best efforts, the Eagles struck back. Flanker Claire Godwin scored two tries to take the game away from Almond's side. USA won 19-6 and USA captain Mary Sullivan became the first player to lift the trophy.

Off the field, the WRFU would be dogged by the financial losses accrued during the tournament for years to come but Griffin, Cooper, Dorrington and Forsyth were not despondent, having ushered the women's game into the spotlight.

"A few months ago no one would have believed we would have 12 countries competing in Wales for a World Cup," said Griffin afterwards. "We've done the ground work."

Above: The 1991 England Women's World Cup squad who participated in the first tournament in Wales

Left: Gill Burns reaches for a lineout ball during the World Cup Final against the USA in Cardiff

Top: Burns battles gale force weather and the Spanish opposition in the pool game in Swansea

Above: England scrum half Emma Mitchell looks to release her backs to attack the USA defence in the final

6 April 1991
England 12 Spain 0
Swansea

8 April 1991
Italy 9 England 25
Llanharan

POOL 4	P	W	D	L	F	A
England	2	2	0	0	37	9
Spain	2	1	0	1	13	19
Italy	2	0	0	2	16	25

Semi-final
12 April 1991
England 13 France 0
Cardiff Arms Park

Final
14 April 1991
England 6 United States 19
Cardiff Arms Park
Attendance: 2,800

England J Mitchell – C Stennett, S Robson, C Willietts, D Francis – K Almond*, E Mitchell (G Prangnell) – S Ewing, S Dorrington, J Watts – S Wenn, H Stirrup – J Ross, G Burns, C Isherwood

USA MG Sullivan* – P Jervey, C Orsini, J Crawford, K McFarren – C Harju, P Connell – A Flavin, V Sullivan, M Sorensen – T Breckenridge, T Flanagan – C Godwin, K Flores, M Whitehead

ENGLAND 21 FRANCE 19

16 March 1991, Twickenham

England celebrate their first Grand Slam since 1980

All paths led to Twickenham on 16 March 1991. Both England and France could win the Grand Slam and the French were formidable adversaries, with a backline renowned for its initiative and pace. After an opening penalty goal, Simon Hodgkinson lined up a second penalty attempt, which floated narrowly past the upright on the wrong side. What happened next has entered rugby legend.

Scrum half Pierre Berbizier caught the ball behind his own line and started running. The ball passed through the hands of full back Serge Blanco, right wing Jean-Baptiste Lafond, fly half Didier Camberabero and the great centre Philippe Sella, who returned the ball to Camberabero. He ran up the right wing and, when challenged after catching his own short kick ahead, crosskicked towards the England posts. Philippe Saint-André, the French left wing, had been following the movement and he ran to collect the ball. After checking his pace, he picked up the bouncing ball and ran 20 metres to score a sensational try underneath the posts.

A superb example of French flair had lit up Twickenham and England knew they were in a contest. Showing great resolve, they worked their way back into the game and established an 18-9 lead at

half-time through a drop goal by Rob Andrew, a 27th international try for Rory Underwood and two further penalty goals and a conversion from Hodgkinson.

But France kept coming back. Camberabero scored a short-range unconverted try after a mix-up on the English line before Hodgkinson kicked another penalty goal to give him a record 60 points in that year's Championship. The French revival continued, with another stunning long-range try in the 77th minute by centre Franck Mesnel, following vital lead-up play by Blanco and Sella.

Camberabero converted this try to narrow England's winning margin to two points, but the English pack remained steadfast.

Spurred on by the crowd, Carling's side held on through the tense closing minutes to win England's ninth Grand Slam. Their success was hard earned and well deserved after 11 long years and the disappointment of Murrayfield the previous year.

England SD Hodgkinson – NJ Heslop, JC Guscott, WDC Carling*, R Underwood – CR Andrew, RJ Hill – J Leonard, BC Moore, JA Probyn – PJ Ackford, WA Dooley – PJ Winterbottom, D Richards, MC Teague

France S Blanco* – J-B Lafond, F Mesnel, P Sella, P Saint-André – D Camberabero, P Berbizier – G Lascubé, P Marocco, P Ondarts – M Tachdjian (M Cecillon), O Roumat – L Cabannes, A Benazzi, X Blond

The England Greats

JEREMY GUSCOTT

Born 7 July 1965
England career 1989-1999, 65 caps
Position Centre **Club** Bath

Jeremy Guscott was a powerful, elusive, running centre from Bath who won 65 caps for England in a 10-year international career. After playing in Bath's winning team in the Pilkington Cup Final in April, his England career started sensationally in May 1989 when he scored three tries on his debut against Romania in Bucharest. He then played in the second and third Tests of the British & Irish Lions tour of Australia, in which he scored a vital try in the second.

Guscott cemented his place in the England centre, alongside Will Carling, throughout the 1989-90 season, in which he scored four tries in five matches and was a key member of the 1991, 1992 and 1995 Grand Slam sides. He scored 30 tries and two drop goals in his England career and twice scored four tries in a match. His partnership with Carling spanned a world record 45 matches, including one Test for the Lions. Their pairing combined flair, genuine pace and power and helped give England an attacking edge that the side had not possessed for many years.

Guscott played in the 1991 World Cup Final at Twickenham and the 1995 semi-final defeat to the All Blacks at Newlands, Cape Town, making 13 appearances across three World Cups and scoring four tries, including two in his final international against Tonga at Twickenham in the 1999 tournament. He toured Australia and New Zealand in 1993 and South Africa in 1997 with the British & Irish Lions, played in eight Lions Tests and scored the series-winning drop goal in the second Test against the Springboks at King's Park, Durban.

A one-club man whose career spanned the amateur and professional eras, Guscott played in four Pilkington Cup-winning sides and more than 260 matches for Bath between 1984 and 2000.

Regarded as one of the most exciting centres England has ever produced, he represented the Barbarians on nine occasions and thrilled crowds with his scintillating running and accomplished distribution skills. Since his retirement, he has been a regular and insightful broadcaster and commentator on rugby for the BBC.

"HIS GRACE AND PACE EARNED THE PLAUDITS OF EVERY DISCERNING FAN"

David Llewellyn in The Year of the Rose

THE FINAL HURDLE

England approached the second Rugby World Cup with genuine optimism. The competition was being held in the UK and France in October and November 1991, with England scheduled to play their three pool games at Twickenham. Grand Slam winners in the 1991 Five Nations Championship, despite being defeated by Australia on their summer tour, England had the basis of a very settled team under the captaincy of Will Carling.

The opening match of the World Cup saw England lose 18-12 to New Zealand, having led 12-9 at half-time, although the All Blacks dominated the forward exchanges and scored the only try of the match. Expected victories followed in England's two remaining pool matches against Italy (36-6) and the USA (37-9), which left them as runners-up to New Zealand in Pool 1.

England's reward was a quarter-final against France, winners of Pool 4, in Paris at Parc des Princes. It was an explosive match, which eventually ended in England's favour 19-10, after they had led 10-6 at half-time. The French backs always threatened but the England pack, with wing forward Micky Skinner to the fore, proved indomitable. Jonathan Webb kicked three penalty goals and converted the second of the England backline's tries to see England through to the semi-final.

Scotland awaited England at Murrayfield in the semi-final, after they had beaten Western Samoa convincingly in their quarter-final. Home advantage was expected to be decisive after Scotland's defeat of England at Murrayfield in a Grand Slam decider only 18 months earlier. It was a tense, dour and try-less match in which the superior kicking of fly half Rob Andrew, allied to another powerful performance by the English pack, saw England through 9-6.

Only Australia now stood in England's way in the final at Twickenham on 2 November 1991. Australia had beaten New Zealand handsomely in their semi-final the weekend before in Dublin and their team contained some outstanding players, but England had home advantage and a crowd of 56,208 saw an enthralling match full of incident.

England elected to play a more expansive game in the belief that they would not win

with a gameplan based solely on a powerful pack, supported by the kicking of Rob Andrew at fly half. Australia started strongly and scored the only try of the match midway through the first half, with fly half Michael Lynagh adding a penalty goal to lead 9-0 at half-time. Webb and Lynagh traded penalty goals in a tense second half remembered primarily for a controversial knock forward by star Wallaby winger David Campese, which prevented a potentially try-scoring pass to Rory Underwood. Despite England's efforts, the Australian defence held firm in the closing stages to give them victory 12-6 and the Rugby World Cup for the first time.

England JM Webb – SJ Halliday, JC Guscott, WDC Carling*, R Underwood – CR Andrew, RJ Hill – J Leonard, BC Moore, JA Probyn – PJ Ackford, WA Dooley – MG Skinner, MC Teague, PJ Winterbottom

Australia MC Roebuck – DI Campese, JS Little, TJ Horan, RH Egerton – MP Lynagh, NC Farr-Jones* – AJ Daly, PN Kearns, EJA McKenzie – RJ McCall, JA Eales – SP Poidevin, T Coker, V Ofahengaue

Left: Will Carling celebrates after scoring a late try against France to take his team to the semi-finals

Above: It's joy for England as the final whistle goes at the end of the semi-final at Murrayfield

AUSTRALIA
ENGLAND
The Final

Left: Will Carling introduces his players to the Queen before the final at Twickenham

Below: Dejection for England as they lose the final to Australia

3 October 1991
England 12 New Zealand 18
Twickenham
Attendance: 57,200

8 October 1991
England 36 Italy 6
Twickenham
Attendance: 30,000

11 October 1991
England 37 USA 9
Twickenham
Attendance: 45,000

POOL 1	P	W	D	L	F	A	Pts
New Zealand	3	3	0	0	95	39	6
England	**3**	**2**	**0**	**1**	**85**	**33**	**4**
Italy	3	1	0	2	57	76	2
USA	3	0	0	3	24	113	0

Quarter-final
19 October 1991
France 10 England 19
Parc des Princes, Paris
Attendance: 48,500

Semi-final
26 October 1991
Scotland 6 England 9
Murrayfield
Attendance : 60,000

Final
2 November 1991
England 6 Australia 12
Twickenham
Attendance: 56,208

ENGLAND 17 USA 6

8 June 1993, Fletcher's Field, Markham

The Canada Cup was an opportunity for the best European and North American sides to compete ahead of the 1994 Rugby World Cup. England, captained by experienced fly half Karen Almond, went into the tournament looking to measure their progress against the USA, the reigning world champions. The format was unrelenting, three games in five days in two locations spread across Greater Toronto in Ontario, Canada.

Above: Jane Mangham, Jayne Molyneux, assistant coach Steve Peters and Gill Burns, who played on with a broken nose and two broken cheekbones, hold the Canada Cup
Top right: Victory over the USA in the mud and fog

The Red Roses would face the USA first. As in 1991, the Eagles retained a slight athletic advantage and were particularly dangerous in broken play and running from deep. England, however, planned to implement a traditional English gameplan by keeping the ball and starving their skilful opponents of possession.

The USA began strongly in muddy conditions and went into a 6-0 lead after 20 minutes through two penalty goals from their fly half Jos Bergmann. England increasingly came into the game and manufactured tries by winger Val Blackett and a penalty try from a powerful scrum surge. Both tries were converted by captain Karen Almond, who added a penalty to give England a half-time lead of 14-6. The second half

was hard-fought, but the USA made numerous errors and failed to take their chances. The sole score was a second penalty goal by Almond which gave England a convincing 17-6 victory over the world champions.

England J Mitchell – V Blackett, J Edwards, G Mather, A Cole – K Almond*, E Mitchell – J Mangham, S Dorrington, S Ewing – S Wenn, H Stirrup – J Ross, G Burns, G Shore

USA K McFarren – P Jervey, J Crawford, J Drustrup, A Westerman – J Bergmann, P Connell – C Fahey, J Gray, M Sorensen – T Breckenridge, J Rutkowski – M Whitehead, K Flores, T Flanagan

The England Greats

NICKY PONSFORD

Born 6 October 1967 **England career** 1987-2002, 50 caps
Position Hooker **Clubs** Loughborough University, Waterloo, Clifton

Nicky Ponsford's contribution to the Red Roses cannot be overstated. As both player and administrator she has walked every step of the journey from 1987 onwards.

Born in Leamington Spa, Ponsford began playing rugby at Loughborough University in 1986. The following year, she was selected at hooker for England's inaugural match against Wales. On graduation from university, she briefly took time off from the game to sail for Great Britain in 1989, before returning to Waterloo and England.

During the first World Cup in 1991 she demonstrated her versatility and nous by operating as an emergency loose-head prop against Italy, while in 1994 she was instrumental in the dominant scrummaging that allowed England to lift the Rugby World Cup for the first time. Two years later, she was injured in the second match of the inaugural Home Nations Championship, which England went on to win. She became a National Development Officer with the RFU the same year.

Ponsford played in her third World Cup in 1998, after recovering from a torn calf muscle in time to make the squad. She was awarded an OBE in 2001 and remarkably earned the last of her 50 caps in 2002. By then, she had become Head of Women's Performance for the RFUW, as it further integrated into the RFU.

Since then, she has overseen an extraordinary period of success for the Red Roses that included another World Cup victory in 2014. More recently, she helped launch the Premier 15s, which she hopes will become a breeding ground for female coaches.

"OVER MORE THAN 30 YEARS, NICKY PONSFORD HAS LEFT HER MARK ON WOMEN'S RUGBY IN ENGLAND"

World Rugby

History in the making

RUGBY WORLD CUP SEVENS 1993

Sevens famously originated in the Scottish Borders in the town of Melrose in 1883. It was fitting, therefore, that the inaugural Rugby World Cup Sevens tournament should take place in Scotland. In April 1993, 24 nations arrived at Murrayfield to contest the Melrose Cup.

England had selected a mixture of youth and experience. Harlequin Andrew Harriman was a veteran of the Middlesex Sevens, while Lawrence Dallaglio, Tim Rodber, Nick Beal and Damian Hopley were all talented youngsters at the beginning of their careers.

England came through the first group stage in second place, enough to qualify for the quarter-final group stage in which they would face New Zealand, South Africa and Australia. Harriman got them off to a flyer against New Zealand and England led 21-0 at half-time, holding on for a 21-12 victory.

A Chester Williams try put South Africa ahead in their next match before captain Harriman struck again and England won 14-7. An Australia side that included Michael Lynagh and David Campese won the final pool match, but

Lawrence Dallaglio fends off David Campese in the Melrose Cup Final

England had done enough to reach the semi-finals.

There they met tournament favourites Fiji and the outstanding Waisale Serevi. Fiji took the lead before Harriman scored in response. A sidestep from Dallaglio then put England in front, before a famous tackle by Dave Scully allowed Adedayo Adebayo to send Harriman away for England's third try. The match finished 21-7 and England were in the final for a rematch against Australia.

Having defeated England already and in the XVs World Cup two years earlier, Australia went into the final as clear favourites. England, however, were inspired and Harriman caught the opposition out in the first minute with a searing run from deep in his own half. Dallaglio added a second try from the restart and Rodber another to put England into an almost unassailable 21-0 lead.

Australia fought back valiantly but England eventually prevailed 21-17 and Harriman became the first player to lift a World Cup for England, a victory he immediately dedicated to Queen, country and his parents.

Melrose Cup Final
18 April 1993
England 21 Australia 17
Murrayfield, Edinburgh

England AA Adebayo, ND Beal, JPS Cassell, LBN Dallaglio, MJS Dawson, AT Harriman*, DP Hopley, TAK Rodber, D Scully, CMA Sheasby

Australia MC Burke, DI Campese, R Constable, J Fenwicke, JA Flett, G Lodge, MP Lynagh, V Ofahengaue, IS Tabua, SHS Taupeaffe

ON TOP OF THE WORLD

The second iteration of the Women's Rugby World Cup was to be held in the Netherlands. As the International Rugby Board (IRB) hadn't endorsed the tournament, New Zealand decided not to compete. An eleventh-hour intervention by the Federation of International Amateur Rugby caused the Netherlands to withdraw and the tournament was without a host.

Refusing to squander their work to date, the WRFU rebranded the tournament as a 'World Championship' and Scotland stepped in as hosts. Twelve teams were divided into four pools, including Kazakhstan and Scottish Students, who replaced Spain on the tournament's eve.

The USA once again arrived as favourites but were given a stern test by Wales' utilisation of the rolling maul. England had retained the core of the 1991 side but Karen Almond, Emma Mitchell and Gill Burns had grown as players and were bolstered by a superb tight-five that included a front row of Jane Mangham, Nicky Ponsford and Sandy Ewing.

A focused England side defeated Russia, hosts Scotland and Canada, to set up a semi-final with France. A much tighter game

Far left: England on the way to a comfortable win against Russia in their first game

Left: A second pool stage victory for England, this time against the tournament hosts in Edinburgh

Right: Gill Burns battles for possession with the French at a lineout during the semi-final win at Galashiels

11 April 1994
England 66 Russia 0
Boroughmuir

15 April 1994
Scotland 0 England 26
Boroughmuir

POOL B	P	W	D	L	For	Ag
England	2	2	0	0	92	0
Scotland	2	1	0	1	51	26
Russia	2	0	0	2	0	117

Quarter-final
17 April 1994
England 24 Canada 10
Galashiels

Semi-final
20 April 1994
England 18 France 6
Galashiels

followed but England did their best to control possession and booked their place in the final with an 18-6 victory.

The final between England and USA, a repeat of the 1991 tournament, would be held at one of rugby's great spiritual homes, Raeburn Place in Edinburgh, where the first international match between Scotland and England had taken place back in 1871.

As in 1991, the American side retained a level of athleticism that England would struggle to match. England had, however, beaten them in the Canada Cup the previous summer and this time captain Almond felt that the English pack had the measure of the Eagles up front.

So it proved in a first half in which the

Far left: Scrum half Emma Mitchell urges her pack forward

Below: Jacquie Edwards bursts through to score the final try of the match

Left: England captain Karen Almond (left) and Sarah Wenn crack open the bubbly after their historic win

Below: Gill Burns' winners' medal

Right: Sandy Ewing, Gill Burns, Paula George, Giselle Prangnell and Genevieve Shore celebrate with the World Cup trophy

English pack was dominant. Every time the Americans wheeled or collapsed, the Red Roses simply opted to scrum again. The result was two penalty tries and a commanding 25-metre pushover by Burns to give England the lead.

The Eagles inevitably struck back with two tries from Jen Crawford and one each from Elise Huffer and Patty Jervey, but a breakaway try from England centre Jacquie Edwards settled things in favour of the Red Roses by 38-23. Almond became the first English player to lift a fifteen-a-side Rugby World Cup.

Unlike in 1991, the tournament itself was a commercial success, yielding a £30,000 profit for the Scottish Rugby Union who pledged to reinvest locally. The next tournament would be officially endorsed by the IRB, who retrospectively did the same for 1991 and 1994 tournaments in 2009.

World Cup Final
24 April 1994
England 38 United States 23
Raeburn Place, Edinburgh
Attendance: 5,000

England J Mitchell – V Blackett, J Edwards (P George), G Prangnell, A Cole – K Almond*, E Mitchell – J Mangham, N Ponsford, S Ewing – S Wenn (J Chambers), H Stirrup – J Ross, G Burns, G Shore

USA J Crawford – K McFarren, C Orsini, E Huffer, P Jervey – J Bergman, P Connell – A Flavin, J Gray, M Sorensen – J Rutkowski, T Flanagan – S Hunt, B Bond*, L Spicer-Bourdon

Karen Almond's 1994
World Cup-winning
jersey and the front
page of The Times
on 25 April 1994,
showing Almond
celebrating England's
victory alongside
her teammates

The England Greats

KAREN ALMOND

Born 18 December 1962 **England career** 1987-1994, 24 caps
Position Fly Half **Clubs** Loughborough University, Wasps, Saracens

Karen Almond arrived at Loughborough University as a middle-distance athlete. She fell in love with rugby at once, appreciating the freedom it offered and, although she started her first game on the wing, she finished it at fly half and never again played any other position.

In 1986, she was selected at 10 for the first Great Britain side. The following year, she was included in the very first Red Roses team that took on and defeated Wales at Pontypool Park. By then she had developed into the complete footballer who could pass, tackle, kick and run, with a knack of understanding which to deploy when.

In the earliest days of the Red Roses, the English game plan was built around Almond's eye-catching lines of running and attacking intent. Constantly singled out for praise, respected journalist Chris Thau soon anointed her the "top female player in the country".

In 1988, Almond assumed the England captaincy for the first time and would remain captain for six years. In 1990, she helped Wasps to a league and cup double, before leading England to the final of the inaugural Rugby World Cup in 1991.

By 1993, she had joined Saracens and claimed a treble of league, cup and sevens titles, but the ultimate prize still eluded her. That changed in 1994, when she led England to a World Cup Final for a second time. Again, England had played well to get there but this time Almond felt they had something in reserve.

In her diary, she wrote: "The day has finally arrived. We know what we have to do to win and it's up to us to do it". A display of controlled forward dominance followed and England ran out 38-23 winners. Almond, therefore, became the first English player to lift a fifteen-a-side World Cup, which she described as her "proudest moment".

She relinquished the England captaincy following the tournament, hoping to give the next captain time to build. On 9 May she arrived at an RFU dinner with the World Cup trophy under her arm. She was given a standing ovation by all in attendance.

"Karen Almond was a true inspiration. Her calm and collected personality rubbed off on her teammates and her undeniable knowledge of all things rugby meant she was able to control games and bring the best out of the players around her. As a new member of the squad in 1988, Karen immediately made me feel welcome and discreetly boosted my confidence – which improved my performance accordingly – and I was always eager to learn from her.

"In the 1994 World Cup Final England were underdogs but Karen's sublime performance that day was the major contributory factor to our win. 'Toasted Almond' was the headline in the *Guardian* the morning after and their report added: 'Almond, who controlled play with a series of beautifully judged kicks, weighed in with 13 points from a penalty and five conversions.' She, as ever, credited the win to her teammates, who all played a part, but it would never have happened without her at the helm.

"Karen was ahead of her time, totally humble and a wonderful leader. She deserves recognition for the massive part she played in helping to grow the women's game during those early years."

Gill Burns

OVER AND OUT

England's preparations for the 1995 Rugby World Cup were unorthodox to say the least. An off-hand but well-publicised remark by Will Carling had led to him being briefly stripped of the captaincy, before being reinstated by popular demand.

South Africa, having been readmitted to the international fold in 1992, were granted the task of hosting the tournament. England approached the tournament as Five Nations Grand Slam winners and with a highly experienced team. Their opponents in Pool B were Argentina, Italy and Western Samoa and, although England never really found their true form, the strength of their pack, allied to excellent line and place kicking saw them safely through to a quarter-final match against Australia.

Australia unexpectedly lost to South Africa in the group stage but progressed nonetheless. Amidst huge media interest across the world, it was the All Blacks who did most to capture the public's attention with 15-man rugby and a sensational young giant of a wing called Jonah Lomu, who was proving almost impossible to stop once in full flow.

England's quarter-final against Australia was intensely exciting, with the lead changing

hands on numerous occasions. Both sides scored one try and Australia led by 22 points to 19 with six minutes of the match remaining. Rob Andrew then kicked a penalty to level the scores and went on to kick a sensational long-range drop goal in injury time to win the match, exact revenge for 1991 and take England into the semi-final with a 25-22 victory.

New Zealand awaited England at Newlands, Cape Town, having overwhelmed Scotland in their quarter-final a week earlier. The winners would meet the hosts South Africa, narrow victors over France, in the final in Johannesburg.

England were confident of their chances but were overrun by an All Black onslaught in the first half, which effectively knocked them

out of the competition by half-time. The score after 50 minutes was 35-3 to the All Blacks and the rampaging Lomu had scored three tries. England rallied and scored four tries of their own through Will Carling and Rory Underwood but Lomu scored a fourth and the All Blacks went through to the final as winners 45-29.

England lost their third-place play-off match against France in Pretoria four days later 19-9, and the stage was set for the historic final between South Africa and New Zealand in front of President Nelson Mandela at Ellis Park. In a very tight match, South Africa defended heroically, countered the threat of Lomu and beat the All Blacks with a drop goal in extra-time from fly half Joel Stransky to win the World Cup for the first time.

Above: Rob Andrew and Jeremy Guscott turn away to celebrate the winning drop goal against Australia in the quarter-final

27 May 1995
England 24 Argentina 18
Kings Park, Durban; Attendance: 35,000

31 May 1995
England 27 Italy 20
Kings Park, Durban; Attendance: 45,093

4 June 1995
England 44 Western Samoa 22
Kings Park, Durban; Attendance: 35,000

POOL B	P	W	D	L	For	Ag	Pts
England	3	3	0	0	95	60	9
W. Samoa	3	2	0	1	96	88	7
Italy	3	1	0	2	69	94	5
Argentina	3	0	0		69	87	3

Quarter-final
11 June 1995
England 25 Australia 22
Newlands, Cape Town; Attendance: 35,000

Semi-final
18 June 1995
New Zealand 45 England 29
Newlands, Cape Town; Attendance: 51,000

Third-place play-off
22 June 1995
France 19 England 9
Loftus Versfeld, Pretoria
Attendance: 44,000

Final
24 June 1995
South Africa 15 New Zealand 12
Ellis Park, Johannesburg
Attendance: 60,000

Top: England face New Zealand, and Jonah Lomu, in the World Cup semi-final

Left: Will Carling congratulates the

All Blacks after their impressive victory

Above: History is made as Nelson Mandela presents the World Cup trophy

Pioneering spirits

Trailblazing England captains Gill Burns and Emily Scarratt have witnessed a revolution in the women's game over the course of their glittering careers, so who better to explain the evolution of the sport as well as exactly what it takes to win a World Cup?

By Sarah Mockford, Editor, *Rugby World*

"It's like having a blanket of rugby memories wrapped around you."

That's how Gill Burns describes walking down the stairs in her house, which is a veritable treasure trove of rugby memorabilia. She has hung framed photos, shirts and ties from her playing days on the walls either side of her staircase, as well as positioned shelves to hold balls and trophies she has collected over the years. It's almost like her own stairway to heaven.

Burns is an iconic figure in women's rugby history whose England journey began back in 1988, travelled into the next century and included a World Cup win in Edinburgh in 1994. Rewind to her international debut against Sweden and her recollections centre more on activities off the field than on it. That's because Burns organised the Test herself!

It's hard to imagine Dean Richards – Burns' No 8 counterpart in the England men's team at that time – ordering kit, putting on a dinner, selling tickets and arranging match officials for one of his own matches, but Burns did all that and much more besides to stage the fixture at her local club, Waterloo.

Top left: Gill Burns (left) on her induction to the IRB Hall of Fame in 2014, and Emily Scarratt with her 2019 World Rugby Player of the Year award

Left: Burns claims a lineout during the 1994 Women's Rugby World Cup Final

Right: Emily Scarratt runs in her team's fourth try against Ireland at Donnybrook Stadium in 2017

"I'd got into the England squad and someone said, 'Sweden want a fixture, would anyone like to host it?' I put my hand up. I was just being young and keen and enthusiastic," explains Burns. "My then partner, Steve Peters, played for Waterloo and he knew the practicalities of big fixtures, so the two of us did everything. I was rushing around doing things to get the fixture ready right up until kick-off."

Such was the hectic build-up that the emotions of the occasion, the magnitude of playing her first match for her country, only hit her as she stood for the anthems. She'd had no chance to contemplate what it would mean before she stood facing the stands for the singing of *God Save The Queen*.

That first cap, along with the 1994 World Cup final victory over the USA, remain her rugby highlights. There were significant moments post-match, too. The vocal spectators. The profit generated (only a few hundred pounds but notable all the same). The changing of people's perceptions. That last point is arguably the most important.

"One of the old alickadoos came up to me afterwards and said he had an admission to make," says Burns. "He said, 'I came here to watch tits and bums but after five minutes I realised I was watching a bloody good game of rugger.'"

Emily Scarratt made her England debut 20 years after Burns – and won a World Cup 20 years after her, too. Two decades may have separated their careers but many of Scarratt's early experiences are similar to those of Burns.

There were the ill-fitting shirts designed for men that had to be reworn for several matches, the crowds that consisted mainly of players' families and friends, the negative stereotypes that surround women's sport, the less-than-salubrious pre-match accommodation.

Both players have stories to tell on that latter aspect. There have been numerous studies on the importance of sleep to sportspeople, its value in ensuring the body can hit peak

"I'd got into the England squad and someone said, 'Sweden want a fixture, would anyone like to host it?' I put my hand up" Gill Burns

performance, but England's women's teams have not always found their quarters conducive to a good night's rest.

During the 1991 World Cup in Wales, Burns and her England team-mates had to move out of their rooms for a night and sleep on Z-beds elsewhere at the hotel while a conference took place. Before her first Great Britain match, she stayed in a youth hostel with a handful of other players based outside of London and they all had to perform chores – cleaning toilets, washing dishes and the like – before heading to the match. Oh, the glamour of being an international sportswoman.

On Scarratt's first tour, to Canada in 2009, the squad stayed in facilities similar to a university halls of residence. She and five others slept in a room with three sets of bunk beds and she says: "Whenever someone in the top bunk moved you could feel the whole room shake!"

Hardly ideal. Neither is having to sew a sponsor's badge onto a shirt the night before a tournament, but Scarratt recalls hearing of the sevens squad having to do exactly that early in her career.

At the start, rugby was more likely to cost women's players money than make any for them. Burns says she "worked to play", with the money she earned going on kit, travel and so on. She wouldn't change it, she cherishes those memories – the wins and the losses, the forging of lifelong friendships and the socialising, of course. It was worth it because she "had a ball on and off the field".

Women's rugby transformed in 2014, though, and took a major step forward. Following that year's World Cup win, the RFU brought in professional contracts for sevens players ahead of the sport's return to the Olympics at Rio 2016. Deals followed for 15-a-side players in the 2016-17 season as the squad built for their world title defence and became a permanent fixture at the start of 2019, when 28 players were contracted.

Players may already have been 'professional' in terms of attitude

Players may already have been 'professional' in terms of attitude and commitment, but being financially compensated for it makes a massive difference

and commitment, in terms of the training they did in their own time, but being financially compensated for it makes a massive difference. They no longer had to juggle their day jobs with their sporting life, as Burns did throughout as a teacher and Scarratt did at the start of her career.

It's all about time and having more of it to focus on rugby or even just recover from rugby. Rather than the old routine of a team run the day before a match, the match itself and a review the day after before having to quickly switch attention back to their work or study, the contracts allow the squad to train together every week to nail down tactics and improve skills.

"It's the time to spend doing whatever you want from a rugby point of view," says Scarratt. "When you're working, you can't practise your goalkicking three or four times a week because you don't have the time. It's the same with extra conditioning work, rehab work and so on; when you're working something has to go as you don't have time whereas now it makes you a lot more of an all-round athlete."

Burns predicted the women's game would turn professional when appearing as the first female guest on *Rugby Special* in the late 1990s. She knew that development would come, albeit too late for her, and recognises the rise in standards since she retired in 2002 as the player base has grown across England. "Strength in depth is what makes the women's game now," says Burns. "When I played, because the player pool was smaller, you did get a range of ability at international level. Now everybody is very good."

The growth of women's rugby is a familiar story across the world – World Rugby reported a 28 per cent increase in the number of registered female players in 2018 – and with the game's stars afforded more visibility, whether on TV, social media, online or print, they can help to inspire the next generation.

Scarratt says: "It's definitely important that people can see role models. If I look back to when I was growing up, Kelly Holmes was probably the only person female-wise to look up to. For me, other than tennis players and those in really high-profile sports, they were few and far between."

With greater exposure has come greater crowds, and they have changed not only in size but make-up. The family and friends of those in action on the pitch remain but have been bolstered by everyday rugby fans who want to support their country. More than 10,000 people packed out Sandy Park and the Twickenham Stoop in 2019 and 2020 respectively for Women's Six Nations matches, which is a far cry from Scarratt's England debut.

Far left: Gill Burns in the thick of the action as England take on Wales in 1996

Left: Scarratt poses for a selfie with fans after England claimed the Grand Slam at Twickenham in 2019

"It's awesome to see the crowds there now – you want to play in front of big crowds, it makes things more exciting" Emily Scarratt

"My first cap was at Esher Rugby Club. I couldn't tell you how many fans were there but it was made up of people's parents and a few friends. It's awesome to see the crowds there now – you want to play in front of big crowds, it makes things more exciting. There are genuine independent supporters who love coming to watch a women's game; when you get thousands of those people who want to come to wherever you're playing, it's so good."

Those are the moments that Scarratt will always look back to, just as Burns recalls the singing and dancing at Waterloo in 1988. The shirts may fit better, the skill levels may have improved, the stereotypes may be breaking and the crowds may be growing, but much remains the same – the team spirit, the friendships, the love of the game… those are the bonds that bind women's rugby players together and will continue to do so.

9

THE PROFESSIONALS

1996-2000

A NEW BALL GAME

The professional era began with matches against world champions South Africa and Samoa at Twickenham. Wasps' openside Lawrence Dallaglio won his first cap from the bench against South Africa and would start and score a try the following month against Samoa, a match in which Paul Grayson and Matt Dawson also began their England careers.

The Red Roses went into the inaugural Home Nations Championship under the leadership of Gill Burns. In their opening fixture their pack overwhelmed Wales as they ran in seven tries, the last a stunning solo run from Paula George, for a 56-3 victory. Scotland provided the sternest test, holding England 0-0 at half-time and being narrowly outpointed 12-8 in the second half. The Red Roses then secured the Championship

Previous pages: Lawrence Dallaglio makes his point during the match against South Africa in December 1998

Below: England coach Clive Woodward watches on as England struggle during the 1998 'Tour from Hell'

by defeating Ireland 43-8. For good measure, they had also beaten France away earlier in the year in front of a crowd of 3,000.

England men's first Five Nations of the professional era began with defeat to France but they rallied to win the Triple Crown and Championship in what would be the final season under the captaincy of Will Carling. Rory Underwood earned the last of his 85 caps in 1996 and retired with a record 49 tries. Jason Leonard was made captain in the autumn against Argentina and duly scored the only try of his England career in a 20-18 win.

The Red Roses started 1997 by snatching victory from the jaws of defeat against Spain, with a late converted try from Emma Mitchell. Mitchell scored again against Scotland in a 23-3 victory, which England followed up by beating Ireland 32-0 in Limerick. A hat-trick of tries for Gill Burns contributed to a 22-14 victory against Wales and confirmed a second successive Championship. They were comfortably beaten by New Zealand over the summer, but won the European Championship in Nice.

Saracens flanker Richard Hill came into the England men's side in 1997, under the captaincy of Phil de Glanville. Carling and de Glanville scored tries against Scotland in a 41-13 victory at Twickenham, and away wins in Dublin and Cardiff proved enough to retain the Triple Crown. However France, inspired by Christophe Lamaison, denied England the Championship by prevailing 23-20 at Twickenham. Carling then retired with 72 England caps, having overseen English rugby's most successful period since the 1920s.

Clive Woodward inherited a squad in transition when appointed coach later in the year. He made Dallaglio his captain and gave debuts to five players against Australia in his first match. The following week he recalled Neil Back and, for the first time, picked a back row of Back, Dallaglio and Hill. A patchy autumn series culminated in an entertaining 26-26 draw against New Zealand at Twickenham.

The Red Roses began 1998 with another friendly win against France. Burns returned from injury in a 29-12 victory over Wales, but England lost to Scotland 8-5 at Inverleith. England defeated Ireland, 62-8, in their final match. Prolific wing Jayne Molyneux finished as top try-scorer, but

CARLING RETIRED WITH 72 ENGLAND CAPS, HAVING OVERSEEN ENGLISH RUGBY'S MOST SUCCESSFUL PERIOD SINCE THE 1920s

Left: The England team huddle up before the Five Nations match against Wales at Wembley in April 1999

Below: The Red Roses celebrate with the Five Nations trophy in April 2000

Scotland took the Championship. Unfortunately, the Red Roses World Cup defence ended at the semi-final stage with defeat to New Zealand.

England were unable to beat France in their opening match of the men's Championship in 1998. Woodward's side recorded the first victory of his tenure, 60-26 against Wales, and went on to win the Triple Crown for the fourth consecutive year, but France won the Grand Slam for the second consecutive year. In the summer, England embarked on a tour marked by ignominy. The 'Tour from Hell' consisted of seven straight defeats, including a record 76-0 defeat to Australia in Brisbane, which also marked Jonny Wilkinson's first start for England.

France joined the Home Nations in 1999 and the women's Five Nations Championship began. Scrum half Emma Mitchell took over as captain for the final game against Wales after Burns stood down, and wings Nicky Crawford and Sue Day came into the squad. At Richmond, 2,500 people turned out to see England defeat Scotland, before a comfortable 56-0 win in Dublin. France were improving quickly but the Red Roses managed to defeat them 13-8, before a third Grand Slam in four seasons was secured with an emphatic 83-11 victory in Swansea. However, England were then surprisingly defeated by both France and Scotland in the European Championships.

Dallaglio, Leonard, Hill, Back and Martin Johnson all returned to the England men's side in 1999. Wilkinson played alongside the experienced Guscott at centre, with Mike Catt and Matt Dawson at half back. Wilkinson's reliable kicking was the difference as England defeated Scotland 24-21. Tries from Tim Rodber and Matt Perry then helped England beat Ireland, before Wilkinson kicked all 21 points in a victory against France to set up a Grand Slam decider with Wales at Wembley.

Dan Luger opened the scoring after two minutes and England led by seven at the break. Wilkinson's boot kept England ahead until the final minute when Scott Gibbs' jinking run split the England defence to score. The conversion ensured a memorable 32-31 win for Wales and the Championship for Scotland. England exited the World Cup at the quarter-final stage that summer but the RFU opted to persevere with the coaching structure.

With Mitchell injured, George took over the captaincy of the Red Roses in 2000. Spain replaced Ireland but were comfortably beaten 31-7. A late try from Chris Diver, converted by Claire Frost, delivered victory over France, before Burns celebrated her 50th cap with a win over Wales. The Grand Slam was confirmed with an emphatic 64-9 victory over Scotland in Edinburgh. In a full calendar, the Red Roses also competed in both the European Championships and Canada Cup but were unable to win either.

The Six Nations era began with the addition of Italy to the men's tournament. England gave debuts to Mike Tindall and Ben Cohen, both scoring tries in a 50-18 victory over Ireland. Wins against France, Wales and Italy set up a Grand Slam decider for the second year running but once again England were undone, this time during a physical encounter in the rain at Murrayfield. Despite the 19-13 loss England were champions for the first-time during Woodward's tenure.

History in the making

REPEALING THE AMATEUR REGULATIONS

Commercial innovation had begun to seep into the RFU's practices in the 1980s with corporate hospitality, advertising hoardings and retail. Though resolutely amateur, the Union's decisions marked a changing perception of the role of money in the sport's development.

The advent of the Rugby World Cup accelerated the process. The 1991 tournament raised the game's global profile considerably and, in turn, introduced new possibilities around advertising, sponsorship and broadcasting.

On the eve of the 1991 Rugby World Cup Final, England fly half Rob Andrew publicly questioned the separation of players from the already evident commercial exploitation of the game. Players began exploring ways to monetise their public image, both overtly and covertly, as the unions

Right: England in 1995, the end of the amateur era
Inset: Will Carling's first professional contract, 1996

struggled to keep up with the sport's changing landscape. Despite the strict enforcement of amateur regulations, the term 'shamateur' was increasingly used to describe amateur players accepting gifts, money and other inducements to play or use branded equipment.

As the 1995 Rugby World Cup was in process, businessmen began to approach star players with professional contracts. Two days before they met in the final, the unions of South Africa and New Zealand agreed a multi-million-pound deal with News Corporation. Threatened with takeover by a rival organisation, on the 27 August 1995 the International Rugby Board voted to repeal amateur regulations and declare the sport open. Though the RFU voted against the measure, the vote was carried and 100 years of top-class amateur rugby came to an end.

DATED   1996

RUGBY FOOTBALL UNION   (1)
and
WILLIAM DAVID CHARLES CARLING   (2)

Player Appointment Agreement
relating to the England International Squad

Wragge&Co

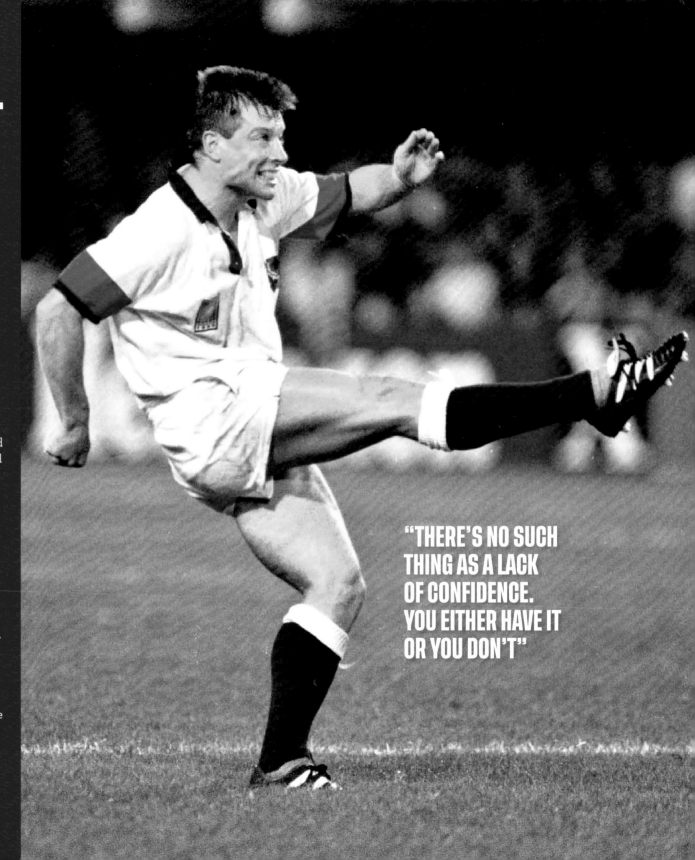

ROB ANDREW

Born 18 January 1963
England career 1985-1997, 71 caps
Position Fly Half/Full Back **Clubs** Cambridge University, Nottingham, Wasps, Toulouse, Newcastle

A key player and administrator in the development of English rugby, Rob Andrew was the principal England fly half between his debut in 1985 and his final appearance, against Wales at Cardiff in 1997. An outstanding sportsman, he attracted attention both as a rugby player and a cricketer while a student at Cambridge University, appearing in three Varsity Matches.

Andrew made his England debut in January 1985 against Romania, scoring 18 of England's 22 points, and went on to score a total of 396 points in 71 international matches – including a then-record 21 drop goals – and play as fly half in the three Grand Slam sides of 1991, 1992 and 1995.

A supremely organised player with a sharp rugby brain, he appeared in three Rugby World Cups, reaching the final in 1991. His memorable long-range drop goal in the final minute of the quarter-final knocked Australia out of the 1995 competition in South Africa. Captain of England on two occasions, he toured twice with the British & Irish Lions in 1989 and 1993, playing in five Tests, and was awarded the MBE in 1995.

After leaving Cambridge, he played primarily for Wasps, with seasons at Nottingham and Toulouse, and was appointed Director of Rugby at Newcastle Falcons in 1995 as the game transitioned into the professional era. He continued playing until 1999 and left Newcastle in 2006 to become Director of Elite Rugby at the RFU, where he remained for 10 years.

"THERE'S NO SUCH THING AS A LACK OF CONFIDENCE. YOU EITHER HAVE IT OR YOU DON'T"

BUILDING THE FORTRESS

Although it had served Twickenham well, Archibald Leitch's North Stand was in need of an upgrade by the middle of the 1980s. Architect Terry Ward was approached about a replacement and implicit in the requirements was the ability to also expand the East and West Stands.

The three-tier North Stand opened in 1991, in time for Twickenham to host its first Rugby World Cup. Ward then stated his ambition to create a stadium so imposing that it would give England a five-point advantage at the start of every game. A sharp intake of breath accompanied the news that the new East Stand would be more than 100 feet in height. RFU Grounds Committee Chairman Tony Hallett steadied the nerves by saying: "We're big men, we're doing a big job. Let's go for it."

Above: Twickenham as it looked from the North Stand before the 1991 World Cup Final

The East and West Stands were complete by the end of 1995 and attention turned to the South Stand that had been installed in 1981. Underneath the East Stand, a permanent home for the national treasure that is the Calcutta Cup was created in the shape of the Museum of Rugby, later renamed the World Rugby Museum in 2007. In the West, a purpose-built gym, dressing rooms and players' tunnel were created on the ground floor, while above the Spirit of Rugby complex was unveiled with catering and member facilities.

The South Stand interior opened in 2006, bringing the stadium's capacity up to 82,000. While the North, East and West Stands were functional in appearance, the South Stand complex was far more elaborate. It opened in 2008 and houses the Rugby House RFU offices, Marriott Hotel, Virgin Active Gym, Rugby Store and, since 2018, the new World Rugby Museum.

In 2010 the iconic Core Values statue was unveiled on the South Piazza. In 2014, the England dressing room was redeveloped under the supervision of coach Stuart Lancaster, who included tributes to historic England players and achievements as a motivational tool for his players.

The East Stand was extended outwards and reopened in 2018, with six further floors of catering and events space added.

Above: Three phases of stadium evolution evident in 1991; facing is the massive new North Stand; on the flanks the traditional East and West Stands; and in the foreground the South Stand built in 1981

Above left: The new East Stand in 1995

Left: An architect's model of the ground, including the 2006 South Stand development

Right: Twickenham Stadium after its 2018 upgrade

The England Greats

EMMA MITCHELL

Born 13 April 1966 **England career** 1988-2002, 52 caps
Position Scrum Half
Clubs Loughborough University, Saracens

Scrum half Emma Mitchell is another in the long production line of international rugby players to graduate from Loughborough University. Mitchell came into the England team in 1988 and would remain for the following 14 seasons. An outstanding No 9, her darting runs and accurate delivery allowed her to form a lethal partnership with Karen Almond that would take England to the first two Rugby World Cup Finals.

Almond retired after lifting the trophy in 1994 and Mitchell forged a new midfield partnership with Giselle Prangnell. The two were instrumental in delivering the inaugural Home Nations Championship in 1996 and Mitchell herself scored the first try of a successful defence the following season.

A founding member of Saracens Women, Mitchell helped her club side to a league, cup and sevens treble in 1997. She first captained England against Holland in 1997 and did so again during the 1998 Rugby World Cup and the 1999 European Championships. She missed the 2000 season with injury but returned the following year against France.

In 2002 Mitchell played in her fourth and final Rugby World Cup at the age of 36 and was one of the stand-out performers in a semi-final against Canada which took England to a third World Cup Final. She finally retired after the tournament with 52 caps for England and five for Great Britain.

"ENGLAND WOMEN'S RUGBY IS IN HER DEBT, BEHOLDEN TO AN ALMOST UNIQUE ABILITY TO BE WORLD-CLASS AS A PLAYER AND QUIETLY BUT DEVASTATINGLY EFFECTIVE AS AN AMBASSADOR"

Stephen Jones

FAMOUS GAMES

ENGLAND 56 WALES 3

England v Wales

at Leicester FC
Kick-off at 2.30 pm
Sunday 4th February 1996

4 February 1996, Welford Road, Leicester

The Women's Home Nations Championship began in 1996. After nine annual contests, England and Wales would face each other for their opening fixture at Welford Road, Leicester. England, captained by Gill Burns, had retained several of the pack that had proved so formidable at the World Cup two years earlier. Flanker Helen Clayton had come into the team and Clifton lock Karen Henderson was now a regular starter alongside Saracen Janis Ross.

Giselle Prangnell had replaced Karen Almond at fly half. Waterloo's Jayne Molyneux would start on the wing with Wasps' Paula George at full back and rugby league convert Julie Twigg, of Liverpool St Helens, at centre. The Red Roses were well-prepared, having spent the week training in Army barracks.

A crowd of 1,200 turned out to watch them and a focused England took the lead with a try from Burns in the 11th minute. Three more tries were scored before half-time, the last following a superlative interception and a 60-metre sprint by Twigg. The Red Roses continued their dominance into the second half. Eight tries were scored in total with Emma Mitchell, Clayton, George and Leeds' Andrea Wallace scoring once, while Molyneux crossed the line twice as England ran out emphatic winners.

Scotland would hold England to 0-0 at half time before the Red Roses prevailed 12-8 in Edinburgh, and the Championship was secured with a convincing victory over Ireland at Sunbury.

"That first game of the 1996 Home Nations really stands out," Burns later said. "It was the first time that people from outside the players' circles, their families and friends, took an interest in the women's game."

England P George – J Edwards, J Twigg, A Wallace, J Molyneux – G Prangnell, E Mitchell – J Mangham, N Ponsford, E Scourfield – S Wenn, K Henderson – J Ross, G Burns*, H Clayton

Wales K Richards – A Rothera, R Williams, L Rickard, K Yau – A Bennett, B Evans – B Trotter, N Griffiths, J Studley (S Gibbard-Jones) – A Dent, S James (L Jones) – S Ellis*, L Burgess, J Morgan

Above: Helen Clayton scores one of eight England tries
Right: Gill Burns lifts the Rice Challenge Cup, awarded to the winners of the England v Wales fixture

ENGLAND 26 NEW ZEALAND 26

6 December 1997, Twickenham

Clive Woodward took over as the England coach in the autumn of 1997. A draw with Australia was followed by defeats to New Zealand in Manchester and South Africa at Twickenham before the All Blacks arrived at HQ. Woodward's side, captained by Lawrence Dallaglio, had increasingly gelled across the previous three matches but the tourists started as heavy favourites.

A magnificent first 40 minutes saw England lead 23-9 at half-time. A stunning try from right wing David Rees, who chipped over his opposite number Jonah Lomu's head and picked up to score in the corner, was followed by a try by Richard Hill after a scything break from centre Will Greenwood. New Zealand replied with a penalty before Dallaglio added a third English try, converted by fly half Paul Grayson, to give England a 17-3 lead. Two further penalties for each side brought half-time with England 14 points in the lead.

Smarting at the break, the All Blacks came back with tries from Andrew Mehrtens and Walter Little. After 17 unanswered points in 20 minutes, they moved into a 26-23 lead with 18 minutes to go. England stemmed the tide and Grayson kicked his third penalty to level the scores at 26-26. The All Blacks missed with a last-gasp drop goal attempt and the match ended a draw, leaving the crowd breathless after a fantastic contest. It remains the only draw in more than 40 matches between two historic rivals.

Right: David Rees (No 14), Lawrence Dallaglio and Phil de Glanville combine to bring down Jonah Lomu

England MB Perry – DL Rees, WJH Greenwood, PR de Glanville (TRG Stimpson), AS Healey – PJ Grayson, KPP Bracken (MJS Dawson) – J Leonard, R Cockerill (MP Regan), DJ Garforth – MO Johnson, GS Archer – NA Back (CMA Sheasby), RA Hill, LBN Dallaglio*

New Zealand CM Cullen – JW Wilson, FE Bunce (SJ McLeod), WK Little (CJ Spencer), JT Lomu – AP Mehrtens, JW Marshall* – MR Allen, NJ Hewitt, OM Brown – ID Jones, RM Brooke – TC Randell, ZV Brooke, JA Kronfeld (CE Riechelmann)

The England Greats

NEIL BACK

Born 16 January 1969
England career 1994-2003, 66 caps
Position Wing Forward **Clubs** Nottingham, Leicester

Neil Back was an exceptionally fit open-side flanker with outstanding handling skills who overcame a perception that he was not tall enough to become an essential part of the England side in the years leading up to their World Cup triumph in 2003.

Back began his career playing for Nottingham but moved to Leicester in 1990 for whom he played more than 330 matches and scored 215 tries, a record for a Leicester forward. He made his international debut in 1994 and played in the 1995 and 1999 Rugby World Cups. After serving a six-month ban for pushing the referee at the end of the 1996 Anglo-Welsh Cup Final, he went on to become a regular in Clive Woodward's England side, and a tally of 66 caps yielded 83 points from 16 tries and a drop goal.

Part of a uniquely balanced back-row partnership with Lawrence Dallaglio and Richard Hill across 37 internationals, Back captained England to four victories in 2001 and 2002 and played his last England match in the World Cup Final in Sydney. He appeared in five Test matches for the British & Irish Lions between 1997 and 2005.

He played in three Heineken Cup Finals for Leicester, winning in 2001 and 2002. A key member of Leicester's squads in their four successive Zurich Premiership victories from 1999 to 2002, he played his final rugby match in the Premiership Final against Wasps in May 2005.

Since his retirement he has become a rugby coach, commentator, author and motivational speaker.

LAWRENCE DALLAGLIO

Born 10 August 1972
England career 1995-2007, 85 caps
Position Back Row **Club** Wasps

Lawrence Dallaglio OBE was an outstanding back-row forward whose England career lasted from 1995 to 2007. He came to early prominence as a member of England's winning sevens team in the 1993 Rugby World Cup Sevens tournament in Edinburgh, won his first cap in the England XV against South Africa in the autumn of 1995 and went on to captain England in 22 of his 85 internationals and score 17 tries – a record for an English forward.

He appeared in the 1999, 2003 and 2007 World Cup campaigns and was the only player to feature in every minute of England's matches throughout their victorious winning campaign in Australia in 2003. It was his run from the back of the scrum in the first half of the final that started the passage of play that would lead to Jason Robinson scoring his crucial try, while his back-row partnership with Neil Back and Richard Hill, affectionately known as the 'Holy Trinity', is regarded as one of the finest combinations in English rugby history.

A one-club man with Wasps throughout his long career, Dallaglio toured three times with the British & Irish Lions and played three Tests against South Africa in 1997. His final appearance for England was as a substitute in the 2007 World Cup Final against South Africa.

He retired from rugby in May 2008 after leading Wasps to the Premiership title with victory over Leicester Tigers at Twickenham and has subsequently carried out extensive charity work and become a respected media pundit and rugby commentator.

"THE MOST IMPORTANT THING ABOUT WINNING IS BELIEVING THAT YOU CAN, NO MATTER WHO YOU ARE PLAYING"

The England Greats

RICHARD HILL

Born 23 May 1973
England career 1997-2004, 71 caps
Position Back Row **Club** Saracens

Richard Anthony Hill was a supremely gifted if unassuming back-row forward who played with distinction for England in 71 internationals between 1997 and 2004. His entire career was spent with Saracens, for whom he appeared more than 280 times, during his 16-year career. He established a deserved reputation for his versatility, positional skills and rock-like defence, and was a vital force in an exceptionally balanced back row alongside Lawrence Dallaglio and Neil Back in 34 England matches.

The 'Holy Trinity' of Back, Dallaglio and Hill is widely considered to be England's greatest back row

Hill played throughout the 1999 World Cup tournament and in 30 consecutive matches between 1998 and 2001. After playing in England's defeats of New Zealand and Australia in the summer of 2003, a hamstring injury threatened to keep him out of the ensuing World Cup and he only appeared against Georgia in the pool stages of that tournament, but recovered in time to play a commanding role in the semi-final against France and the epic finale in Sydney.

After the World Cup victory, Hill captained an England XV against New Zealand Barbarians at Twickenham and played throughout the 2004 Championship and the summer southern hemisphere tour. He scored 12 tries in his England career, as well as representing the British & Irish Lions in five Tests on their tours to South Africa, Australia and New Zealand. A knee ligament injury in the first half of the opening Lions Test in Christchurch in June 2005 ended his international playing career, although he played on for Saracens until his retirement in 2008.

Hugely respected throughout the game, he became the England manager working with Eddie Jones in September 2016.

THE END OF THEIR REIGN

The IRB formed a Women's Rugby International Committee at the end of 1994. Rosie Golby was appointed as RFUW representative and plans were made for a first 'official' Rugby World Cup in 1998. The Netherlands would host the tournament, as was intended in 1994 before the competition was hurriedly cancelled, rescheduled and moved to Scotland.

As reigning world champions, the Red Roses went into the tournament as one of the favourites to win but expectations were tempered. New Zealand had shocked everyone by defeating England 67-0 in the summer of 1997 and England had lost their Home Nations crown to Scotland in 1998.

As a result, scrum half Emma Mitchell believed England to be underdogs. Several players from 1994 were still involved in the squad, including Mitchell, Giselle Prangnell, Janis Ross and captain Gill Burns. Others, such as Paula George and Maxine Edwards, had been squad players in 1994 but were now starters.

The Red Roses progressed from the pool stage with ease, having defeated Canada and Sweden comfortably. The quarter-final against Australia was tougher but England prevailed to progress to the semi-final. There they were comfortably beaten by New Zealand, who went on to lift the trophy for the first time by beating the United States in the final.

In the third-place play-off, the Red Roses fielded several of their younger players, such as 19-year-old scrum half Jo Yapp and Wasps' wing Sue Day, and Day rewarded her coaches' faith with four individual tries in a 31-15 victory over Canada in Amsterdam.

Below left: Trudi Collins in action during the pool match against Canada in Amsterdam

Below: Emma Mitchell gets the ball away before being brought down by a Canadian defender

Far left: Linda Uttley is tackled by Anna Richards of New Zealand during the World Cup semi-final

Left: Sue Day evades the tackle of Annaleah Rush

Below: Paula George runs in a try against Canada during the third-place play-off

2 May 1998
England 75 Sweden 0
Amsterdam

5 May 1998
Canada 6 England 72
Amsterdam

POOL A	P	W	D	L	F	A	Ladder
England	2	2	0	0	147	6	2nd
Canada	2	1	0	1	22	79	8th
Netherlands	2	1	0	1	51	16	10th
Sweden	2	0	0	2	0	139	15th

Quarter-final
9 May 1998
Australia 13 England 30
Amsterdam

Semi-final
12 May 1998
England 11 New Zealand 44
Amsterdam

Third-place play-off
16 May 1998
Canada 15 England 31
Amsterdam

Final
16 May 1998
New Zealand 44 United States 12
Amsterdam

GILL BURNS

Born 12 July 1964 **England career** 1988-2002, 73 caps
Position Back Row **Club** Waterloo

Gill Burns' mother ran a group of dancing schools across Merseyside. Her daughter credits her early years as a dancer for her fast feet and agile turning, attributes she put to good use as an explosive No 8 for her club, Waterloo. Burns' rise as a player was rapid – within a year of playing her first game at Liverpool Polytechnic she was playing for England. Her international debut came in 1988 against Sweden, a match that England won 40-0 and her impact was immediate.

A smothering defender and devastating ball-carrier, with the capacity to take out half the opposition defence, Burns quickly developed into one of the Red Roses' most potent assets. As the inaugural Rugby World Cup approached, she added technical skills in the lineout and a rugby brain that allowed her to exert influence in all areas of the field. Her try in the semi-final against France helped England to the final, where they ultimately fell short against the USA.

After the defeat, Burns' passion was an inspiration – becoming world champions was the goal and her determination to succeed was reflected in her commitment to the national side. Despite having a full-time job as a schoolteacher in Liverpool and commuting long distances for training, her dedication to the sport never wavered.

In 1994, she was integral to the England side that realised that dream. In a repeat of the 1991 final, Burns and England this time made use of their forwards to control the field and deny the Americans attacking space.

She captained the national side for the first time in 1993 and replaced Karen Almond in the role full-time at the end of 1994. She proceeded to lead England to a Grand Slam in the inaugural Home Nations Championship of 1996 and repeated the feat in 1997, scoring a hat-trick of tries in the Championship decider against Wales.

England's world title defence ended at the semi-final stage in 1998 and Burns stood down as captain after retaining the 1999 Five Nations. She was back in the side by 2001 and sparked England into life at the semi-final stage of the 2002 Rugby World Cup with a match-winning performance at the age of 37. She retired at the end of the tournament with 73 caps.

Rugby writer Stephen Jones perhaps said it best when he described Burns as "a genuine, 24-carat English sporting heroine".

"I USED TO IMAGINE SINGING THE NATIONAL ANTHEM WHILST WEARING MY INTERNATIONAL KIT BUT I NEVER DREAMED THAT THE SPORT I COULD PLAY WOULD BE RUGBY. HOW WRONG I ONCE WAS!"

COMING UP SHORT

Wales were the hosts of the 1999 Rugby World Cup, although many of the matches took place in grounds around the UK and France, including both semi-finals which were played at Twickenham. The tournament had been expanded to include 20 countries and there were five pools of four teams, with play-offs to decide the other three sides to join the winners of the five pools in the quarter-finals.

England warmed up for the tournament by playing matches against USA and Canada at Twickenham in August. They had a settled side under the captaincy of their second-row forward Martin Johnson and impressive reserve strength in their overall squad.

England were drawn in Pool B, alongside Italy, Tonga and New Zealand, with all their matches scheduled to be played at Twickenham. They opened with a very convincing 67-7 victory over Italy in which young fly half Jonny Wilkinson scored an English record of 32 points in a World Cup match. Their next match against New Zealand was less successful, with Jonah Lomu scoring a vital try midway through the second half to take the All Blacks into a lead which they never relinquished, emerging as 30-16 winners. England then overwhelmed Tonga 101-10 to finish second in Pool B, behind the All Blacks.

England's play-off match against Fiji, runners-up in Pool C, produced a comfortable 45-24 victory, with Wilkinson scoring 23 points. This took England into the quarter-final where they faced South Africa at Stade de France in Paris. The first half was closely fought and ended 16-12 to the Springboks. The second half was a rout. England had no answer to the marksmanship of the Springbok fly half Jannie de Beer. Consistently set up by his forwards, de Beer kicked a world record five drop goals to end with a personal tally of 34 points in South Africa's 44-21 victory, which knocked England out of the competition.

France memorably came back to defeat New Zealand in their semi-final but Australia went on to win their second World Cup by beating South Africa in their semi-final and then overpowering France in the final in Cardiff.

Left: Jeremy Guscott breaks through the Italian defence as England make a strong start to the World Cup

Above: England struggle to contain New Zealand wing Jonah Lomu in their Pool B encounter

Left: England watch the Fijians perform the Cibi before their quarter-final play-off victory at Twickenham

Below: Lawrence Dallaglio gets the ball back to his teammates, but despite England's best efforts the Springboks ran out comfortable winners in the quarter-final at Stade de France

2 October 1999
England 67 Italy 7
Twickenham
Attendance: 70,244

9 October 1999
England 16 New Zealand 30
Twickenham
Attendance: 73,500

15 October 1999
England 101 Tonga 10
Twickenham
Attendance: 75,000

POOL B	P	W	D	L	F	A	Pts
New Zealand	3	3	0	0	176	28	9
England	3	2	0	1	184	47	7
Tonga	3	1	0	2	47	171	5
Italy	3	0	0	3	35	196	3

Quarter-final play-off
20 October 1999
England 45 Fiji 24
Twickenham
Attendance: 55,000

Quarter-final
24 October 1999
South Africa 44 England 21
Stade de France, Paris
Attendance: 80,000

Final
6 November 1999
Australia 35 France 12
Millennium Stadium, Cardiff
Attendance: 72,500

COMMERCIAL BREAKS

The short-lived Twickenham South Stand that opened in 1981, came with new opportunities. Tucked away at the back of a stand that had been designed for a racecourse were 12 corporate boxes. This prompted a rethink around the commercial and corporate use of the ground and the appointment of the RFU's first full-time Marketing Manager.

Over the course of the decade, a series of innovations including, but not limited to, matchday hospitality, sponsorship packages, brand development and pitch-side advertising were incorporated into the Twickenham matchday experience for the first time. Revenues derived would help fund the upkeep of Twickenham Stadium,

Above: The first corporate boxes in the Twickenham South Stand in the 1980s

the introduction of national youth programmes and grassroots investment, including club renovations.

The early success of this process allowed for the rebuilding of the North Stand, and new corporate facilities were included in the design. As the game became professional in 1995, the process of commercialisation intensified. BT Cellnet, later rebranded O2, became England's first jersey sponsor and a tiered partner structure was implemented.

The additional corporate hospitality facilitated by the development of the East and West Stands saw Twickenham Experience Limited (TEL) come into existence, in partnership with Compass Group. TEL would manage and deliver all corporate functions within the stadium. In time TEL's operations would grow to surpass both ticketing and broadcasting as a source of revenue.

Also included in the East Stand was the Museum of Rugby, later rebranded the World Rugby Museum, that, together with Twickenham Stadium Tours, would see Twickenham become a successful year-round visitor attraction for members of the public from 1996 onwards.

Above: Phil de Glanville wearing a sponsored England shirt in 1997

The 1981 South Stand was demolished in 2005 and its replacement was completed by 2008. The elaborate new complex added large conferencing, banqueting and exhibition venues to TEL's portfolio, a four-star Marriott

hotel, Virgin Active Gym with Olympic-sized swimming pool and the Rugby House RFU offices.

With corporate space still at a premium, an extra layer of six floors of event and catering space was planned and installed around the East Stand in 2017-18. It included the ground-floor Union Ale House, a bar for the debenture holders whose predecessors had first funded the development of the ground in the 1900s. On the top floor of the development was the British Airways Rose Garden, named in reference to the RFU's most recently acquired tier one partner. British Airways' name and logo would soon be visible from the roof of the stadium to the thousands of air travellers flying in and out of nearby Heathrow Airport.

As a non-profit organisation, the money that the RFU raises in revenue is reinvested back into the sport of rugby. In recent years, the All Schools programme has seen rugby introduced to an additional 750 English state secondary schools. Grassroots rugby clubs also benefit from grants for training kit, coaching courses and ground development.

"QUICK, BRAVE AND WITH THAT UNSHAKEABLE CONFIDENCE ALL GREAT SCRUM HALVES NEED"

Stuart Barnes

The England Greats

MATT DAWSON

Born 31 October 1972
England career 1995-2006, 77 caps
Position Scrum Half **Clubs** Northampton, Wasps

The quicksilver scrum half Matt Dawson won 77 caps in an 11-year career and was one of the key players in England's World Cup-winning side in Australia in 2003.

A member of the England Sevens team that won the World Cup at Murrayfield in 1993, Dawson made his full Test debut against Western Samoa in December 1995 and then shared the national scrum half responsibilities with Bristol and Saracens number 9 Kyran Bracken over the next eight years.

Dawson enjoyed an outstanding tour of South Africa with the British & Irish Lions in 1997, playing in all three Tests and scoring two tries. He toured again with the Lions in Australia in 2001 and New Zealand in 2005, playing in seven Tests overall.

He captained England nine times, including on the southern hemisphere tour of 1998 and throughout the inaugural Six Nations Championship in 2000. His pace frequently surprised opposition defences and he scored a record 16 tries as an England scrum half. His game management was shown to greatest advantage in the World Cup Final in Sydney in 2003, where his partnership with Jonny Wilkinson was to prove the decisive factor in England's victory.

Born in Birkenhead, Dawson joined Northampton in 1991 in the last stages of the amateur era and played for them until the end of the 2004 season, after which he joined Wasps. He played for Wasps in their Premiership Cup Final victory over Leicester Tigers in May 2005 and retired a year later. He has since forged an active media career and supported numerous charitable initiatives.

10

ALL CONQUERORS

2000-2003

THE ROAD TO GLORY

O ver the summer of 2000, Woodward's England travelled to South Africa. They lost the first Test but defeated the Springboks in Bloemfontein to tie the series. World champions Australia then visited Twickenham in November only to lose to their hosts for the first time since 1995. England then consolidated their place at the top table of world rugby by defeating Argentina and South Africa over consecutive weekends.

Above: The England squad huddle up under the watchful eye of Clive Woodward

Right: Sue Day in action in 2002

The Red Roses began their 2001 campaign with wins against Wales and Spain. Sue Day scored the first try against Scotland but was later stretchered from the field with a serious injury. England went on to win 39-0. The deciding fixture would be played against France in Northampton and captain Paula George celebrated her 50th cap by scoring the first try, while Nicky Crawford added a hat-trick as England secured a comfortable 50-6 win and a third consecutive title.

After finishing third in the European Championship, the Red Roses embarked on a tour of Australasia. Two victories against Australia were followed by a 15-10 defeat to New Zealand in Rotorua. England then won the second Test 22-17, Emily Feltham's last-minute try helping to defeat the Black Ferns for the first time.

Martin Johnson's men's side opened the defence of their Championship title in Cardiff, in the recently opened Millennium Stadium, and a hat-trick of tries from Will Greenwood helped them to a 44-15 victory. Rugby league convert Jason Robinson made his debut from the bench against Italy and England scored 10 tries to win 80-23, while Lawrence Dallaglio and Iain Balshaw contributed two tries each in a 43-3 victory against Scotland, which was followed by an equally impressive win against France.

With England in such imperious form, it seemed that it would take an 'Act of God' to prevent them gaining a Grand Slam in Dublin. The game was duly suspended until October, after an outbreak of foot and mouth disease. A distracted England eventually lost 20-14 to Ireland but retained the Championship.

Later that autumn, England extended their winning sequence against southern opposition by defeating Australia and South Africa at Twickenham, with fly half Wilkinson the chief architect in both matches. In between, Neil Back captained England to a record 134-0 victory over Romania, in which Robinson scored his first four international tries, and Charlie Hodgson scored a record 44 points on his debut.

The Red Roses began their 2002 World Cup year with five tries and a 35-8 victory over Scotland. With six teams now contesting the title, they defeated Ireland 79-0, before losing 22-17 to France. They bounced back with a 40-0 victory over Wales. In Madrid, Sue Day scored three tries from the bench after returning from injury and

England won 53-14 in Emma Mitchell's 50th appearance. England were back in Spain over the summer and were beaten finalists in the 2002 Rugby World Cup.

England men secured a record 29-3 victory at Murrayfield in the opening match of their 2002 Championship campaign. Against Ireland, Wilkinson produced perhaps his finest performance in an England jersey. His jinking runs, fast hands and creative footwork repeatedly unlocked the Irish defence for a 45-11 victory that took England to the top of the world rankings.

They were brought back down to earth with a bump at Stade de France. At 17-0 down after 15 minutes, they fought back but France eventually won 20-15. Regrouping, they returned to winning ways against Wales and beat Italy in Rome, but it wasn't enough to prevent a French Grand Slam.

New Zealand arrived at Twickenham in the autumn with an eye on the scalp of a side that claimed to be the world's best. Lewis Moody touched down in injury time of the first half to give England the lead. A Wilkinson-inspired England then systematically dismantled the All Blacks, two converted tries taking them to a 31-28 victory despite a determined fight back late in the game from the visitors. Subsequent wins against Australia and South Africa confirmed England's dominance over her southern hemisphere rivals for perhaps the first time in her history.

The Red Roses opened their 2003 Six Nations campaign with a red-letter day at Twickenham. Captained by Maxine Edwards, the side marked

Above: Maggie Alphonsi, a Red Roses debutant in 2003

Below: Richard Hill (centre) and the England players acknowledge the crowd after finally winning the Grand Slam at Lansdowne Road in 2003

WITH ENGLAND IN SUCH IMPERIOUS FORM IT SEEMED THAT IT WOULD TAKE AN 'ACT OF GOD' TO PREVENT THEM GAINING A GRAND SLAM IN DUBLIN

their first appearance at the national ground by running in nine tries in a 57-0 win against France. They ran in 69 points against both Spain and Wales, before beating nearest challengers Scotland 31-0 at the Stoop. Eighteen-year-old Danielle Waterman replaced Susie Appleby against Ireland to become England's youngest player and England rounded off a dominant Grand Slam with a 46-3 victory to bring their points tally to a record 272, for only 10 conceded.

In the summer, they travelled to Vancouver to compete in the inaugural Churchill Cup. Youngsters Margaret Alphonsi and Rochelle Clark came into the squad and they brought the trophy home after wins against Canada and USA.

The men's side continued their commanding form, with a workmanlike 25-17 defeat of champions France at Twickenham. Comfortable wins over Wales, Italy and Scotland followed, with Steve Thompson impressing at hooker and Robinson a constant threat from the wing. Their final match took place in Dublin, with both sides seeking a Grand Slam. Johnson's England proved famously immovable and ran in five tries for a superb 42-6 victory. It was England's first Grand Slam since 1995 and the first of the Clive Woodward era.

In preparation for the World Cup, England travelled south for matches against New Zealand and Australia. Wilkinson kicked England into a 9-6 lead against the All Blacks before Back and Dallaglio were both shown yellow cards. Demonstrating immense physical and mental resilience, England defended with 13 men before Wilkinson stretched their lead to 15-6. A converted New Zealand try brought the scores to 15-13 but England held on for their first away victory against New Zealand since 1973.

A 25-14 win over Australia in Melbourne would prove to be a precursor to the victorious World Cup Final later in the year. The summer victories had given England the self-belief they needed to become world champions for the first time. A World Cup and Grand Slam in a calendar year signalled England's finest hour in 150 years of international men's rugby.

ENGLAND 22 AUSTRALIA 19

18 November 2000, Twickenham

England captain Martin Johnson consoles his Australian counterpart John Eales after an incredible match

World champions Australia arrived at Twickenham in the autumn of 2000 with a side containing some of the greats of the era: full back Chris Latham, wings Matt Burke and Joe Roff, centre Stirling Mortlock, John Eales in the second row and Toutai Kefu in the back row, alongside George Smith in his first international season. Despite home advantage, Clive Woodward's side, captained by Martin Johnson, went into the match as underdogs.

A tense encounter followed, with numerous infringements leading to penalties. Jonny Wilkinson and Matt Burke shared three each, before Wilkinson added a drop goal at the end of the first half to give England a 12-9 lead at the break. Three minutes into the second half, a superb break by Joe Roff down the left wing took him close to the England line. Matt Perry, the England full back, tackled him but Roff was able to pass inside to the supporting Burke, who scored and then converted his own try. A further penalty six minutes later by Burke gave the Wallabies a 19-12 lead which they held until Wilkinson kicked his fourth penalty goal five minutes later to bring the scores to 19-15.

The game see-sawed for 30 minutes, until injury time when substitute winger Iain Balshaw made a searing break through the Australian defence. The move was halted but in the ensuing melee Australian flanker Matt Cockbain was yellow-carded for preventing release of the ball. A short penalty was taken, Johnson drove towards the Australian posts and substitute scrum half Matt Dawson passed to Balshaw. He kicked ahead and chased the ball into the in-goal area, where it bounced into the hands of left wing Dan Luger who touched down just before the ball rolled into touch. After confirmation of the try, all that remained was for Wilkinson to kick the conversion and England had won a famous victory 22-19.

This match demonstrated that at the dawn of the 21st century, Woodward's England had the capability to take on and defeat the strongest sides in the world.

England MB Perry – AS Healey (IR Balshaw), MJ Tindall, MJ Catt, DD Luger – JP Wilkinson, KPP Bracken (MJS Dawson) – J Leonard, PBT Greening (MP Regan), PJ Vickery (DL Flatman) – MO Johnson*, DJ Grewcock – RA Hill, LBN Dallaglio, NA Back

Australia CE Latham – MC Burke, DJ Herbert, SA Mortlock, JW Roff – RB Kafer (NP Grey), SJ Cordingley – WK Young, MA Foley (JA Paul), FJ Dyson (GM Panoho) – DT Giffin (MJ Cockbain), JA Eales* – GB Smith (PR Waugh), RST Kefu (MR Connors), RW Williams

FAMOUS GAMES

NEW ZEALAND 17 ENGLAND 22

16 June 2001, North Harbour Stadium, Albany

The Black Ferns went into their match against England in June 2001 on the back of a 26-game winning run that stretched all the way to the 1991 World Cup. The Red Roses, under coach Geoff Richards and the captaincy of full back Paula George, were looking to measure their progress against the world champions after running them close the previous week in Rotorua.

The match, at the North Harbour Stadium, began badly for England as New Zealand fly half Anna Richards fed full back Tammi Wilson for a try, which Richards effortlessly converted. New Zealand led 7-0 after five minutes.

The Red Roses struck back almost immediately with a try from Nicky Crawford to make the score 7-5, before Vanessa Cootes extended New Zealand's lead in the 19th minute. A penalty from fly half Shelley Rae kept England in contention with the score 12-8 to New Zealand at half-time.

England opted to use their experienced tight five in the second half. It worked and a try by Rae put England in the lead for the first time, with 20 minutes remaining, only for Annaleah Rush's try to once again restore New

Paula George (left) celebrates leading her team to victory against world champions New Zealand

Zealand's lead. With the scores 17-15 it looked like the home side had once more done enough.

The Red Roses disagreed, however, and in the dying moments of the game George set Emily Feltham away in space. From deep in her own 22, Feltham ran in to score between the posts and Rae converted for a famous 22-17 victory.

New Zealand T Wilson – V Cootes, AM Rush, S Shortland, ET Shelford – AM Richards, MJ Hirovanaa – R Sheck, FR Palmer*, R Liua'ana – FJ King, V Heighway – MC Robinson, CM Waaka, RL Martin (Replacements: S Yates, A Marsh, T Mulipola, P Paasi)

England P George* – N Crawford, A De Biase, S Rudge, E Feltham – S Rae, J Yapp – N Huxford, A Garnett, T O'Reilly – J Sutton, T Andrews – G Stevens, G Burns (C Frost), H Clayton

JONNY WILKINSON

Born 25 May 1979 **England career** 1998-2011, 91 caps
Position Wing/Fly Half/Centre **Clubs** Newcastle, RC Toulon

The iconic Jonny Wilkinson will forever be synonymous with English rugby, and his career will always be defined by his historic right-footed drop goal in the final minute of the 2003 World Cup Final against Australia in Sydney, which gave England men their first Rugby World Cup title.

On leaving school at the age of 18, Wilkinson joined Newcastle Falcons in 1997 as a professional rugby player playing at fly half and centre. His outstanding footballing talent was quickly recognised. He made his first appearance for England as a replacement wing against Ireland in the final match of the 1998 Five Nations Championship, before being fully blooded as a fly half in two Tests on the ill-fated 1998 tour of the southern hemisphere. He played in the centre through the 1999 Five Nations before moving to fly half, where he played in all but one of his remaining matches in a 91-Test career spanning 13 years.

An outstanding reader of the game and a prolific left-footed kicker, he scored a record 1,179 points in his England international career, including a world record 36 drop goals. He appeared in four World Cup tournaments and was instrumental in guiding England to two World Cup Finals, in 2003 and again in France in 2007, where they lost to South Africa. His final international appearance was in a losing cause against France in the quarter-final of the 2011 Rugby World Cup in Auckland.

A tourist with the British & Irish Lions in Australia in 2001 and New Zealand in 2005, he played in six

Lions Tests, scoring a record 67 points. In the final phase of his illustrious career, he moved to France in 2009 and played in two European Cup-winning sides for RC Toulon in 2013 and 2014, before retiring from rugby after leading Toulon to the Top 14 title against Castres in May 2014.

One of the most dedicated players to ever pull on an England shirt, Wilkinson was appointed CBE in 2015 for services to rugby union.

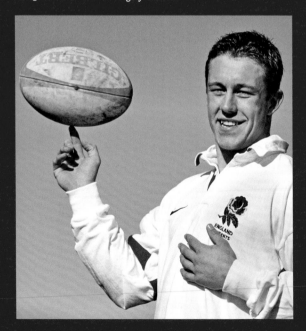

iRB
RUGBY
WORLD CUP
'03

"WHAT I AM PROUD OF IS I HAVE SEARCHED
FOR THE BEST OF ME AND I HAVE BEEN
A TEAM MAN WITHOUT FAIL"

PAULA GEORGE

Born 20 October 1968 **England career** 1994-2005, 75 caps
Position Full Back **Clubs** Richmond, Wasps

Paula George's rise to the top of international rugby is a tale of extraordinary resilience. At the age of 12 she was living in a foster home in Wales, but her single-minded determination took her to Cardiff University, where she was introduced to rugby for the first time.

It was love at first sight for George, who appreciated the mental side of the game as much as the physical, and quickly developed into a fast, attacking back, blessed with both poise and guile.

Her path to becoming a Red Rose, however, was unusually complicated. She played five times on the wing for Wales and featured in the inaugural Rugby World Cup in 1991, before growing disillusioned.

On moving to London, she joined Richmond and then Wasps. In 1994, after a two-year mandatory exile from international rugby, she was selected to play for England. Later the same year she and England became world champions for the first time.

In 1997 she helped London win the regional title and was given player of the match for the Red Roses against Scotland. Rob Drinkwater, the RFUW Development Manager, described George as "a true world-class professional in terms of her attitude and focus" and, in 2000, she was installed as England captain.

In George's first year as captain, she delivered England a Grand Slam, secured by Chris Diver's winning try in injury time against France. Her 50th cap came against France in 2001, where she scored the game's opening try and set England on a path to an unprecedented third Grand Slam in three seasons. Later that year, she captained England to a first-ever win against the Black Ferns, describing the 22-17 win as "the greatest moment of my life".

She was unable to repeat the feat in the final of the 2002 Rugby World Cup and was left out of the side in 2003. Showing characteristic tenacity, she forced her way back into the side and regained the captaincy in 2005, before retiring at the age of 36.

"I DIDN'T KNOW I WANTED TO BE A WARRIOR UNTIL I TASTED IT"

FAMOUS GAMES

ENGLAND 31 NEW ZEALAND 28

9 November 2002, Twickenham

Back-to-back wins over both South Africa and world champions Australia meant that England were in a position to lay claim to being the world's pre-eminent side in the autumn of 2002. One team stood in their way. England hadn't beaten New Zealand since 1993 and had only beaten them four times in 23 attempts before their arrival at Twickenham in November 2002.

Captained by the redoubtable Martin Johnson, the fulcrum of the side was the half-back pair Jonny Wilkinson and Matt Dawson, with Will Greenwood, Ben Cohen and the effervescent Jason Robinson running lines from deep. Lewis Moody was preferred to Neil Back in the back row alongside Lawrence Dallaglio and Richard Hill, the latter leading the side out to mark his 50th appearance for England.

Wilkinson was enjoying the form of his career. Accurate and reliable kicking from his boot and a try from Moody, deep into injury time, helped England to a 17-14 half-time lead. In eight electrifying second-half minutes, England scored two converted tries, the first a dazzling chip and run in which Wilkinson started and finished a superb solo try. Cohen then consolidated the lead by adding the second with a surging run from deep (*right*).

At 31-14 down New Zealand did not give up. The great Jonah Lomu sparked the revival and two converted tries brought them within reach, at 31-28, with three minutes remaining. Sensing blood the All Blacks probed the English defence but a 79th minute try-saving tackle from Cohen was enough to confirm victory.

England J Robinson – JD Simpson-Daniel (AS Healey), WJH Greenwood (JB Johnston), MJ Tindall, BC Cohen – JP Wilkinson, MJS Dawson – TJ Woodman, SG Thompson, PJ Vickery – MO Johnson*, DJ Grewcock (BJ Kay) – LW Moody, LBN Dallaglio (NA Back), RA Hill

New Zealand BA Blair – DC Howlett, TJF Umaga, KR Lowen (MP Robinson), JT Lomu – CJ Spencer (AP Mehrtens), SJ Devine (DD Lee) – JM McDonnell, AK Hore, KJ Meeuws – AJ Williams, KJ Robinson (BM Mika) – TC Randell*, SR Broomhall, MR Holah

WITHIN TOUCHING DISTANCE

If the 1998 World Cup had indicated a gulf in class between first-time winners New Zealand and the rest, the Red Roses were not about to accept it lying down. Former Australian international full back Geoff Richards took over as coach in the 2000/01 season with one intention. "Our goal is to win the 2002 World Cup," he said and highlighted back play as key to the team's improvement.

By the summer of 2002, it was clear that England had indeed caught up. They inflicted a first defeat since 1991 on the Black Ferns when they tied a two-Test series in New Zealand. Strong showings were expected from Canada and also France, who had beaten England to the 2002 Six Nations.

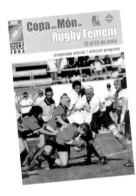

Left: Team captain Paula George with coach Geoff Richards at the World Cup squad announcement at Twickenham

Right: George (centre) with teammates (from left) Shelley Rae, Jenny Sutton, Nicki Jupp and Sue Day

The 2002 Rugby World Cup would be hosted by Spain in Barcelona. The England squad had an intriguing mixture of youth and experience, with Helen Clayton, Gill Burns, Emma Mitchell, Nicky Ponsford and captain Paula George all still very much involved, while big things were expected from a pack that included Georgia Stevens and Selena Rudge and a front row that featured the likes of Teresa O'Reilly, Maxine Edwards and hooker Amy Garnett. Rae and Jo Yapp were the creative half-back pairing and wings Sue Day and Nicky Crawford were among the most prolific try-scorers in the game.

A comfortable group stage began for England with a 63-9 victory over Italy. After topping the group, they faced hosts Spain in the quarter-final and found themselves 5-0 down before a moment of individual brilliance from centre Nicky Jupp triggered a revival that ended in a 13-5 victory for the Red Roses.

Against Canada in the semi-final, it was the veterans Burns and Mitchell who sparked the Red Roses into life. A hat-trick of tries from Day helped England to a 53-10 victory and, suddenly, the side looked like champions in waiting.

The Black Ferns awaited them in the final and, perhaps chastened by their defeat in the summer, began the game with four props, determined to play for territory and keep the English backs out of the game.

England were shoved off the ball at the first scrum, but the physicality of the Black Ferns resulted in a string of penalties, allowing Shelley Rae to kick England into a 9-6 lead in the 24th minute. Eventually, New Zealand's attritional play began to pay off and two tries gave them a commanding lead. Black Ferns indiscipline gave England hope in the second half but it was not to be. Deservedly, New Zealand won their second World Cup 19-9.

So ended the storied international careers of Burns and Mitchell, although a standing ovation awaited them and the rest of the squad when they paraded their runners-up medals at Twickenham at half-time during the England v Barbarians men's match.

Left: Sue Day dives over to score a try in the semi-final against Canada in Girona

Above: New Zealand women celebrate beating England in the final at the Olympic Stadium in Barcelona

13 May 2002
England 63 Italy 9
Cornella de Llobregat

18 May 2002
Spain 5 England 13
Cornella de Llobregat

POOL C	P	W	D	L	F	A	Pts	
England	2	2	0	0	76	14	6	3rd
Spain	2	1	0	1	67	13	4	6th
Italy	2	1	0	1	39	66	4	12th
Japan	2	0	0	2	3	92	2	15th

Semi-final
21 May 2002
Canada 10 England 53
Girona, Barcelona

Final
25 May 2002
England 9 New Zealand 19
Olympic Stadium, Barcelona
Attendance: 8,000

England P George* – N Crawford, N Jupp, S Rudge (A de Baise), S Day – S Rae (S Appleby), J Yapp – M Edwards (T O'Reilly), A Garnett, V Huxford – K Henderson, T Andrews (G Burns) – J Phillips (H Clayton), C Frost, G Stevens

New Zealand T Wilson – DMT Kahura, AM Rush, S Shortland (HJ Myers), A Marsh – AM Richards, MJ Hirovanaa – R Sheck (H Va'aga), FR Palmer*, R Liua'ana – MM Codling, VL Heighway – CM Waaka, RL Martin, AP Lili'i (MC Robinson)

ENGLAND 57 FRANCE 0

15 February 2003, Twickenham

'Dream, Believe and Achieve' was the Red Roses' motto in 2003, and the year began with the realisation of an ambition. Carol Isherwood had been pushing for England to play at Twickenham for some time, and had been backed by Clive Woodward and a supportive rugby press, among which *Rugby World* magazine had been actively campaigning for women's international matches to be played at the national ground. The moment finally arrived on 15 February 2003.

Reigning Six Nations champions France would be the opposition and might even have been favourites as they took the field. Such thoughts were not entertained by England prop Maxine Edwards who, at 35, would be captaining England for the first time.

Selena Rudge was one of several players who had played at Twickenham before in the National Cup Final. A degree of pressure must have been on the shoulders of full back Chris Diver, who had been selected ahead of outstanding former captain Paula George.

Perhaps inspired by the occasion, England completely overran the French to score nine tries in a 57-0 victory, and Diver repaid the faith shown in her by scoring three of them. Not to be outdone, wing Sue Day scored three of her own. On the full-time whistle, Day remarked: "It's an honour to play here and if you can score a try it's even better".

No-one was happier than coach Geoff Richards, who savoured the spectacle as the culmination of considerable hard work. England would go on to secure the Grand Slam by a record margin.

England C Diver – N Crawford, N Jupp, A De Biase (K Andrew), S Day (S Marsh) – S Rae, J Yapp (S Appleby) – M Edwards*, A O'Flynn (S Rudge), V Huxford (S Whitehead) – J Sutton, C Green (A Pilkington) – G Stevens (H Durman), C Frost, H Clayton

France E Sartini – C Devilliers, D Plantet, C Le Duff, M Talayrac (C Lemazurier) – M Hans (S Agricole), S Provost (J Pujol) – D Roussel, O Sorel*, F Gelis (D Irazu) – M Bonnin, A Massacand (C Devroute) – A Sagols, C Flaugere, S Serres

MAXINE EDWARDS

Born 28 July 1966
England career 1991-2004, 45 caps
Position Prop **Club** Saracens

Born in Beckenham, Kent, Maxine Edwards attended Lewisham School and Hackney College, taking on an electrical apprenticeship before studying at Greenwich University and later training as a teacher. She began playing rugby, aged 19, with Bromley Women's Rugby Football Club, which later became Blackheath Women's Rugby Club. Initially a flanker, she developed into a reliable and uncompromising prop.

Edwards made her debut for the Red Roses against Wales in 1991 and competed at the inaugural Rugby World Cup. She then took time out as a mother, before returning to the national set-up later in the decade. In 1994, England became world champions and, although Maxine was absent, her sister Jacquie, a centre, scored a try in the final. From 1997-98 Maxine was ever present in the national side and established herself as a key player in a team that won three consecutive Grand Slam Five Nations Championships between 1999 and 2001.

Wearing the Red Rose, Edwards reached the semi-finals of the 1998 Rugby World Cup before going one better in 2002. Part of the pioneer generation, she had huge strength of character and was made captain of England, at the age of 35, in 2003. Her first duty was to lead the Red Roses out at Twickenham for the first time. They won the game – a brutal demolition of the reigning Six Nations champions France – and went on to complete the Grand Slam. She retained the captaincy in 2004, which proved to be her final season.

Edwards earned 45 caps in all and was awarded an MBE in 2010.

RUGBY WORLD CUP 2003

REACHING FOR THE SKIES

England went into the 2003 Rugby World Cup as the world's number one side. In the preceding years, they had defeated every major rugby playing nation, both home and away, and in doing so built a formidable reputation. Led by Martin Johnson, with the impressive trio of Lawrence Dallaglio, Neil Back and Richard Hill in the back row, the talismanic Jonny Wilkinson kicking every penalty and conversion that came his way, and livewire rugby league convert Jason Robinson at full back, they were rightly considered favourites.

Three warm-up internationals against Wales and France in August and September had shown the strength in depth of the squad, and when the World Cup started in October, England had won 15 out of 16 internationals since March 2002.

A key strength of their side lay in a well-balanced backline, orchestrated by Wilkinson and scrum half Matt Dawson, with strike runners such as Robinson, Ben Cohen and Josh Lewsey across the back three, in support of a centre pairing drawn from Will Greenwood, Mike Tindall or Mike Catt. The English forwards were rightly admired and feared, a powerful front row drawn from Phil Vickery, Trevor Woodman or Jason Leonard alongside hooker Steve Thompson; a strong and mobile second row that included Johnson and Ben Kay; and one of the all-time great England back rows in Back, Hill and Dallaglio.

England were drawn in Pool C and they opened their campaign at the Subiaco Oval in Perth with an 84-6 victory over Georgia, before beating South Africa, their principal rivals in the pool, convincingly 25-6. Their next opponents, Samoa, at the Telstra Dome in Melbourne, proved a major obstacle and were leading 22-20 with 15 minutes of the match remaining. Helped by a Jonny Wilkinson drop

Above: The 2003 England squad heads for Australia

Left: The team gathers around skipper Martin Johnson in Sydney prior to the semi-final

goal, England regained the initiative in time and pulled away with two further tries to win 35-22. Uruguay, at the Suncorp Stadium in Brisbane, were the final opponents in the pool but had no answer to the skill and power of the England side. Victory by 111-13 with 16 tries and Josh Lewsey equalling the England record of five tries in an international, secured their position at the top of the pool.

A rejuvenated Wales side that had put in a strong showing in a losing cause against the All Blacks awaited England in the quarter-final at the Suncorp Stadium. Wales began the match in the same style and led England 10-3 at half-time. A vital try early in the second half for Greenwood, after Robinson had cut open the Welsh defence with a long, winding run, turned the tide. Intelligent kicking and positioning allowed England to pull away, with five penalty goals and a drop goal from Wilkinson securing a 28-17 win. England were through to the semi-finals but concerns remained that their strike runners were not quite firing on all cylinders and their defence was falling short of their previous standards – indeed Wales had outscored them by three tries to one.

England entered their semi-final against France at the Telstra Stadium in Sydney knowing that, if they won, their opponents in the final would be host nation Australia. Although France scored a try early in the first half to take a 7-3 lead, they scored no further points and the remainder of the match belonged to England. There was no need for tries as Wilkinson had a supreme afternoon with the boot, scoring all 24 points – including five penalty goals and three drop goals – to seal a 24-7 victory. After a gap of 12 years, England were back in the World Cup Final.

Top left: Mike Tindall touches down during England's comfortable first match victory against Georgia in Perth

Bottom left: The English team clap the Wales side off the field after their quarter-final clash in Brisbane

Right: Fly half Jonny Wilkinson prepares to convert yet another penalty during the semi-final against France in Sydney

12 October 2003
England 84 Georgia 6
Subiaco Oval, Perth
Attendance: 25,501

18 October 2003
South Africa 6 England 25
Subiaco Oval, Perth
Attendance: 49,922

26 October 2003
England 35 Samoa 22
Telstra Dome, Melbourne
Attendance: 50,647

2 November 2003
England 111 Uruguay 13
Suncorp Stadium, Brisbane
Attendance: 46,233

POOL C	P	W	D	L	F	A	BP	Pts
England	**4**	**4**	**0**	**0**	**255**	**47**	**3**	**19**
South Africa	4	3	0	1	184	60	3	15
Samoa	4	2	0	2	138	117	2	10
Uruguay	4	1	0	3	56	255	0	4
Georgia	4	0	0	4	46	200	0	0

Quarter-final
9 November 2003
England 28 Wales 17
Suncorp Stadium, Brisbane
Attendance: 45,252

Semi-final
16 November 2003
France 7 England 24
Telstra Stadium, Sydney
Attendance: 82,346

AUSTRALIA 17 ENGLAND 20

22 November 2003, Telstra Stadium, Sydney

The Telstra Stadium was packed to the rafters for what promised to be a titanic clash. England made one change to their winning semi-final side by bringing Mike Tindall in at centre and moving Mike Catt to the bench. Australia had a strong side and would have partisan support in front of their home fans, but the power of the England pack was expected to be decisive.

A rugby classic followed. Australia gained an early advantage when Lote Tuqiri scored an unconverted try after five minutes. Wilkinson replied with three penalty goals, before Robinson scored a superb try in the left-hand corner just before half-time following interplay between Dallaglio and Wilkinson. In an increasingly tense second half, Australia came back into the game. Their sole scorer was nerveless centre Elton Flatley, who kicked three penalty goals, including one in the final minute of the half, to secure a 14-14 draw and take the game into extra-time.

Both sides brought on replacements, with Leonard's arrival in the front row helping to stabilise the English scrum. Wilkinson put England ahead with a penalty in the 82nd minute but Flatley equalised with his fourth penalty in the 96th minute. Just four minutes of the match remained, with a draw looking increasingly inevitable.

In the final minute, substitute Lewis Moody received a lineout in England's half. A sniping break by Dawson allowed England to drive up the middle of the field, before Johnson gained further metres with a drive of his own. Dawson passed back to Wilkinson just outside the 22-metre line. His pass reached Wilkinson just out of reach of the Australian back row, giving him enough time and space to kick from his weaker foot and for the briefest of moments time seemed to stand still for thousands of English rugby fans around the world.

With a clean strike, Wilkinson cleared the posts with his right foot. His drop goal gave England a 20-17 lead and, with no time for Australia to come back, all that remained was for England to receive the Australian kick-off and boot the ball from the park. Mike Catt did the honours and England had won.

After returning with the Webb Ellis Cup on a chartered British Airways plane called 'Sweet Chariot', the team were received by 10 Downing Street and Buckingham Palace. Thousands lined the streets of central London to celebrate an open-top bus parade. In 150 years of rugby, this was England's finest hour.

Left: Jason Robinson touches down during the final
Above: The most famous drop goal in English rugby history
Right: The players are transfixed as the ball sails goalwards

World Cup Final
22 November 2003
Australia 17 England 20 (after extra-time)
Telstra Stadium, Sydney
Attendance: 82,957

Australia MS Rogers – WJ Sailor (JW Roff), SA Mortlock, EJ Flatley, LD Tuqiri – SJ Larkham (MJ Giteau), GM Gregan* – WK Young (MJ Dunning), BJ Cannon (JA Paul), AKE Baxter – JBG Harrison, NC Sharpe (D Giffin) – GB Smith, DJ Lyons (MJ Cockbain), PR Waugh

England OJ Lewsey (IR Balshaw) – JT Robinson, WJH Greenwood, MJ Tindall (MJ Catt), BC Cohen – JP Wilkinson, MJS Dawson – TJ Woodman, SG Thompson, PJ Vickery (J Leonard) – MO Johnson*, BJ Kay – NA Back, LBN Dallaglio, RA Hill (LW Moody)

The final whistle blows as Martin Johnson (above, centre) and Jonny Wilkinson (right) are engulfed by their teammates

Australia		England
1	Tries	1
0	Conversions	0
4	Penalties	4
0	Drop Goals	1
17	**Score**	20

Extra Time

The moment of victory for England's fans in the stadium in Sydney (left and below left)

Below: Will Greenwood knows he's become a World Cup winner and Lewis Moody's World Cup winners' medal

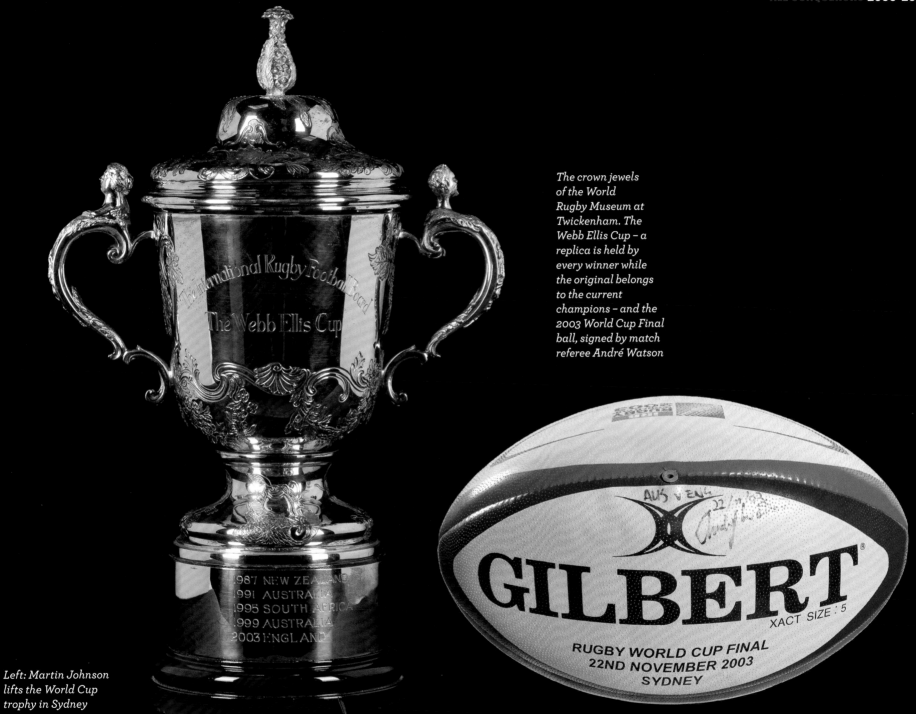

The crown jewels of the World Rugby Museum at Twickenham. The Webb Ellis Cup – a replica is held by every winner while the original belongs to the current champions – and the 2003 World Cup Final ball, signed by match referee André Watson

Left: Martin Johnson lifts the World Cup trophy in Sydney

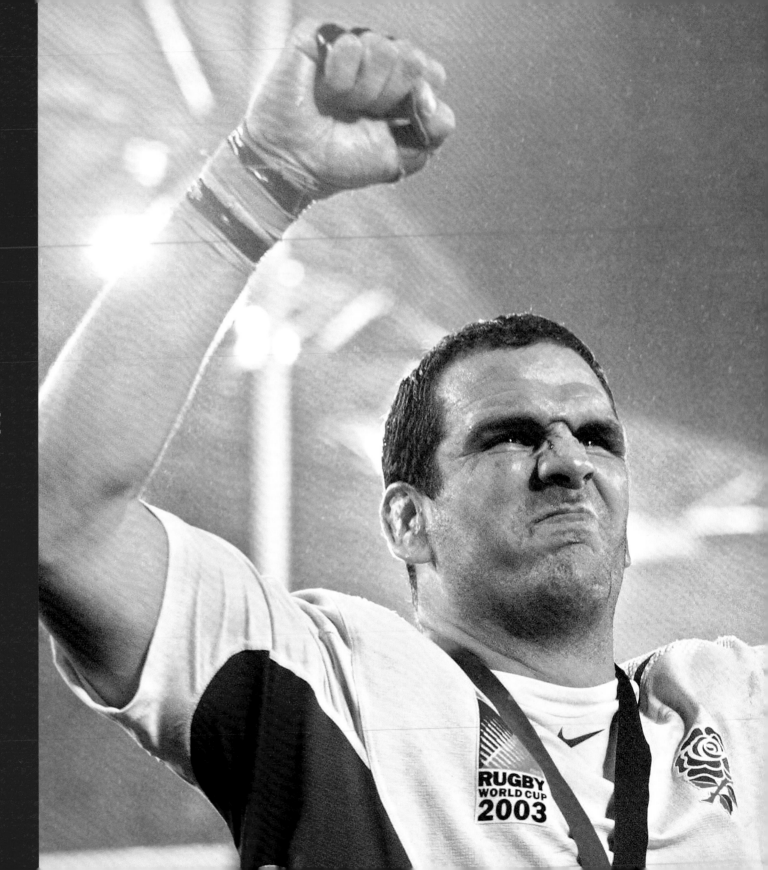

"IT'S ABOUT US GOING OUT THERE TRYING TO IMPOSE OUR GAME ON THEM AND THEM TRYING TO DO THE SAME TO US AND WHOEVER DOES BEST WILL COME OUT ON TOP"

The England Greats

MARTIN JOHNSON

Born 9 March 1970 **England career** 1993-2003, 84 caps
Position Second Row **Club** Leicester

Martin Johnson, a towering presence on and off the field and widely considered one of rugby's greatest-ever forwards, played his last England international in that historic match in Sydney which delivered the England men's team a World Cup for the first time.

Johnson won almost every honour in the game and earned 84 England caps in all. He made his debut against France in 1993 at Twickenham and appeared in three World Cup tournaments. He played throughout England's Grand Slam campaign in 1995 – during a run of 24 consecutive internationals – and scored his two tries against Italy in 1996 and USA in 1999.

England captain in 39 matches, 34 of them victories, Johnson also memorably led England to a Grand Slam in 2003. Despite very limited captaincy experience at the time, he was chosen to lead the British & Irish Lions on their victorious tour of South Africa in 1997, after which he was awarded an OBE. He became the first player to captain the Lions on two successive tours when he also led the touring party to Australia in 2001.

His club career was no less distinguished. He played for Leicester Tigers from February 1989 through to his retirement in 2005, except for a two-year break in New Zealand, where he played for King Country on the recommendation of Sir Colin Meads. He was highly rated and represented the New Zealand Under-21 XV in three matches in 1990, alongside a number of future All Blacks.

On his return to England, Johnson led Leicester during their greatest period of success. They were Pilkington Cup winners in 1997, Premiership winners for four seasons from 1999 to 2002 and European Cup winners in 2001 and in 2002. His final competitive match was the 2005 Premiership final against Wasps. He said farewell as a player by leading a star-studded Northern Hemisphere XV against Jonah Lomu's Southern Hemisphere XV at Twickenham in June 2005.

After a brief break from rugby, he became England team manager in 2008, winning the 2011 Six Nations before standing down following the World Cup later that year. He was appointed CBE in 2004, and in 2009 was voted England's Player of the Century.

United nation

England had finally conquered the world. Martin Johnson's team, expertly coached by Clive Woodward, had seen off all comers to beat Australia in the World Cup Final. The game would never be the same again

By Mick Cleary, Chief rugby writer, *The Daily Telegraph*

O ne by one they came shuffling through, elated if tired, still bruised, perhaps even a touch hungover – and who could begrudge them the odd tipple in celebration? But Australia was far behind them already and the party was over.

If there was one thing that the England squad did get wrong in winning the Rugby World Cup in 2003 it was the notion that the party had come to an end as their British Airways plane landed back in London. Boys, it was only just starting.

You can attempt to evaluate the success of Martin Johnson's team by itemising their various wins during the tournament, the typically hard-nut 25-6 victory over the Springboks in the Pool C game in Perth or the lung-bursting effort against Wales in the quarter-final and, yes, of course, the swing of the ever-faithful Jonny boot that secured the spoils on a rainy night under the Telstra Stadium lights in Sydney. All triumphs of the soul as much as of skill, England

displaying togetherness as much as talent in their varying manners of performance – crucial Jason Robinson breaks and tries, hard-hitting back-rowers in Richard Hill, snafflers like Neil Back, and Jonny, always Jonny. 'Is That All You've Got?' mocked an Australian newspaper about England's prime weapon, Wilkinson. The *Sydney Morning Herald* had the good grace to print a tongue-in-cheek full-page apology on the Monday after the final.

Yet ordinary match analysis does not do the occasion justice. The thousands greeting those weary heroes at Heathrow on that November morning told a tale, as did the multitudes on the surrounding approach roads, unable to get into the terminal itself as it was already overcrowded at 6am. On and on went the crowds, as did the cheers, even from the hotel staff as they returned to their base at Pennyhill Park, ready to collect their belongings as well as a changed sense of reality.

The party was in full flow for days, even if the usual suspects such as captain Martin Johnson were turning out for their clubs the following weekend. If the players were intent on sticking to their same old routines, they too could not help but be affected by the country's reaction to the World Cup victory.

Rugby is a popular sport in England, yet it is markedly not football in terms of its profile and reach. But for those madcap few months English rugby did sample the sort of acclaim that is usually the preserve of the national football team, or global sporting brands such as Manchester United and Liverpool.

The official celebration parade in London was a monumental affair, akin to a Royal Wedding

Martin Johnson shows off the World Cup to an ecstatic crowd at Trafalgar Square in December 2003

Above: Martin Johnson arrives at Heathrow airport with a very important piece of baggage

Right: Clive Woodward, architect of England's victory, gets his hands on the trophy after the final in Sydney

The official celebration parade in London a few weeks later was a monumental affair, akin to a Royal Wedding as two open-topped buses inched their way around Mayfair and into Trafalgar Square. Everyone wanted a slice of the action. It was not as if the rugby players were celebrity-chasing individuals trying to force their way into the limelight. Whoever managed to persuade Jonny Wilkinson to appear on Michael Parkinson's television chat show deserved a pay rise as England's favourite son, the points-scoring machine of the World Cup, would rather walk across hot coals than willingly submit to interview. Yet appear he did and Parkinson was later to relate that of all the hundreds of guests who have appeared on his award-winning programme, no-one – not even one of Hollywood's finest – had received such a standing ovation as they came down the stairs on the TV set to be interviewed. If you wanted a snapshot of what England's World Cup victory meant to the country then that was it, even if Jonny was probably wishing that the staircase would open up and swallow him whole such was his embarrassment.

The England squad deserved the adulation that came their way, their sponsorship endorsements, too, their various awards in the Honours' Lists, the knighthood for Clive Woodward, the architect of so much and over such a long period of time. The seven matches at the tournament itself almost took care of themselves although even those best-laid plans almost went awry at different junctures, right through to the final itself when England simply could not shake off those pesky Aussies or knock Wallaby fly half Elton Flatley out of his goal-kicking stride right until the very last minutes, despite apparent dominance, at which point Johnson's team drew on all the savvy and know-how accumulated over the last six years under Woodward. That is why Woodward was so feted and still is today.

The former Lions and Leicester centre professionalised an amateur set-up. It was a root and branch operation that took years of near-misses and no little amount of money. But the RFU investment which ran into millions of pounds had its return as the post-World Cup interest levels show. England were box office, on the streets of London as well as in the commercial market place.

The contrast with 1999 could not have been starker. Back then, England had slunk home from Paris after their dispiriting defeat by South Africa in the quarter-final, Jannie de Beer's five drop goal haul the centre-piece of a shattering 44-21 victory. There was no-one, bar a few loved ones, to greet England as they stepped off the Eurostar that following Monday.

Yet by the time Woodward's men headed to their initial World Cup base in Perth in early October 2003, their stock had risen enormously. They had real presence on the English sporting landscape. The likes of Johnson and

Wikinson, as well as Lawrence Dallaglio, Matt Dawson, Neil Back, Will Greenwood, Jason Robinson and others, were recognisable figures – their exploits the stuff of pub conversations up and down the land.

Woodward's England may have had too many unsuccessful tilts at Grand Slams for comfort among their supporters until finally nailing one in some style against Ireland at Lansdowne Road six months before the start of the tournament, but they ruled the roost over the vaunted southern hemisphere teams – New Zealand, South Africa and Australia – in the build-up to the tournament, the victory over Eddie Jones' Wallabies in the 2003 final marking England's 12th in succession over the 'Big Three' from south of the equator.

That is why England were box office, the number one seeds, testimony to their prowess across three years. It is legitimate to argue that they played their best rugby of 2003 just prior to the World Cup, their 42-6 Grand Slam-securing victory in Dublin followed up by a ground-breaking

England were box office, on the streets of London as well as in the commercial market place

tour of New Zealand and Australia. The All Blacks were beaten in Wellington 15-13, despite Johnson's side being reduced to 13 men at one point with Dallaglio and Back in the sin bin, a landmark victory that was matched seven days later with England's first ever win over the Wallabies on Australian soil, an emphatic 25-14 victory in Melbourne.

Hopes were high as was the interest throughout the country. Woodward's team were dominating the back pages and had a fair old presence up the front end of the papers, too, thanks to the enthusiastic support of Prince Harry, who had been welcomed into camp on several occasions and was also there to lend his backing in Australia.

The 2003 World Cup was a tremendous success on so many levels. Even if only by default (New Zealand had been due to be co-hosts but had those rights taken away from them by the International Rugby Board), it took place in one country – as had happened in South Africa eight years earlier – and was the better for it.

The Aussies really got behind the event, adopting countries such as Namibia and Georgia and Uruguay as their second team, a practice that was to become the norm in later tournaments. Rugby union is well down the pecking order of sports in Australia but such was the splendid marketing of the event the code was to be the talk of the country for seven weeks, the self-styled 'Greatest Show on Turf,' a fitting follow-up to the successful Sydney Olympics of three years earlier. The Telstra Stadium, sited in the Olympic Park on the outskirts of the city at Homebush, was to stage seven matches, all of which drew crowds in excess of 75,000.

From such humble, ad-hoc beginnings in 1987, the World Cup had become a global event, reaching a TV audience of almost four billion across 200 territories. The action was to take place at 11 venues in 10 cities round the country.

The Wallabies did their bit in reaching the final, their barnstorming 22-10 win over joint favourites New Zealand in the semi-final the high point of a successful campaign.

England had to fend off a stirring Welsh performance in the quarter-final in Brisbane to come through to face France in the semi-final, Steve Hansen's side defying pre-tournament form to give England a real scare. Wales had lost 13 of their last 15 encounters with England, yet as they went down the tunnel of the Suncorp Stadium at half-time with a 10-3 lead no-one begrudged them their advantage. It took (yet another) moment of magic from Jason Robinson to help turn the tide England's way, although the 28-17 final score line did not do justice to the cleverness and energy of Wales's play.

France did not manage to trouble England anything like as much in a rain-drenched semi-final. There was a 20°C drop in temperature between the two semi-finals, a despondent meteorological backdrop to what was to prove a glorious seven days for England followers. Nothing, but nothing could dampen their spirits. They flooded the city. Some 40,000 of them danced in the rain as Wilkinson once again delivered in the 24-7 semi-final win, landing five penalties and three drop goals.

"It is the dream final," said Clive Woodward as he looked forward to meeting the Wallabies. And so it proved. The excitement levels cranked up, with England barely able to set foot outside their hotel in Manly. It comes to something when the away team is at least as well supported as the hosts but that is the way it was. The Telstra Stadium was a sea of (rather wet) white shirts and that backing was to prove uplifting as England battled to win the favour of referee Andre Watson and subdue the Wallabies.

It took a final upfield drive with Johnson and Dawson leading the charge, and a swing of Wilkinson's right boot to land a wonky drop goal. It may not have been a thing of beauty but it was enough to bring the World Cup home.

It was quite an occasion, bedlam throughout the city and throughout the night, with scenes of celebration from the travelling army. It was party time, a joyous mood that was to last for weeks as the country fell in love with new-found heroes.

Above: Prince Harry enjoys England's semi-final win over France

Below: Celebrations begin in earnest amongst the England fans lucky enough to be at the Telstra Stadium in 2003

11

THE RISE OF
THE ROSES

2004-2011

IN TRANSITION

Newly appointed England men's coach Andy Robinson recorded wins against Canada and South Africa at the start of the 2004-05 season, as prop Andrew Sheridan earned the first of his caps. England then suffered their worst start to a Six Nations campaign since 1987 by losing their first three matches. Martin Corry subsequently took over as captain and led England to wins against Italy, Scotland, Australia and Samoa.

Paula George's Red Roses opened the 2005 Six Nations with a crushing 81-0 victory in Cardiff over Wales but were beaten for a third consecutive time by France, who topped the table. In the summer England recorded a 101-0 victory against South Africa, but lost two Tests in New Zealand.

The 2006 men's Championship began with a six-try victory over Wales and victory in Rome but finished with three defeats. In the autumn, England lost to New Zealand, Argentina and South Africa. Andy Robinson was dismissed as coach and replaced by Brian Ashton, while World Cup winners Matt Dawson and Ben Cohen called time on their careers.

The Red Roses went into the 2006 Championship determined to improve and began with a 38-15 win over Wales. The crucial match against France would be played in Paris. This time a dominant English pack steered England to a 28-0 win, with lock Jenny 'TJ' Sutton proving crucial at set-pieces. The Grand Slam was confirmed with a 29-10 victory over Ireland, but their World Cup campaign ended with defeat in the final once again.

Prop Phil Vickery was Ashton's choice for captain and the 2007 season began promisingly with wins over Scotland and Italy, but Ireland proved too strong in an emotional fixture at Croke Park. Victory against France meant England were one of four teams still in contention on the final weekend but defeat to Wales left them in third place. In the autumn, they reached their second consecutive World Cup Final but couldn't overcome a potent Springboks side. Following the final, both Dallaglio and Corry announced their international retirements.

Several experienced Red Roses retired at the end of 2006. A clutch of younger players stepped up, including Katy Mclean and Sarah Hunter. Sue Day replaced Jo Yapp as captain as England blasted out of the blocks under her leadership, scoring 18 tries in three matches without conceding a point. In the Six Nations they beat nearest rivals France 38-12 and defeated Wales 30-0 to secure back-to-back Grand Slams, before beating France again in the European Championships Final and seeing out an unbeaten year with victory against the USA – after which Day brought the curtain down on her illustrious career as England's record tryscorer.

The 2008 men's Six Nations began with Wales winning at Twickenham for the first time in 20 years, before victories on the road against Italy and France. Jonny Wilkinson became the highest-scoring

With Lawrence Dallaglio back as captain, England began their 2004 campaign with away wins in Rome and Edinburgh before losing at home against Ireland. They remained in Championship contention but lost narrowly to France in their final match. It was the first of four consecutive defeats, after which Clive Woodward stood down as coach. It was the end of an era.

The Red Roses won their first four games comfortably but were also undone by France – 13-12 – in Bourg-en-Bresse. France beat them again in the final of the European Championships, and their Churchill Cup defence ended at the same stage against New Zealand. Nicky Crawford and Vanessa Huxford both earned their 50th caps in the calendar year.

Above: England celebrate a crucial victory in France on the way to the Grand Slam in 2006

Previous pages: Heather Fisher, Catherine Spencer, Maggie Alphonsi and Karen Jones celebrate their Grand Slam win in 2010

player in the history of international rugby in the match against Scotland but couldn't stop England slumping to defeat at Murrayfield. England responded by defeating Ireland for the first time since 2003.

Gary Street took over from Geoff Richards as Red Roses coach and England continued their dominance by defeating Wales 55-0 in the first game of the 2008 Six Nations. Emily Scarratt made her debut and England cruised through the campaign, securing a record third consecutive Grand Slam with a 17-7 victory over Ireland. They had added the European Championships and Nations Cup before the year was out.

Caretaker coach Rob Andrew made Steve Borthwick captain during an unsuccessful tour of New Zealand and new coach Martin Johnson retained him in the role for the 2009 Six Nations. Defeats to Wales and Ireland followed as the Irish claimed a first Grand Slam since 1948. Defeats during the year to Argentina, New Zealand and Australia confirmed that England remained in transition.

The Red Roses quest for a fourth consecutive Grand Slam faltered in the second round when they lost 16-15 to Wales for the first time since their rivalry began in 1987. They recovered and took the Championship on points, with Scarratt and Fiona Pocock ending the season as joint top tryscorers. England won the Nations Cup in the summer, before hosting New Zealand for a two-match series, and Catherine Spencer celebrated her 50th cap by leading England to a 10-3 victory in the second.

England's men began 2010 in retro jerseys as they beat Wales in a match that commemorated 100 years of Test rugby at Twickenham, with Lewis Moody taking over as captain after defeats against Ireland and Scotland. A tied summer series in Australia followed, before Chris Ashton's 80-yard run secured a memorable 35-18 win over the Wallabies at Twickenham.

The Red Roses won their first four matches of 2010, and a 64th-minute penalty from Mclean was the difference in Rennes as England beat

Above: A familiar face took charge of the men's team in 2009 in the shape of former captain Martin Johnson

Right: Chris Ashton scores a phenomenal 80-metre try against Australia in November 2010

Left: England captain Catherine Spencer poses with the Women's Six Nations trophy in 2008, the year her team completed a third consecutive Grand Slam

France 11-10, to complete the Grand Slam. Unfortunately for Spencer's side, their 2010 season ended with defeat in the World Cup Final.

Johnson's England began 2011 by defeating Wales in Cardiff for the first time since 2003. Ashton landed six tries in the opening two rounds, before hard-fought wins against France and Scotland set up a Grand Slam decider in Dublin. Ireland spoiled the party, but England won the Championship for the first time since 2003.

With Mclean installed as captain, the Red Roses bounced back from their World Cup disappointment with the most commanding Grand Slam in Six Nations history. They added the Nations Cup in the summer, before defeating New Zealand twice and drawing once in a three-Test series in November.

THE RED ROSES BOUNCED BACK FROM WORLD CUP DISAPPOINTMENT IN 2010 WITH THE MOST COMMANDING GRAND SLAM IN SIX NATIONS HISTORY

CLOSE ENCOUNTERS

Edmonton in Alberta, Canada, would be the venue for the first women's edition of the Rugby World Cup to be held outside Europe. In a sign of the growing status of the tournament, competitors would have their expenses paid by the IRB for the first time.

New Zealand were once again favourites, having beaten England across a two-match series in 2005. England, however, were Grand Slam champions for the first time since 2003

and veteran openside Helen Clayton believed that the side was stronger than the one that had won the tournament in 1994.

England had an experienced pack with Jenny 'TJ' Sutton back alongside Jenny Lyne in the second row and Vanessa Gray doing the lifting in the lineouts. Selena Rudge and Georgia Stevens were still involved but the squad was flush with talented younger players, such as wing Charlotte Barras, Rochelle Clark, Maggie Alphonsi, Amy Turner and back row Catherine Spencer, who had recently been named player of the year.

Prolific wings Nicky Crawford and Sue Day were setting English records, and there were plenty of options at fly half, with Shelley Rae and Karen Andrew competing for the jersey to partner their influential captain Jo Yapp at scrum half.

The tournament format had been shortened, with only 12 teams participating, meaning that a first round defeat might well be terminal. England were handed three tough matches against USA, South Africa and France. A disciplined performance saw them past USA 18-0, and this was followed by a comprehensive defeat of South Africa and a controlled and impressive victory against France to set up a semi-final with the hosts. Canada provided the stiffest test of the tournament so far, but the Red Roses stuck to their game plan and prevailed.

As in 2002, the Black Ferns awaited in the final. Despite the results of 2005, Yapp and the England coaches were confident that they had the players and strategy to win.

England began the match with a ferocious intensity, charging down two kicks in the opening minute. Moments later, the Red Roses took the lead with a penalty from Andrew, and they maintained the pressure for most of the first half. However, they were unable to build the score and allowed New Zealand to strike back with a Monalisa Codling try that gave the Black Ferns a 10-3 half-time lead.

Another New Zealand try in the opening minute of the second half stretched their lead before the English scrum delivered a penalty try for Yapp's side. Replacements Rae and Clayton brought England within three points at 20-17 in injury time, before the Black Ferns scored again to see out the match 25-17.

As in 2002, England had gone close and, with a young squad of developing players, the Red Roses could look to the future with cautious optimism.

Above: Helen Clayton (left) and Maggie Alphonsi (right) nurse their injuries alongside teammate Karen Andrew after they defeated France 27-8

Left: England's Jenny Sutton battles for lineout ball against Jen Crouse in the match against the USA

Cross-pool matches

31 August 2006
England 18 United States 0
St Albert Rugby Park, Alberta

4 September 2006
England 74 South Africa 8
Ellerslie Rugby Park, Edmonton

8 September 2006
England 27 France 8
St Albert Rugby Park, Alberta

POOL B	P	W	D	L	F	A	Pts
England	3	3	0	0	119	16	14
Australia	3	1	0	2	88	42	6
Ireland	3	0	0	3	48	67	5

Semi-final
12 September 2006
Canada 14 England 20
Ellerslie Rugby Park, Edmonton

Final
17 September 2006
England 17 New Zealand 25
Commonwealth Stadium, Edmonton

England C Barras – D Waterman, S Day, K Oliver (A Turner), K Shaylor – K Andrew (S Rae), J Yapp* – R Clark, A Garnett, V Gray (V Huxford) – J Sutton, J Lyne (T Taylor) – G Stevens, C Spencer (H Clayton), M Alphonsi

New Zealand A Marsh – C Richardson (HJ Myers), HR Manuel, ET Edwards, SA Mortimer – AM Richards, EM Jensen – FDL Maliukaetau, FR Palmer*, CJ Robertson – MM Codling, VL Heighway – MJ Ruscoe, RL Martin, LF Itunu (S Willoughby)

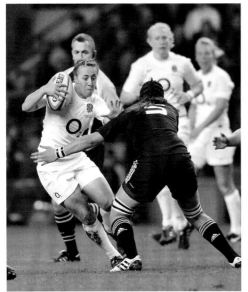

Top: England face the Haka before the final in Edmonton

Far left: Katy Mclean tries to find a way through the Black Ferns defence

Left: Monalisa Codling consoles Karen Andrew after New Zealand claimed a 25-17 victory and with it the World Cup trophy

SUE DAY

Born 29 October 1972
England career 1997-2007, 61 caps
Position Wing/Centre **Club** Wasps

Sue Day discovered rugby while in Spain on a placement year with Oxford University. An explosive runner, she saw gaps and exploited them. Blessed with fast feet and fast hands, she was both a creator and scorer of tries.

Day made her England debut in a match against Spain in 1997, was part of the 1998 Rugby World Cup squad and helped England to a Grand Slam in 1999. Her versatility meant that she could play across the back three or at centre and she swiftly became a regular starter.

After scoring the opening try against Scotland in 2001 she was stretchered from the field with a dislocated ankle. So severe were her injuries that at one point she was told that she would not play rugby again. Challenge accepted, Day was back with the squad in 2002 and a hat-trick of tries against Spain began a remarkable run of scoring form that carried into the 2002 World Cup.

During the 2002 tournament, Day scored six tries in the group stage and another hat-trick in the semi-final – allowing England to go one better than in 1998 – and she finished the tournament as top tryscorer with nine tries.

In 2003, Day marked the Red Roses' first appearance at Twickenham with three tries against France. In 2005, she captained Wasps to a third successive Premiership and, having moved to full back, went into the 2006 Rugby World Cup as a crucial component in one of the most potent backlines in world rugby. She scored four tries against South Africa and another two against France. Victory against Canada followed, before a narrow defeat to New Zealand in the final.

In 2007 she was installed as England captain. A Grand Slam was duly delivered, and her calm encouragement is credited with instilling belief in a group of young players who would dominate the Six Nations for years to come. Her influence on the game did not end there. In 2013, Day became the first female president of Wasps and in 2017 she joined the RFU as Chief Financial Officer, before becoming Chief Operations & Financial Officer.

Day's remarkable career can perhaps be best summed up by her tally of 59 tries at international XVs level – in 150 years, no England player has scored more.

"I AM JUST ONE OF A WHOLE MOVEMENT OF PEOPLE WORKING INCREDIBLY HARD TO DRIVE THE PROGRESS OF WOMEN'S SPORT AND WOMEN'S RUGBY"

The England Greats

PHIL VICKERY

Born 14 March 1976
England career 1998-2009, 73 caps
Position Prop **Clubs** Gloucester, Wasps

Phil Vickery was a proud Cornishman who anchored the England scrum in 73 internationals over 11 years and played in two World Cup Finals. Vickery played his early rugby for Bude and then Redruth in Cornwall, before moving to Gloucester in 1995, from where he was first capped for England, against Wales at Twickenham in February 1998. He went on to play in four Tests on the 'Tour from Hell' to the southern hemisphere later that summer and quickly established himself as an essential member of the England pack.

After playing three Tests in Australia for the British & Irish Lions in 2001, Vickery played a pivotal role in England's Grand Slam team in 2003. Forming a formidable front-row partnership with hooker Steve Thompson and his fellow Gloucester prop Trevor Woodman – supported by the evergreen Jason Leonard – he played a major part in England's World Cup victory in Sydney in November 2003.

Although injury at times limited his international appearances over the next few years, he moved to play for Wasps in October 2006 and was appointed captain of England for the 2007 season, which culminated in England's run to the World Cup Final in Paris.

Nicknamed 'Raging Bull', Vickery remained captain of England the following season and ended with 10 victories from his 15 matches in charge. He finished his England career at the end of the Six Nations Championship in 2009, after which he toured South Africa with the Lions, playing in the first and third Tests.

"RUGBY STIRS SO MANY AMAZING EMOTIONS, FEAR AND PASSION, THOSE ARE THINGS THAT NO ONE CAN TAKE AWAY"

DEFYING THE ODDS

England entered the 2007 Rugby World Cup in France as cup holders but with a less impressive pedigree than their 2003 predecessors. They had come third in the 2007 Six Nations and lost a chastening two-Test series in South Africa, before beating Wales and losing to France in two warm-up internationals at Twickenham.

Under the leadership of prop Phil Vickery, England could call on Jason Robinson, Josh Lewsey, Mike Catt and Jonny Wilkinson in the backline and Mark Regan, Ben Kay, Simon Shaw, Martin Corry, Lewis Moody and

Lawrence Dallaglio among their forwards. That level of experience was to prove vital in what was a far from straight-forward progression for England through the tournament.

Pool A produced some familiar adversaries and England began their title defence against the USA. After leading 21-3 at half-time, they managed a further converted try before allowing the USA a late try to make the final score 28-10 in England's favour. Their next opponents, South Africa, showed why they were among the most fancied teams with a 36-0 demolition of Brian Ashton's side at the Stade de France in Paris.

England were boosted by the return from an ankle injury of Jonny Wilkinson at fly half for their match against Samoa and he duly delivered by scoring 24 points, including two drop goals, in England's 44-22 victory. Their final pool match against Tonga produced a 36-20 victory, with Wilkinson kicking 16 points and providing much-needed game management.

England met their 2003 final opponents Australia in the quarter-final at the Stade Velodrome in Marseilles. Australia led 10-6 at half-time but Wilkinson steered England home with his third and fourth penalty goals to secure a vital, if slender, victory 12-10. The unexpected victory of France over the All Blacks the same day in Cardiff meant that England faced France at the Stade de France

in the first of the two semi-finals. England scored the only try of the game through Josh Lewsey in the second minute. Although France went into a 9-5 lead shortly after half-time, the accurate kicking of Wilkinson, with two penalties and a drop goal, gave England a 14-9 victory and ensured a second consecutive appearance in the final.

South Africa were to be their opponents, having overcome Argentina in the other semi-final. England made just one forced change to their side, with Mark Cueto replacing the injured Lewsey on the left wing.

Despite losing comprehensively to the Springboks earlier in the tournament, the match was much closer than anticipated. If a potential try by Mark Cueto after a magnificent break by centre Matthew Tait early in the second half had not been ruled out, the momentum might have swung England's way.

Above: Lawrence Dallaglio consoles Matt Giteau after the quarter-final between Australia and England

Left: Olly Barkley looks for support during England's match against the USA in Lens

8 September 2007
England 28 USA 10
Stade Felix Bollaert, Lens
Attendance: 36,755

14 September 2007
England 0 South Africa 36
Stade de France, Paris
Attendance: 77,523

22 September 2007
England 44 Samoa 22
Stade de la Beaujoire, Nantes
Attendance: 47,022

28 September 2007
England 36 Tonga 20
Parc des Princes, Paris
Attendance: 45,085

POOL A	P	W	D	L	F	A	BP	Pts
South Africa	4	4	0	0	189	47	3	19
England	4	3	0	1	108	88	2	14
Tonga	4	2	0	2	89	96	1	9
Samoa	4	1	0	3	69	143	1	5
USA	4	0	0	4	61	142	1	1

Quarter-final
6 October 2007
Australia 10 England 12
Stade Velodrome, Marseilles
Attendance: 59,102

Semi-final
13 October 2007
England 14 France 9
Stade de France, Paris
Attendance: 80,000

Final
20 October 2007
England 6 South Africa 15
Stade de France, Paris
Attendance: 80,340

Although Wilkinson immediately kicked a penalty to reduce the deficit to 6-9, the power of the Springbok pack won through and two further penalty goals saw South Africa ease home as 15-6 winners.

England JT Robinson (DJ Hipkiss) – PA Sackey, MJ Tait, MJ Catt (TGAL Flood), MJ Cueto – JP Wilkinson, ACT Gomersall – AJ Sheridan, MP Regan (GS Chuter), PJ Vickery* (MJH Stevens) – SD Shaw, BJ Kay – ME Corry, NJ Easter (LBN Dallaglio), LW Moody (JPR Worsley/PC Richards)

South Africa PC Montgomery – JPR Pietersen, J Fourie, FPL Steyn, BG Habana – AD James, PF Du Preez – JP Du Randt, JW Smit* (BW Du Plessis), CJ Van der Linde – JP Botha, V Matfield – SWP Burger, DJ Rossouw (JL Van Heerden), JH Smith

Above: England and South Africa prepare to scrum during the World Cup Final in Paris

Left: Jonny Wilkinson walks off the pitch as the Springboks celebrate

JASON ROBINSON

Born 30 July 1974
England career 2001-2007, 51 caps
Position Wing/Full Back **Club** Sale Sharks

Born in Leeds, Jason Robinson was an exceptionally gifted rugby league player who changed codes when rugby union went professional in the late 1990s. Equally gifted on the wing or at full back and with devastating footwork, he had a stellar career in rugby league for Wigan, England and Great Britain and played in the 1995 Rugby League World Cup Final.

He played briefly for Bath during the 1995-96 season and returned to rugby union full-time by signing for Sale Sharks in November 2000. England coach Clive Woodward fast-tracked him into the national squad and he made his international debut against Italy as a replacement in February 2001. His mesmeric close-range try for the British & Irish Lions later that year showcased his extraordinary talent. Dubbed 'Billy Whizz', he quickly became a regular starter and firm favourite with the Twickenham crowd.

A key member of the 2003 England World Cup-winning side, picked on the right wing, he scored the sole England try in the final in the left-hand corner after Lawrence Dallaglio and Jonny Wilkinson had breached the Australian defence. He toured for the second time with the Lions in 2005 in New Zealand and appeared in the first two Tests. He captained England seven times, becoming the first black male to lead the fifteen-a-side team. His international career came to a close in the World Cup Final defeat to South Africa in 2007.

Robinson's remarkable scoring record included 28 tries for England and two for the Lions in a total of 56 internationals. He was awarded an OBE in 2008.

Jason Robinson
England v Australia
22nd November 2003
28th Cap

"WHAT DO YOU REMEMBER ABOUT JASON ROBINSON? HIS FEET. HE COULD GO ROUND YOU IN A PHONE BOX"

Brian O'Driscoll

Simon Shaw's match-worn jersey from the centenary game at Twickenham

ENGLAND 30 WALES 17

6 February 2010, Twickenham

In February 2010, one hundred years after 20,000 spectators watched the first international match at Twickenham, England once again played Wales, this time in front of a crowd of 81,406 on the opening weekend of the Six Nations Championship. With England attired in sponsor-free heritage jerseys, this was the 119th match between the two countries, the overall record standing at 53 wins each and 12 draws since 1881.

England were captained by the Saracens second-row forward Steve Borthwick. The backline contained impressive firepower with Delon Armitage at full back and Mark Cueto and Ugo Monye on the wings. A skilful forward pack included Simon Shaw in the second row, alongside Borthwick, with a highly competitive and mobile back row of James Haskell, Lewis Moody and Nick Easter. The Welsh selectors picked a very experienced team, with 11 British & Irish Lions, under the captaincy of Ryan Jones.

After an exchange of penalties, the first half ended 13-3 in England's favour when Haskell drove over for his first try on the stroke of half-time, following intense pressure in the Welsh 22. Fly half Jonny Wilkinson converted the try.

The second half opened with a converted try for scrum half Danny Care, who produced one of his trademark dummies to scythe through the Welsh

England and Wales go head-to-head at Twickenham, 100 years since their first encounter on the same turf

defence to score at the posts. Wales were not out of the match, however, recovering their poise to score two converted tries, one from a magnificent weaving break by centre James Hook as the England lead was reduced to three points with just 10 minutes of the match remaining.

The defining score of the game was James Haskell's second try in the 74th minute. A Welsh backline move broke down in the England half and Armitage and centres Toby Flood and Matthew Tait stormed upfield into the Welsh 22, finding Haskell in support on the right. He went over to score, and Wilkinson added the conversion and kicked a penalty

goal four minutes later to give England a deserved 30-17 victory. A delighted Twickenham crowd looked forward to another 100 years of Test rugby.

England DA Armitage – MJ Cueto, MJ Tait, TGAL Flood (DJ Hipkiss), UCC Monye – JP Wilkinson, DS Care (PK Hodgson) – TAN Payne, DM Hartley (SG Thompson), DG Wilson (DR Cole) – SW Borthwick*, SD Shaw (LP Deacon) – JAW Haskell, NJ Easter, LW Moody (SE Armitage)

Wales LM Byrne – TE James (SL Halfpenny), JW Hook, JH Roberts, SM Williams – SM Jones, GJ Cooper (RS Rees) – P James, GJ Williams (H Bennett), AR Jones – LC Charteris (BS Davies), AW Jones – ME Williams, RP Jones*, AT Powell (J Thomas)

BACK ON HOME GROUND

RFUW Managing Director Rosie Williams had been disappointed when the IRB awarded the hosting of the 2006 Rugby World Cup to Canada and determined that the 2010 edition would be held in England.

Having supported the RFUW for so long, the RFU threw its full weight behind 'England 2010'. A launch event for the England squad was hosted by the World Rugby Museum, whose special exhibition celebrating the history of the women's game would be displayed at all the matches.

Gary Street had taken the reins as Red Roses coach in 2007. Catherine Spencer was now captain and Street had singled out Danielle Waterman as a key player. In the press, Rocky Clark was being described as the "world's best prop" and Maggie Alphonsi was being pushed by tenacious ball-carrier Heather Fisher in a

back row that now included the dynamic Sarah Hunter. A creative centre combination of Emily Scarratt and Rachael Burford could be relied on to create chances, and at fly half Katy Mclean was an assured kicker.

In 2009, England had demonstrated the extent of their development by defeating New Zealand 10-3 at Twickenham and Clark, for one, was feeling confident, commenting: "I'd have put everything on us winning in 2010."

In the group matches England began by defeating both Ireland and Kazakhstan, without conceding a point. As anticipated, the USA was a stiffer test but a magnificent jinking run and try from 'Nolli' Waterman helped the Red Roses to a 37-10 victory.

Another try for Waterman and one for captain Spencer helped England ease past Australia 15-0 in the semi-final, setting up a clash with New Zealand in the final for the third consecutive time. A bumper crowd of 13,253 awaited on 5 September on a bright, cool day that was perfect for rugby.

The Black Ferns began the stronger side, with only a crucial interception from Waterman preventing a certain try for Kelly Brazier. The rolling maul allowed England a way back into the game, before a jinking run from New Zealand wing Carla Hohepa cut open the Red Roses defence for a try, converted by Brazier to give New Zealand a 7-0 half-time lead.

Mclean and Brazier then traded penalties either side of an outstanding tackle from Joanna McGilchrist that prevented the flying Hohepa from taking the game out of reach. Showing true grit and resolve, Amy Turner surged forward in the 56th minute before releasing the ball to Charlotte Barras, who crossed the tryline to level the game at 10-10 amid deafening roars from the crowd.

Alas, the fightback seemed to have taken too much out of the Red Roses. New Zealand were able to confine them to their own half and Brazier kicked another penalty to secure a narrow 13-10 victory. The Black Ferns were able to celebrate winning the Rugby World Cup for a fourth consecutive time, but a young England team had shown that they were destined for greater things.

Above: The respective team captains pose for the cameras at Tower Bridge

Far left: England's Sarah Beale attacks Kazakhstan in their pool game

Below: England celebrate beating Australia in the semi-final

Right: Victoria Heighway claims the lineout despite the best efforts of Becky Essex during the final

Top right: Victoria Grant evades Danielle Waterman's diving tackle

Far right: A distraught Waterman (left) is consoled by her teammate La Toya Mason after the game

20 August 2010
England 27 Ireland 0
Surrey Sports Park, Guildford

24 August 2010
England 82 Kazakhstan 0
Surrey Sports Park, Guildford

28 August 2010
England 37 United States 10
Surrey Sports Park, Guildford

POOL B	P	W	D	L	F	A	BP	Pts
England	3	3	0	0	146	10	3	15
Ireland	3	2	0	1	59	42	2	10
United States	3	1	0	2	73	59	1	5
Kazakhstan	3	0	0	3	3	170	0	0

Semi-final
1 September 2010
England 15 Australia 0
Twickenham Stoop

Final
5 September 2010
New Zealand 13 England 10
Twickenham Stoop
Attendance: 13,253

England D Waterman – C Barras, E Scarratt, R Burford (A Richardson), K Merchant (A Penrith) – K Mclean, A Turner (LT Mason) – R Clark (C Purdy), A Garnett (E Croker), S Hemming – T Taylor (B Essex), J McGilchrist – S Hunter, C Spencer* (S Beale), M Alphonsi

New Zealand VE Grant – CG Hohepa, HR Manuel, KA Brazier, RWM Wickliffe (TR Hina) – AM Richards, EM Jensen – KR McKay, F Fa'amausili, M Bosman (S Te Ohaere-Fox) – VJ Robinson, VL Heighway – MJ Ruscoe*, CJ Robertson (LF Itunu), J Lavea (JL Sione)

The England Greats

LEWIS MOODY

Born 3 June 1978
England career 2001-2011, 71 caps
Position Wing Forward **Clubs** Leicester, Bath

Lewis Moody joined Leicester Tigers in 1996 while a student at De Montfort University and won a reputation over a long career as a ferocious marauding flanker.

Moody won his first cap on the North American tour of 2001 and became the most capped flanker in English rugby history, winning 71 caps and scoring nine tries between 2001 and 2011. He started in three matches of England's 2003 World Cup campaign and was a replacement in the other four, notably winning a crucial lineout ball in the lead up to Jonny Wilkinson's drop goal in extra-time of the final. A first-choice wing forward for England from the autumn of 2004, he toured New Zealand with the British & Irish Lions in 2005, playing two Tests and scoring a try in the third Test.

In the 2007 World Cup, Moody played in all seven matches, starting in the final four matches including the defeat against South Africa in the final in Paris. He took over the England captaincy at the end of the 2010 Six Nations and captained England in his final 11 internationals, ending with the defeat to France in Auckland at the 2011 World Cup.

Alongside Neil Back and Martin Corry he was part of an exceptional back row for Leicester and appeared in the club's Heineken Cup triumph in Cardiff in 2002 as well as four Premiership finals. He retired in 2012 and between 2014 and 2018 was appointed the RFU's Great War Ambassador. He became an Ambassador for the World Rugby Museum in 2018.

"HE WAS ONE OF THE MOST COMMITTED GUYS I EVER PLAYED WITH AND HAD A COMPLETE DISREGARD FOR HIS OWN PHYSICAL WELLBEING"

Martin Johnson

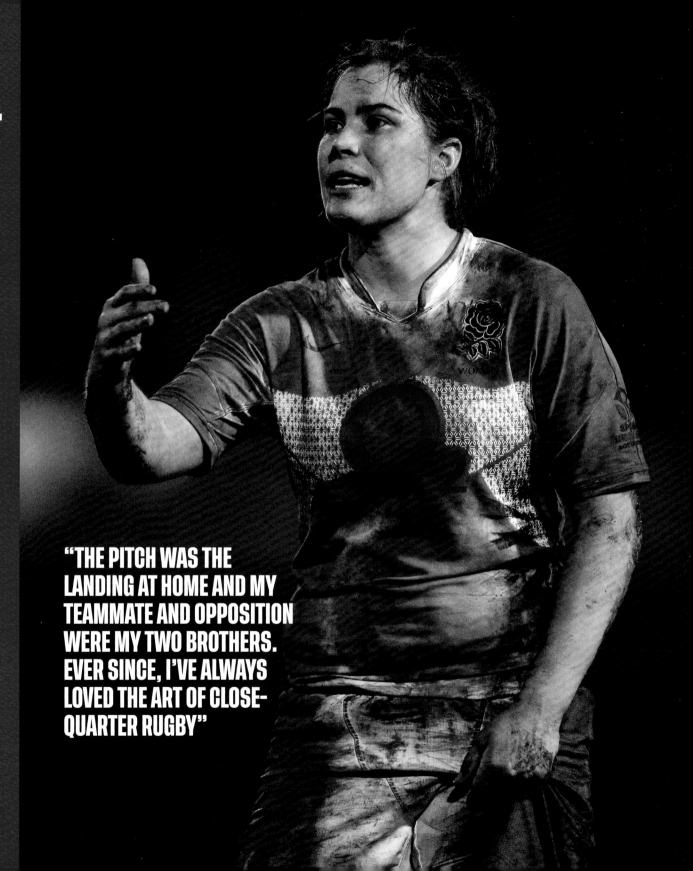

The England Greats

CATHERINE SPENCER

Born 25 May 1979 **England career** 2004-2011, 63 caps
Position Back Row
Clubs Worcester, Bristol, Aylesford Bulls

Catherine Spencer first picked up a rugby ball aged five. She joined Folkestone RFC at the age of nine and progressed from the wing to the forwards before being moved to No 8 while playing for Cardiff University. By the time she was first selected for England in 2004, she had matured into an impactful ball-carrier with a knack for getting over the gain line.

Spencer's Red Rose debut was as a substitute in a 53-3 win over Wales. By 2006 she was a regular starter in a side that claimed England's first Grand Slam since 2003 and reached the final of the Rugby World Cup in Canada.

In 2007 she was appointed captain and maintained her side's dominance to lead the Red Roses to consecutive Grand Slams. In 2009 she celebrated her 50th international appearance with a match-winning try against the Black Ferns in a 10-3 win at Twickenham. It was England's first win over New Zealand since 2001.

The face of 'England 2010', she led her side with distinction during a tournament in which England and New Zealand duly progressed to the final at the Stoop. In an extremely close game, Spencer was substituted with only 10 minutes to go and the scores level at 10-10. She then suffered the heartbreak of watching her side concede the penalty that ultimately cost them the game.

She played on for a final season and helped chalk up her and England's sixth consecutive Championship, before retiring with 63 caps in all.

"THE PITCH WAS THE LANDING AT HOME AND MY TEAMMATE AND OPPOSITION WERE MY TWO BROTHERS. EVER SINCE, I'VE ALWAYS LOVED THE ART OF CLOSE-QUARTER RUGBY"

A STEP TOO FAR

New Zealand had hosted and won the inaugural Rugby World Cup in 1987 but had failed to repeat the feat in the five intervening tournaments before they hosted it a second time in 2011. England, in contrast, went into the tournament having reached two consecutive finals.

Martin Johnson's England side opened their campaign with a 13-9 victory over Argentina in Dunedin. They scored the only try of the game through substitute scrum half

England coach Martin Johnson inspects earthquake damage in Christchurch

Ben Youngs just after half-time and the steady kicking of Jonny Wilkinson provided the necessary margin of victory. They remained in Dunedin for convincing victories over Georgia, 41-10, and Romania, 67-3, with wing Chris Ashton scoring five tries in the two matches.

England moved on to Eden Park, Auckland, for the pivotal match against Scotland. Victory over the Scots would lead to a quarter-final against France but defeat would mean facing the All Blacks – in theory a much more daunting prospect.

England's match against Scotland was a tight encounter and Scotland led 12-3 after 55 minutes. As so often, Wilkinson came to the rescue for England with a drop goal and a penalty goal, before Ashton scored his sixth try of the tournament three minutes before the end of the match to give England a 16-12 victory.

The quarter-final did not go to plan. France played with style and drive and scored two unconverted backline tries in the first half to lead 16-0 at half-time. Full back Ben Foden and wing Mark Cueto scored tries for England in the second half, one of which Wilkinson converted, but the England team was never able to exert enough pressure on an impressive French side to avoid a 19-12 defeat. After beating 14-man Wales in an epic semi-final, France would go on to lose by the narrowest of margins to the All Blacks in the final.

Jonny Wilkinson played his 91st and final international for England in the quarter-final against France. His World Cup record was exceptional. He played 19 matches in four tournaments and scored 277 points, including 58 penalty goals and 14 drop goals – scoring records which remain to this day.

Top: Ben Youngs scores against Argentina in England's first game

Above: A Chris Ashton try secures victory over Scotland

10 September 2011
Argentina 9 England 13
Otago Stadium, Dunedin
Attendance: 30,000

18 September 2011
England 41 Georgia 10
Otago Stadium, Dunedin
Attendance: 20,117

24 September 2011
England 67 Romania 3
Otago Stadium, Dunedin
Attendance: 25,687

1 October 2011
England 16 Scotland 12
Eden Park, Auckland
Attendance: 58,213

POOL B	P	W	D	L	F	A	BP	Pts
England	4	4	0	0	137	34	2	18
Argentina	4	3	0	1	90	40	2	14
Scotland	4	2	0	2	73	59	3	11
Georgia	4	1	0	3	48	90	0	4
Romania	4	0	0	4	44	169	0	0

Quarter-final
8 October 2011
England 12 France 19
Eden Park, Auckland
Attendance: 49,105

Final
23 October 2011
France 7 New Zealand 8
Eden Park, Auckland
Attendance: 61,079

Above: England face up to defeat against France after the quarter-final in Auckland

Left: Jonny Wilkinson, in his last game for England, and Chris Ashton can't stop France's Vincent Clerc

THE RECORD BREAKERS

The Red Roses class of 2011 was several years in the making. Among the most senior members of the squad, Nolli Waterman, Maggie Alphonsi and Rocky Clark had been on the international scene since 2003. Cath Spencer had made her debut in 2004 and Katherine Merchant in 2005. Rachael Burford had broken through in 2006, to be joined by Sarah Hunter, Joanna McGilchrist and Katy Mclean in 2007. Emily Scarratt's debut came in 2008 and Heather Fisher and La Toya Mason's in 2009.

By 2011, coached by Gary Street, they had matured into an outstanding side ready to take on the world. Their Six Nations campaign began at Pandy Park, Caerphilly, where they managed a 19-0 shut-out against Wales. A week later they ran in 11 tries against Italy for a 68-5 win, the potency of the side illustrated by the fact that those tries were scored by eight different players, including two each for Waterman, Fisher and Merchant.

Rocky Clark celebrates her try in the 2011 win over Scotland

France were dispatched comfortably 16-3 before the Red Roses headed to Twickenham. There they ran in 15 tries past a despondent Scotland side for an 89-0 victory. They rounded off the tournament with another whitewash, 31-0, against Ireland.

The 2011 Six Nations side stands alone in the record books for having amassed an amazing 223 points over five games for only eight points conceded.

This was the mid-way point in another trio of Grand Slams. Between 2006 and 2012, the Red Roses won seven consecutive Championships and six Grand Slams, making them the most dominant side ever to have pulled on an England jersey in 150 years of rugby. Indeed, in the history of the Six Nations Championship and its predecessor tournaments, no international side, men or women, has ever emulated the feats of this particular group of players.

They went on to defeat 2010 world champions New Zealand five times in the autumns of 2011 and 2012 to cement their place at the top of the world order. The core of the side became world champions, for only the second time, two years later in France in 2014.

Left: The Women's Six Nations winners' medal from the all-conquering 2011 season

This page: England celebrate their 10-0 victory over New Zealand at Twickenham that same year

"RUGBY MADE ME A BETTER PERSON"

The England Greats

MAGGIE ALPHONSI

Born 20 December 1983
England career 2003-2014, 74 caps
Position Back Row **Club** Saracens

Maggie Alphonsi grew up on a council estate in Edmonton, north London. She admitted having some difficulty at school and was almost expelled at the age of 13. Rescue came through a PE teacher, Welsh international captain Liza Burgess, who encouraged her to give rugby a try.

Try Maggie did and the game quickly gave her the focus she had previously lacked and a reason to develop her powerful physique. Aggressive, strong, a ferocious tackler and line-breaker, she was called up for the inaugural Churchill Cup in 2003 at the age of 19.

Her single mindedness was evident from an early age, as was her steely ambition: "I want to stay in the side and one day be captain of England. I would like to lead England in the World Cup and win it, and I want to make sure I play in a side that beats New Zealand." She slept in her England jersey the night before her first cap.

Initially playing at inside centre, coach Geoff Richards converted her to open-side flanker and she began to feature more regularly. Through the course of the 2006 World Cup, she worked her way into the starting XV and began the final with a committed tackle on her opposite number.

By 2010 Alphonsi was central to English hopes and she became the first woman to win the Rugby Union Writers' Club Player of the Year award. Her performances were outstanding throughout the 2010 World Cup tournament and helped England to another second place.

A knee injury in 2013 kept her from the side but she returned in time for the 2014 World Cup adamant that second place would not be enough this time around.

More than a decade after her international debut she remained crucial to her side, and it was her delayed pass that sent Nolli Waterman over for the first try in the final that would make her a world champion.

She retired after the tournament and continued her work as Divisional Talent Development Officer. She has since been elected to the RFU Council and is a highly respected broadcaster.

12

CORE VALUES

2012-2020

REACHING NEW HEIGHTS

In the 2013 Six Nations, Farrell's reliable kicking contributed to victory against Scotland and a first win in Dublin since 2003. Victories against France and Italy set up a Championship-deciding showdown with Wales, but Cardiff proved a bridge too far as England slumped to a 30-3 defeat in front of a passionate Welsh crowd. Billy Vunipola and Jonny May earned their first caps over the summer and England beat Australia and Argentina before losing to New Zealand.

Several Red Roses were away on sevens duty in 2013 as Vicky Fleetwood and Ceri Large came into the side. Sarah Hunter replaced Mclean as captain, but England suffered defeats to both Ireland and France. They completed the year with an unsuccessful tour of New Zealand and were defeated in the final of the Nations Cup by Canada.

Lancaster's men should have won in Paris in 2014 and did win at Murrayfield. Harlequins trio Robshaw, Danny Care and Mike Brown then combined to defeat Ireland, while a win against Wales secured a first Triple Crown since 2003. They finished 2014 with victories against Samoa and Australia as George Ford earned his first cap.

The Red Roses were close to full strength in 2014 but looked rusty when losing 18-6 to France. They recovered to notch 139 points for just 13 conceded across their remaining four fixtures. Over the summer, they put it all together and deservedly became world champions.

The 2015 men's Six Nations campaign began with a 21-15 victory in Cardiff, but England lost in Dublin. They remained in Championship contention until the final weekend. An immense performance, orchestrated by scrum half Ben Youngs, earned a 55-35 victory over France, but it wasn't quite enough. A disappointing home World Cup ended Lancaster's tenure and Eddie Jones was appointed England's first overseas coach.

Maggie Alphonsi, Joanna McGilchrist and Katherine Merchant retired after 2014. Nicky Ponsford was interim Red Roses coach, before Simon Middleton took over with a win against Scotland. Overall it was a poor year that included defeats to Wales, Ireland and France.

Stuart Lancaster was appointed as the men's head coach, initially on a temporary basis, at the start of the 2012 Six Nations. He selected Harlequins' industrious flanker Chris Robshaw as captain and 20-year-old Owen Farrell came in at fly half.

England might have won the Championship were it not for a late Welsh try at Twickenham and Lancaster was awarded the job on a permanent basis. Setting out to improve the culture of English rugby, his side ended world champions New Zealand's 20-match unbeaten run with a thrilling, record 38-21 victory at Twickenham.

Meanwhile, Katy Mclean's side romped to a sixth Championship. Michaela Staniford finished the series as top tryscorer and Emily Scarratt, having taken over kicking duties, as top points scorer. They also won the European Championships before completing a three-Test whitewash against New Zealand to establish themselves conclusively as the world's best side.

Above: England celebrate winning their sixth Championship in seven years in 2012

Previous pages: A silhouette of the 'Core Values' statue outside Twickenham

Right: Jack Nowell evades the Welsh tacklers in 2014

In 2016, Jones installed experienced hooker Dylan Hartley as captain and duly delivered England's first Grand Slam since 2003. Saracens lock Maro Itoje was outstanding in a 25-21 victory over Wales. Anthony Watson scored tries in four matches and Elliot Daly made his first international appearance. Experienced flanker James Haskell played some of the best rugby of his career in Australia and an almighty 44-40 victory in Sydney confirmed a 3-0 series whitewash.

Vickii Cornborough and Amy Cokayne lined up alongside veteran Rocky Clark in the English front row in 2016. They were denied a Grand Slam in the final match, a 17-12 defeat in Vannes, which allowed the French to take the title on points difference.

In 2017, Eddie Jones' side beat France and then Wales, the latter after quick interplay between Ford and Farrell put Daly in for the winning try. Jonathan Joseph's hat-trick helped England to a 61-21 victory over Scotland, which confirmed a second consecutive Championship with a week to spare. Defeat in Dublin meant there would be no Grand Slam.

The Red Roses overturned a 13-point half-time deficit to defeat France 26-13 at Twickenham. Wing Kay Wilson scored seven tries in a 64-0 victory over Scotland and a first Championship and Grand Slam since 2012 was secured with victory over Ireland in Dublin. They were back in Ireland for the Rugby World Cup where their title defence ended in Belfast in the final.

2018 began for England's men with a try-saving tackle from Sam Underhill that helped England squeeze past Wales at Twickenham, before England suffered a first loss against Scotland since 2008. Defeats against Ireland and France followed. After losing a Test series in South Africa, England narrowly defeated the Springboks at Twickenham, lost to New Zealand by a point after a late Underhill try was ruled out, fashioned a 35-15 win against Japan despite the visitors leading 15-10 at the break, and overwhelmed Australia 37-18.

Hunter scored three tries in a 42-7 Red Roses victory against Italy. Abigail Dow's try put them in front in Grenoble, but a last-minute try gave France an 18-17 win, although England finished second in the table after beating Ireland.

With Farrell now captain and Tuilagi in the starting line-up for the first time in five years, England powered to a dominant 32-20 win against champions Ireland in Dublin in 2019. Tom Curry's try was not enough to beat Wales in Cardiff and England concluded their campaign with a spectacular 38-38 draw against Scotland. Improving all the time, England saw off Australia and New Zealand on their way to the 2019 Rugby World Cup Final.

Above: New boss Eddie Jones supervises training at Twickenham in 2016

Below: Ben Youngs, winning his 100th cap, scores England's second try against Italy in an empty Stadio Olimpico in 2020

ENGLAND MEN BOUNCED BACK TO CLAIM THE TRIPLE CROWN IN 2020 WITH WINS OVER SCOTLAND, IRELAND AND WALES

Sarah Bern returned from injury to line up alongside Hannah Botterman in a new-look Red Roses front row in 2019. Jessica Breach scored two first half tries in a crucial match against France in Doncaster which England won 41-26, and the Grand Slam was sealed with 12 tries against Scotland.

Defeated by a resurgent France in Paris, Farrell's England bounced back to claim the Triple Crown in 2020 with wins over Scotland, Ireland and Wales. They sealed a third Championship in five years by beating Italy in October.

Hunter's Red Roses began their Grand Slam defence in the best possible manner by defeating France 19-13 in Pau. A blizzard impacted the timing of their fixture against Scotland but didn't put off the players who won 53-0. A back-to-back Grand Slam, delayed due to the Coronavirus pandemic, was duly recorded with victory over Italy in November.

The Triple Crown
(left) and the Six
Nations trophy
(right), introduced
in 2006 and 2016
respectively

Left: Ben Youngs gets
his hands on both
pieces of silverware
after the 2016 Grand
Slam win in France

History in the making

CORE VALUES

"Rugby is a great traditional subject for sculptures. The players are like gladiators" – Gerald Laing

Figurative sculptor Gerald Laing's first commission for the RFU was to produce the 'Four Players' that stand across the top of the Rowland Hill Memorial Gates, under which players pass upon entering the stadium. In 2009, Laing and the Black Isle Bronze foundry were commissioned again, this time to produce a piece of public art that would complete the South Stand development.

Featuring five players engaged in a lineout, 'Core Values' (based on an initial sketch, *above*) was unveiled on 1 June 2010. Situated on the corners of both Whitton and Rugby Roads it has quickly become established as the most popular meeting place outside the ground.

Its name refers to the five core values of rugby union: Teamwork, Respect, Enjoyment, Discipline and Sportsmanship. Capturing the ethos of the game at all levels, those values can be found on the walls of rugby clubs around England and inside the England dressing room.

ENGLAND 38 NEW ZEALAND 21

1 December 2012, Twickenham

New Zealand arrived at Twickenham on Saturday 1 December for the final match of their 2012 autumn tour. They had won 12 of 13 Tests in 2012 and were unbeaten in 20 internationals.

England opened their season with victory over Fiji, 54-12 before narrow losses to Australia and South Africa. They were not expected to beat an All Black team that had been bolstered by the return of talismanic fly half Dan Carter.

The England side, under the captaincy of Chris Robshaw and coached by Stuart Lancaster in his first season since being confirmed in the role, contained just 221 caps. In contrast the All Blacks team, who had been crowned world champions a year earlier, had amassed 804 caps, a huge disparity in terms of experience.

England made an impressive start and deservedly led 12-0 at half-time thanks to three penalty goals and a drop goal from fly half Owen Farrell. He added a fourth penalty just after half-time, before the All Blacks came back with tries by powerful wing Julian Savea and No 8 Kieran Read in the 50th minute, both converted by Dan Carter. With the score at 15-14 it was expected that the All Blacks would go on to dominate the match, as in their three previous internationals, but England rose to the challenge and the opposite happened.

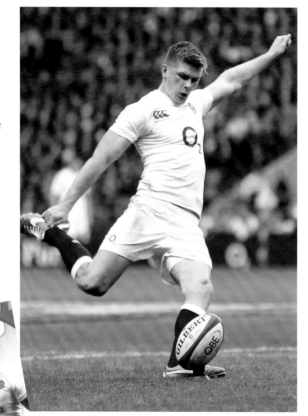

Above: Owen Farrell kicks one of four penalties he scored in the win over the All Blacks
Right: Chris Ashton dives over the line in dramatic fashion as he scores a try in the second half

Brad Barritt broke through the centre and, supported by a powerful surge from rampaging centre Manu Tuilagi, scored an unconverted try in the 53rd minute. Tuilagi then tore through the All Blacks midfield to set up an unconverted try for wing Chris Ashton in the 57th minute and Tuilagi himself intercepted an All Black pass and stormed over for another try, converted by Farrell. Freddie Burns then replaced Farrell in the 64th minute and kicked two penalty goals to give England an unassailable 38-14 lead with just eight minutes remaining.

Shell-shocked, the All Blacks managed to manufacture a third try and the match finished 38-21 to England. It was England's first victory over the All Blacks since 2003 and remains their largest winning margin against them.

England AD Goode – CJ Ashton, MS Tuilagi (JBA Joseph), BM Barritt, MN Brown – OA Farrell (FS Burns), BR Youngs (DS Care) – AR Corbisiero (MN Vunipola), TN Youngs (DJ Paice), DR Cole (DG Wilson) – JO Launchbury (CL Lawes), GMW Parling – TA Wood, BJ Morgan (JAW Haskell), CDC Robshaw*

New Zealand IJA Dagg (BR Smith) – CS Jane, CG Smith, MA Nonu, SJ Savea – DW Carter, (AW Cruden), AL Smith (PAT Weepu) – TD Woodcock (WWV Crockett), KF Mealamu (DS Coles), OT Franks (CC Faumuina) – BA Retallick (L Romano), SL Whitelock – LJ Messam (VVJ Vito), KJ Read, RH McCaw*

History in the making

WORLD RUGBY UNDER 20 CHAMPIONSHIP

The annual World Rugby Under 20 Championship began in 2008. England were the beaten runners-up in the first two editions, while New Zealand claimed each of the first four titles. An England side featuring George Ford, Owen Farrell and Elliot Daly were beaten finalists again in 2011, before England lifted the trophy for the first time in 2013.

The side, featuring hooker Luke Cowan-Dickie, wing Anthony Watson and Henry Slade at fly half, narrowly qualified for the semi-finals as the best runners up after losing to South Africa in the group stage. In the semis they stormed past New Zealand 33-21 to set up a final against Wales. Behind at half-time, Jack Clifford's talented side struck back through tries from Jack Nowell and Sam Hill to win 23-15.

It was to be the start of a dominant period for England, the following year they made the final again with a pack that included Paul Hill and Charlie Ewels under the captaincy of rookie Saracens lock Maro Itoje. Tries for Nathan Earle and Joel Conlon gave

Above: The class of 2013 in the England dressing room after victory v Wales
Right: Joe Marchant scores in the 2016 final

England a 21-20 victory against South Africa at Eden Park.

Beaten finalists in 2015, England reached the final again in 2016 where they met Ireland. A scintillating solo

try from centre Joe Marchant set fly half Harry Mallinder's side on their way to a 45-21 victory and a third title in four years.

England made the final again in 2017 and 2018 as the competition continues to serve as a breeding ground for international rugby players of the future.

The England Greats

DANIELLE WATERMAN

Born 20 January 1985
England career 2003-2018, 82 caps
Position Full Back **Clubs** Wasps, Bristol

Born a stone's throw from Twickenham Stadium into a rugby family, Danielle Waterman's destiny seemed assured from birth. Her father, Jim Waterman, played 416 times for Bath and first gave her the nickname 'Nolli'. A full back, like her father, she spent part of her childhood in New Zealand, where she regularly played rugby with the boys at Palmerston North High School.

Fast, agile and elusive, she combined outstanding footwork with game awareness and a fearsome competitor's spirit. Her rise through the England academy ranks was meteoric and she earned her first cap against Ireland in 2003, aged 20.

A young player in a successful England side, Waterman credits the likes of Shelley Rae and Sue Day with teaching her application and work rate. In the 2006 World Cup, she scored two tries in the crucial group stage match against France.

The following year she contributed eight tries from the wing in England's second of three consecutive Grand Slams and emerged as a key player, dangerous from all areas of the field but particularly in broken play, where her jinking runs could unlock defences.

A cruciate ligament knee injury in the autumn of 2009 was the first of a number of serious injuries but she returned in time for the 2010 World Cup, when she scored an outstanding try against USA and helped England to another final.

In 2014, Waterman went one better and, on reaching the final, scored the opening try in England's 21-9 victory against Canada that confirmed the Red Roses as world

champions for the second time. She helped England Sevens win the Canada Sevens tournament in 2015 and was selected for Great Britain at the 2016 Olympic Games in Rio, where she narrowly missed out on a medal.

In 2016, she scored one of the finest individual tries ever seen at Twickenham (*above*) with a solo run from deep within her own half against Canada. She played in the 2017 Rugby World Cup, her fourth, but injury ruled her out of the final. She retired in 2018 having scored 47 tries in 82 matches.

> ## "ONE OF THE SIGNATURE FIGURES OF THE BOOM YEARS OF THE WOMEN'S GAME"
> *The Times, September 2020*

DATE WITH DESTINY

England went to the 2014 World Cup in France having finished runners-up in three consecutive tournaments. They had improved markedly since 2010, however, and had recorded five victories against rivals New Zealand in 2011 and 2012. Their form had dipped slightly in 2013 and they had finished runners-up in the 2014 Six Nations to France.

Nonetheless, England's squad was packed full of world-class players. Under the captaincy of Katy Mclean, they could call on the experience of Rocky Clark, Sophie Hemming, Maggie Alphonsi and Tamara Taylor; while in Emily Scarratt, Sarah Hunter, Natasha Hunt and Marlie Packer they had players at the peak of their careers. Danielle Waterman, who had been out with injury, also returned to play her part.

Coach Gary Street had described the three months after losing the final in 2010 as the worst of his life and had introduced the concept of 'Toughen-Up Tuesdays', as a means of layering mental toughness onto physical toughness in preparation for the tournament.

As evidence of the growing strength in depth of the competition, England were held to a hard fought 13-13 draw with Canada in the

group stage while New Zealand suffered defeat to Ireland. England in the semi-final then faced a strong Ireland team, who had beaten them the previous year on the way to becoming Six Nations champions.

Clark described the Red Roses as being like wounded animals in the lead-up to the match and it was her dominant scrummaging that

led to consistent turnover ball and eventually a crushing 40-7 victory in which Ireland never threatened. Clark later described the match as being the best of her 95 caps to date.

Before the tournament, the English players had been instructed to bring a personal mascot with them. To take their minds off the coming game they spent time attempting to abduct each others' mascots, whilst guarding their own with their lives. Reminiscent of a similar ploy in 1994, it seemed to work.

They faced Canada in the final at the Stade Jean-Bouin in front of a sell-out French crowd. Canada started strongly but Scarratt's boot gave England the lead. Taylor and Alphonsi then worked an opening for Waterman to extend their lead with a try. Canada came

"I'M SICK AND TIRED OF GETTING THE SILVER MEDAL. I WANT THE RESULT TO GO OUR WAY"

Maggie Alphonsi

Left: England captain Katy Mclean, Sarah Hunter, Rocky Clark, Victoria Fleetwood and Katherine Merchant line-up at the 2014 World Cup in France

Below: Maggie Alphonsi shakes off an Irish tackle during the semi-final clash

Top right: Emily Scarratt of England touches down during the World Cup Final against Canada in Paris

Bottom right: Scarratt is mobbed by her teammates as the celebrations begin

1 August 2014
England 65 Samoa 3
Centre National de Rugby, Marcoussis

5 August 2014
England 45 Spain 5
Centre National de Rugby, Marcoussis

9 August 2014
England 13 Canada 13
Centre National de Rugby, Marcoussis

POOL A	P	W	D	L	F	A	BP	Pts
England	3	2	1	0	123	21	2	12
Canada	3	2	1	0	86	25	2	12
Spain	3	1	0	2	51	81	1	5
Samoa	3	0	0	3	15	148	0	0

Semi-final
13 August 2014
Ireland 7 England 40
Stade Jean-Bouin, Paris

Final
17 August 2014
England 21 Canada 9
Stade Jean-Bouin, Paris
Attendance: 15,000

England D Waterman – K Merchant (C Allan), E Scarratt, R Burford (C Large), K Wilson – K Mclean*, N Hunt (LT Mason) – R Clark, V Fleetwood (E Croker), S Hemming (R Essex) – T Taylor, J McGilchrist (L Keates) – M Packer (A Matthews), S Hunter, M Alphonsi

Canada J Zussman (J Sugawara) – M Harvey, M Marchak, A Burk, J Dovanne (B Waters) – E Belchos, E Alarie – M-P Pinault-Reid (MJ Kirby), K Donaldson (L Russell), H Leith (O DeMerchant) – L Blackwood, M Samson (K Mack) – J Murphy, K Paquin, K Russell*

back at the start of the second half to bring themselves within two points at 11-9 with 20 minutes remaining.

The irrepressible Scarratt would have the final say, adding a penalty, try and conversion in the closing quarter for a 21-9 victory. An ecstatic squad celebrated with abandon at the full time whistle but Waterman took time out to pay tribute to the 2006 and 2010 sides who had gone so close.

After the game, the team stopped at a bar on their way to their hotel, where they found Gill Burns, Emma Mitchell and Nicky Ponsford of the 1994 side. After 20 long years, England were world champions again.

Far left: Katy Mclean lifts the World Cup in Paris as England women are crowned champions for the second time

Left: A delighted crowd greet Mclean and her teammates as they return home to Twickenham with the trophy

Top: The England players wave to their fans in the Stade Jean-Bouin

Above: Katy Mclean's World Cup winners' medal

AN EARLY EXIT

England were the hosts for the 2015 Rugby World Cup in September and October. Twickenham was the principal venue but the 48 matches were spread around England and Wales, with eight being played at the Millennium Stadium in Cardiff and five at the new stadium in the Olympic Park.

England, under their coach Stuart Lancaster, had a young side which had blended well over the two previous years, and had come second in the 2015 Six Nations, losing only to Ireland in Dublin. They were drawn in an exceptionally tough group alongside Australia, Fiji, Wales and Uruguay, from which only two teams would qualify for the quarter-finals.

They began well under the leadership of Chris Robshaw, with a 35-11 victory over a combative Fiji side. Eight days later, Wales came to Twickenham having defeated Uruguay in Cardiff in their opening match. Livewire wing Jonny May opened the scoring to help England to a 16-9 lead at half-time. Three more penalty goals by Owen Farrell stretched their lead to 25-18 but Dan Biggar, the Welsh fly half, who had already kicked three penalties in the first half, kept Wales in the match with penalties.

The turning point came in the 71st minute when the Welsh backs put their replacement wing Lloyd Williams into space just inside the England half. He ran down the left flank and cross-kicked towards the posts where scrum half Gareth Davies won the race to the touchdown. Biggar converted and the score was 25-25 with seven minutes remaining. Three minutes later Biggar kicked a huge penalty goal from just inside the halfway line and Wales were in the lead. England had an opportunity to level the scores with a penalty right at the end but, instead, Robshaw called a kick to the corner for a lineout that Wales defended with ruthless intent. Seconds later, England had lost 28-25 and their place in the tournament was in jeopardy.

England had to win their third match against Australia at Twickenham to reach the quarter-finals. Sadly, they were never really in the match. Down 17-3 at half-time, they conceded a further 16 points to Australia in the second half and succumbed to a convincing 33-13 defeat, ending any hope of reaching the quarter-finals. All that remained was a match against Uruguay in Manchester, which the hosts won 60-3.

Apart from England's exit, the group stage of the tournament was notable for Japan's inspirational defeat of the Springboks in Brighton. New Zealand were the outstanding side, however, with Dan Carter, Richie McCaw, Ma'a Nonu and Sam Whitelock in imperious form. Thrilling victories against France (62-13), South Africa (20-18) and Australia (34-17) in the final resulted in McCaw becoming the first captain to lift the Webb Ellis Cup in successive tournaments and New Zealand the first nation to win the tournament three times.

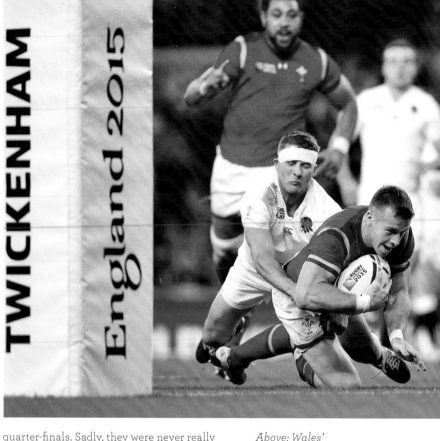

Above: Wales' Gareth Davies scores under the posts as they narrowly defeat England at Twickenham

Left: England's Anthony Watson tries to stop Nemani Nadolo of Fiji scoring in the tournament opener

18 September 2015
England 35 Fiji 11
Twickenham
Attendance: 80,015

26 September 2015
England 25 Wales 28
Twickenham
Attendance: 81,129

3 October 2015
England 13 Australia 33
Twickenham
Attendance: 81,010

10 October 2015
England 60 Uruguay 3
Manchester City Stadium
Attendance: 50,778

POOL A	P	W	D	L	F	A	BP	Pts
Australia	4	4	0	0	141	35	1	17
Wales	4	3	0	1	111	62	1	13
England	**4**	**2**	**0**	**2**	**133**	**75**	**3**	**11**
Fiji	4	1	0	3	84	101	1	5
Uruguay	4	0	0	4	30	226	0	0

Final
31 October 2015
New Zealand 34 Australia 17
Twickenham
Attendance: 80,125

Above: Australia secure the lineout during their pool match clash with England

Far left: Chris Robshaw walks past the World Cup trophy prior to the defeat against Australia

Left: Joe Launchbury tussles with Alejo Duran of Uruguay in England's final pool game

LEST WE FORGET

The RFU approached the centenary commemorations of the Great War with the respect and poignancy of a sport that had lost much to the conflict. Lewis Moody was appointed Great War Ambassador and a committee was assembled to pay tribute to the fallen.

'Forever England' by the artist Shane Record was unveiled inside the West Stand in 2014. It showed the England team that played against France in Paris in 1914 (*see page 69*). Of those selected, every player enlisted and six did not return. In the painting itself Record identifies their sacrifice by darkening the roses on their jerseys.

In 2015, the World Rugby Museum launched its special exhibition 'Lest We Forget' that paid tribute to the 27 fallen England players and many more from nations around the world.

The Rose and Poppy Gates were unveiled in 2016 in the centre of the Rowland Hill Memorial Gates, through which the players pass on matchdays. Designed and constructed by the artist Harry Gray, they feature gunmetal roses, cast in bronze, that rise

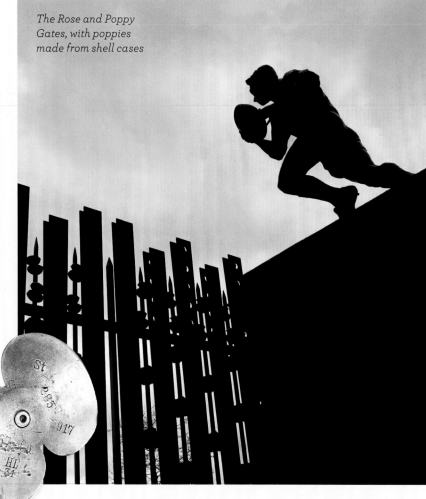

The Rose and Poppy Gates, with poppies made from shell cases

to become poppies. The metal for the poppies is fashioned from shell casings retrieved from the Somme battlefield. The gates have become an official symbol of remembrance.

Finally, the RFU sent a delegation of captains, including Moody, Bill Beaumont and John Spencer, to Ypres to retrieve soil from the grave of 1914 captain Ronald Poulton. Shot and killed by a sniper in 1915, purportedly among his last words were a lament that he would never play at Twickenham again. The soil was returned to Twickenham and buried pitchside close to where the players exit the tunnel.

Ronnie Poulton
1889 - 1915

Above: The pitchside tribute that marks Ronnie Poulton's relaid ashes
Right: 'Forever England' depicts the last team to play before the Great War

ROCKY CLARK

Born 29 May 1981
England career 2003-2018, 137 caps
Position Prop **Clubs** Wasps, Worcester

Rochelle Clark began playing rugby at the age of 15 after an invitation from a friend and was selected for England in 2003 at the age of just 21 and quickly established herself in the team. In the deciding match of the 2006 Six Nations, she scored a try against France as the Red Roses claimed the first of seven consecutive Championships.

In the 2006 World Cup Final, she was part of a pack that threatened to blow New Zealand away in the first half before the Black Ferns came back into the game.

In 2008, *Rugby World* magazine dubbed her England's best-ever prop and Clark was confident that home advantage would help England to win the World Cup in 2010. She didn't dwell on defeat but immediately turned her attention to 2014.

She had her best game in the semi-final of the 2014 World Cup, scoring the opening try and helping England to a dominant 40-7 victory against Ireland. After beating Canada in the final, she was emotional: "After all the heartache – I've been through two horrendous finals, losing by three points in 2010 was heart-wrenching – to finally win the World Cup and be on top was amazing!"

Now widely known as 'Rocky' Clark, the victory did not dampen her appetite. She collected her 100th cap in 2015 (*right*) versus France and went on to become England's all-time record cap holder, with 137 appearances, before her retirement in 2018.

"I WOULD PLAY AN INTERNATIONAL EVERY WEEK IF I COULD! I LOVE PULLING ON THE WHITE SHIRT"

The England Greats

DYLAN HARTLEY

Born 24 March 1986
England career 2008-2018, 97 caps
Position Hooker
Clubs Worcester Warriors, Northampton Saints

Dylan Hartley was born in Rotorua, New Zealand, and came to England as a teenager before going on to forge a remarkable club and international career. Qualified for England through his English mother, he played a season with Worcester Warriors before joining Northampton Saints in 2006, where he remained until retiring in 2019.

His forthright play, combined with excellent lineout work, saw him earn early recognition with five matches for the England Saxons, before winning his first cap as a replacement hooker against the Pacific Islanders at Twickenham in November 2008. He played in the Rugby World Cup tournament in New Zealand in 2011 but indiscipline cost him his place in the British & Irish Lions tour party to Australia in 2013. A further ban resulted in him not being picked in the 2015 England Rugby World Cup squad.

Recognising a tough competitor's spirit in Hartley, new coach Eddie Jones surprised many by choosing him as his captain. His decision was soon vindicated as England, under Hartley's leadership, went on to record their first Grand Slam since 2003 in the 2016 Six Nations (*right*). A historic three-Test victory over Australia in the summer of 2016 followed. He scored four tries in his international career and captained England 29 times, with 24 victories, before his final appearance as a replacement off the bench against Australia in November 2018.

He retired as England's most capped hooker with 97 caps and a record 56 Test appearances at Twickenham.

"SIMPLY ONE OF THE BEST LEADERS. FROM THE ACADEMY TO THE FIRST TEAM HE GAVE HIS TIME TO THE YOUNGEST"

Will Hooley, former teammate

THE GRAND FINALE

The lead then swapped twice, with tries from New Zealand lock Charmaine Smith and a stunning individual score and second try for Thompson. Without pause, Natua regained the initiative for New Zealand, scoring her third try to put New Zealand in front again. Three further tries were shared between the two sides, before New Zealand ran out 41-32 winners in a match that will be remembered for many years to come.

Defending champions England went into the 2017 Rugby World Cup – hosted for the first time by Ireland – as professional players. Coached by Simon Middleton, they were also the world's number one ranking team, having beaten New Zealand 29-21 in June, for the first time since 2001.

Fifteen out of 28 players survived from the 2014 squad, including Rachael Burford, Tamara Taylor, Rocky Clark and Danielle Waterman. Katy Mclean remained at fly half, but 'World Rugby Player of the Year' Sarah Hunter was now the captain. Amy Cokayne and Sarah Bern were growing in influence in the front row

and Emily Scarratt was getting used to being described as the world's best centre.

They comfortably navigated the group stage, with wins against Spain, Italy and USA. The Kingspan Stadium in Belfast played host to their semi-final against France, who they brushed aside 20-3 to set up another final against the Black Ferns.

More than 17,000 fans were in attendance to bear witness to what is generally regarded as the greatest women's World Cup Final to date.

A try from Selica Winiata had given New Zealand an early lead in the first half, before England took control. Dominating possession, their constant pressure resulted in a penalty try, before wing Lydia Thompson went over the line for England's second score. Scarratt, playing full back in the absence of Waterman, then kicked the Red Roses into a 12-point lead.

At 17-5, it looked as though England were fully in control but, demonstrating their own herculean spirit, the Black Ferns hauled themselves back into the game. Tries either side of half-time for Toka Natua made the score 17-17, before a Scarratt penalty put England in the lead once again.

Bottom left: Megan Jones breaks through a tackle against Spain

Left: Simon Middleton debriefs his team following victory over the USA

Below: Sarah Bern crashes over the line in the semi-final against France

9 August 2017
England 56 Spain 5
UCD Bowl, Dublin

13 August 2017
England 56 Italy 13
Billings Park UCD, Dublin

17 August 2017
England 47 United States 26
Billings Park UCD, Dublin

POOL B	P	W	D	L	F	A	BP	Pts
England	3	3	0	0	159	44	3	15
United States	3	2	0	1	93	59	3	11
Spain	3	1	0	2	27	107	0	4
Italy	3	0	0	3	33	102	0	0

Semi-final
22 August 2017
England 20 France 3
Kingspan Stadium, Belfast

Final
26 August 2017
England 32 New Zealand 41
Kingspan Stadium, Belfast
Attendance: 17,115

England E Scarratt – L Thompson
(A Wilson-Hardy), M Jones, R Burford (A Reed),
K Wilson – K Mclean, N Hunt (LT Mason) –
V Cornborough (R Clark), A Cokayne
(V Fleetwood), S Bern (J Lucas) – A Scott,
T Taylor (H Millar-Mills) – A Matthews,
S Hunter*, M Packer (I Noel-Smith)

New Zealand SC Winiata – PL Woodman,
SJAK Waaka (TM Fitzpatrick), KA Brazier,
RWM Wickliffe (CG Hohepa) – VS Subritzky-
Nafatali, KM Cocksedge (KJ Sue) –
TI Natua (SJ Talawadua), F Fa'amausili*
(TR Ngata-Aerengamate), AT Itunu (AP Nelson)
– ES Blackwell, CB Smith (RJ Wood) –
CJ McMenamin (LT Ketu), A Savage, SL Goss

Above: England captain Sarah Hunter climbs highest in the lineout during the World Cup Final against New Zealand

Far left: Lydia Thompson runs in a try in a classic final

Left: The players embrace after an epic encounter ended with victory for the Black Ferns

The England team leave the field after the nail-biting drawn game with Scotland in 2019

ENGLAND 38
SCOTLAND 38

16 March 2019, Twickenham

In the closing match of the 2019 Six Nations Championship, one of the most extraordinary encounters in the history of the Calcutta Cup took place at Twickenham.

The England team, with Owen Farrell as captain, had won three of their four matches but were unable to win the Championship because Wales had beaten Ireland earlier that afternoon. Scotland, in contrast, had endured a poor season and had lost three of their four matches. As they had not won at Twickenham since 1983, they were not expected to trouble a powerful England side.

The first half went as expected, although the extent of the Scottish capitulation was a surprise. Jack Nowell scored England's first try on the right wing, converted by Farrell in the second minute. Forwards Tom Curry and Joe Launchbury scored further converted tries, to give England a 21-0 lead after 15 minutes. A penalty goal from Farrell, and his conversion of a try from left wing Jonny May, meant that England led 31-0 after only 29 minutes. A Scottish rally produced a try after 35 minutes, following a charge-down and long run-in by hooker and captain Stuart McInally. There was no further scoring in the five minutes remaining, leaving the half-time score 31-7, a reflection of England's near total dominance.

George Ford saves England with his last-minute try in a breath-taking match that ended in a draw

The second half was sensational. Scotland were inspired by their fly half Finn Russell and attacked relentlessly. Stunning their hosts with four unanswered tries, three of which were converted, Scotland levelled the score at 31-31 with 20 minutes still to play. With four minutes of the match remaining, a converted Scotland try by centre Sam Johnson gave them a 38-31 lead.

In a frenzied atmosphere and with the crowd roaring them on, England launched attack on attack to save the match. Deep in injury time George Ford, the replacement fly half, cut through to score at the posts and convert his own try. The final score was a breathless 38-38 draw, a new world record for drawn matches in major internationals. Scotland retained the Calcutta Cup and most England fans were left wondering what on earth had happened.

England EF Daly – JT Nowell, HJH Slade, MS Tuilagi (BJ Te'o), JJ May – OA Farrell* (GT Ford), BR Youngs (BT Spencer) – B Moon (E Genge), JE George (LA Cowan-Dickie), K Sinckler (DR Cole) – JO Launchbury (NWJ Hughes), GEJ Kruis – ME Wilson (BDF Shields), VML Vunipola, TM Curry

Scotland SD Maitland (AR Hastings) – D Graham, NJ Grigg (CJ Harris), S Johnson, B McGuigan – FA Russell, AW Price (GD Laidlaw) – AME Dell (GJ Reid), S McInally* (FJM Brown), WP Nel (SA Berghan) – GS Gilchrist (JD Gray), BM Toolis – HFW Watson, MDB Bradbury, SG Skinner (JZ Strauss)

RISING SONS

The 2019 Rugby World Cup was held in the autumn in Japan, the first country outside the traditional rugby union powerhouses to be chosen to host the tournament. Matches were spread throughout the country, with the semi-finals and final played at the 72,000-seater International Stadium in Yokohama.

England were drawn in Pool C, alongside Argentina, France, Tonga and the USA. Their squad was captained by Owen Farrell and combined experience alongside some players very new to international rugby. Their first match, against Tonga at the Sapporo Dome, produced a comfortable 35-3 victory, with Manu Tuilagi scoring two tries and Farrell kicking 15 points. England picked a much-changed side, captained by fly half George Ford, for their second match against the USA at the Kobe

Misaki Stadium and scored seven tries as they won convincingly 45-7.

At the Tokyo Stadium, they dominated Argentina throughout. A half-time lead of 15-3 became 25-3, after 15 minutes of the second half. The Pumas rallied with a converted try but England, with their powerful bench all on the field, scored two more converted tries in the last six minutes to win the match 39-10. Nature intervened before England's final pool match, in the form of the massive typhoon Hagibis, which led to the cancellation of three matches, including England's match against France.

England topped Pool C through their greater number of bonus points and their reward was a quarter-final against Australia at the Oita Stadium. Their inspirational young wing forward duo of Tom Curry and Sam Underhill outplayed their counterparts Hooper and Pocock and, with Owen Farrell kicking 20 points and left wing Jonny May scoring two of England's four tries before half-time, England finished 40-16 winners.

Their next challenge was to face New Zealand, winner of the two previous World Cups, in the semi-final at Yokohama. Within three minutes England had scored a try through Manu Tuilagi, converted by Farrell, and soon established a control which they never relinquished. Despite having two possible tries disallowed by the TMO, England outplayed the All Blacks. George Ford took

over from Farrell and kicked four penalty goals to beat New Zealand – for the first time in a Rugby World Cup – convincingly 19-7.

South Africa, coached by former Springbok Rassie Erasmus, and World Cup winners in 1995 and 2007, awaited England in the final under the inspirational captaincy of Siya Kolisi.

In just the third minute, England were rocked by the loss of rumbustious prop Kyle Sinckler to concussion after an accidental collision. South African fly half Handré Pollard was in fine kicking form and he scored six penalty goals to Farrell's four to give the Springboks an 18-12 lead with 20 minutes to go.

England still had a chance but the Springbok pack, with all its replacements on the field, proved too powerful. The match finished with superb converted tries by the Springbok wingers Makazole Mapimpi and

Above: Jonny May celebrates scoring in the quarter-final win over Australia

Left: Jack Nowell squeezes home a try against Argentina

Top right: An elated Mark Wilson after England's first-ever World Cup win over the All Blacks

Right: Billy Vunipola can't find a way through the South Africa defence in the World Cup Final

Cheslin Kolbe, to leave South Africa as worthy winners 32-12. England had fallen at the final hurdle for the third time.

England EF Daly – AKC Watson, MS Tuilagi, OA Farrell*, JJ May (JBA Joseph) – GT Ford (HJH Slade), BR Youngs (BT Spencer) – MN Vunipola (JWG Marler), JE George (LA Cowan-Dickie), K Sinckler (DR Cole) – OM Itoje, CL Lawes (GEJ Kruis) – TM Curry, VML Vunipola, SG Underhill (ME Wilson)

South Africa WJ Le Roux (FPL Steyn) – C Kolbe, L Am, D de Allende, M Mapimpi – H Pollard, F de Klerk (HJ Jantjies) – TD Mtawarira (S Kitshoff), MT Mbonambi (MJ Marx), JF Malherbe (VP Koch) – E Etzebeth (RG Snyman), L de Jager (FJ Mostert) – S Kolisi* (LF-P Louw), DJ Vermeulen, PS Du Toit

22 September 2019
England 35 Tonga 3
Sapporo Dome, Sapporo
Attendance: 42,000

26 September 2019
England 45 USA 7
Kobe Misaki Stadium, Kobe
Attendance: 27,194

5 October 2019
England 39 Argentina 10
Tokyo Stadium, Tokyo
Attendance: 48,185

12 October 2019
England v France – match cancelled (0-0)
International Stadium, Yokohama

POOL C	P	W	D	L	T	F	A	BP	Pt
England	4	3	1	0	17	119	20	3	17
France	4	3	1	0	9	79	51	1	15
Argentina	4	2	0	2	14	106	91	3	11
Tonga	4	1	0	3	9	67	105	2	6
USA	4	0	0	4	7	52	156	0	0

Quarter-final
19 October 2019
England 40 Australia 16
Oita Bank Dome, Oita
Attendance: 36,954

Semi-final
26 October 2019
England 19 New Zealand 7
International Stadium, Yokohama
Attendance: 68,843

Final
2 November 2019
England 12 South Africa 32
International Stadium, Yokohama
Attendance: 70,103

A NATIONAL HEALTH EMERGENCY

"As soon as I realised it was an option for me to go back into the NHS... it wasn't something we questioned. I contacted the RFU and they were fantastically supportive of it." – Lydia Thompson

Few would have predicted that the RFU would see out its sesquicentenary with tributes to the National Health Service (NHS) but so it came to pass. The Covid-19 coronavirus forced families, businesses and whole nations into lockdown and impacted rugby clubs and their communities at all levels. With both England men and women in contention for the 2020 Six Nations titles, both competitions were suspended with a match to play. Club rugby too ceased across England.

Recognising the gravity of the fast-evolving situation, RFU Chief Executive Bill Sweeney prioritised the safety of the rugby community and took immediate steps to safeguard the financial health of the governing body and community clubs through the period of lockdown and beyond.

As in 1939, Twickenham Stadium was offered into the service of the nation, the West Car Park becoming an

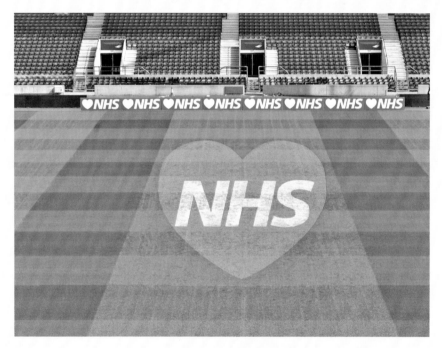

Above: A tribute to the NHS on the field at Twickenham during the 2020 lockdown
Right: A Covid-19 testing centre at RFU HQ

NHS national testing centre. With the backing of the RFU, Red Rose Lydia Thompson applied to return to work for the NHS as an Occupational Therapist. Tom Rees, who had played for England

during the 2007 Rugby World Cup, had retrained as a doctor following injury. He worked on the NHS frontline throughout the crisis, helping patients at Basingstoke Hospital.

Rugby clubs and club members around the country did what they could to support their local communities. Beaconsfield RFC took it on themselves

to deliver prescriptions to households. Alton RFC drew up a roster of volunteer drivers to facilitate home visits for their local surgery. Droitwich Rugby Club began packing and delivering food, while Winchester Rugby Club opened its doors to the NHS Blood and Transport Team. Grimsby Rugby Club even donated their boot bags to their local hospital to be used to hold personal respirators.

"Across the country, grassroots clubs are supporting their local communities: the charities, food banks, hospitals, the elderly and the vulnerable. It is the values of rugby in action and I want to thank them all." – Bill Sweeney

England huddle after the Six Nations victory against Italy at an empty Stadio Olimpico in Rome. It was the first English international match following the suspension of rugby due to the coronavirus pandemic

Modern times

Rugby as a sport has evolved dramatically in recent times, with players fitter, stronger and faster than ever before and coaches able to analyse their side's performance in incredible detail

Owen Slot, Chief rugby correspondent, *The Times*

Left: Ellis Genge is tracked by Billy Vunipola during an England squad training session in 2020

Right: Abbie Ward and Poppy Cleall walk out at England's state-of-the-art Pennyhill Park training facility

I f you are a professional rugby player in the England squad these days, 150 years after England first played Scotland and the whole extraordinary business of international rugby kicked off, you would be required to fulfil the most disciplined of regimes. You would have your skinfolds tested regularly, in eight places; you would have your sleep-quality monitored and you would give regular urine samples in order to have your hydration levels tested. And that is a comparatively light version of player management. Only recently, a player would have to stand on the scales and get weighed before breakfast each morning, but England decided that such information was superfluous. Even in the modern age, winning matches isn't completely solved by data.

Yet at the highest end, the version of professional rugby that we find today is pushing performance to its limits. As Eddie Jones, the England coach, wrote in his autobiography: "There are 10,080 minutes in every week. A game of rugby lasts 80 minutes. How you use the other 10,000 minutes each week is vital. There is never a minute to waste because every idea, word, action and their consequences have to be considered, calibrated and either adopted or discarded. I am an obsessive planner. I work to a clear and deliberate strategy. Even my sleeping patterns are ordered."

When I think how far the game has come, I reflect back to the first rugby story that I ever had published in a national newspaper. It was an interview with a Wasps player called Steve Pilgrim in 1994, back when rugby union was still an amateur game. Pilgrim had played in a trial game in the rival, professional code of rugby league for Leeds Rhinos seconds against Wakefield Trinity reserves. Even though he was not paid, such flirting with the professional code was not permitted and though

At the highest end, the version of professional rugby that we find today is pushing performance to its limits

Pilgrim's name was omitted from the teamsheet for that game (he was down as AN Other), the RFU discovered his skulduggery and deemed it a crime so heinous as to be worthy of a lifetime ban from the sport.

The rumpus that followed resulted in Pilgrim's ban soon being reduced to six months. However, the story is significant here because less than 30 years ago, the game was doing its utmost to hold back professionalism. Today, Eddie Jones et al are at the other extreme. They are forever pushing the limits to see how much further they can go.

In his time as England coach, Stuart Lancaster would educate his squad on the history of the shirt and some of the players who went before them. In particular, they learned of Arthur Harrison, the only England international to win the Victoria Cross, who died in the First World War.

It is a strange family tree that had Anthony Watson in the 2019 World Cup Final wearing the same number 14 jersey as 'The Flying Prince' Obolensky, or that had Jason Robinson wearing it in England's victorious World Cup campaign in 2003.

Modern England players know this, yet their focus is unswervingly on high performance. The game they have to play now is unrecognisable from the one known to their predecessors.

In the first Rugby World Cup in 1987 there was an average of 77 scrums and lineouts per game. By 2019, that had gone down to 39.

Eddie Jones keeps a keen eye on an England training session

Simultaneously, the amount of time that the ball is in play has accelerated significantly, which has led to more action: there were an average of 129 tackles per game in the last World Cup compared to 48 at the first, and 82 rucks compared to 25.

Yet the game is tighter, more intense and also more conservative. Modern players protect the ball better; they give half the number of offloads that they did back when World Cups started.

All this is noted, every game action recorded. The product of it all is the training regime to be found at Pennyhill Park, England's elite training base. Jones and his staff know exactly what the professional player of the modern age should look like and how to optimise preparation to maximise output.

This is Jon Clarke, the former professional rugby league player, who is head of strength and conditioning for the England men's team: "When you are trying to design a player, the first thing you have to look at is what the game is. The international game is very, very quick for short periods of time – and then there are relatively decent rests from ball-out-of-play time."

One key challenge is these short periods of time. On average, each bout of play lasts just under 30 seconds. However, players have to be conditioned for 30 seconds of play – which is like being a 400m runner – and shorter sprints, as well as longer phases. In the 2020 Six Nations, there was one period of play that lasted four minutes, which requires the endurance of a middle-to-long distance runner.

"And we want them to repeat these efforts over and over again," Clarke explains. "That's ultimately what international rugby is: fast, physical and you've got to be able to get up and down off the floor repeatedly, you have got to sprint and tackle repeatedly for anywhere between 15 seconds to four minutes. So we want our lads lean, powerful and fast."

England use the regular skinfold tests to tell them whether the players are delivering this. They measure eight places on the body, upper and lower. The leanest athletes are the outside backs whose total of those eight skinfold sights should not be much more than 50mm. In the modern

What every coach wants to know is when a player's tank is about to run on empty

game, back-rowers are expected to be pretty much as lean as the backs. Only the front-rowers are given minimal leeway; their expected total measurements are 80-100mm.

While the intensity of each phase when the ball is in play is what dictates the England game, huge emphasis is now put on what happens when the ball isn't in play. "You are trying to take lads from a high level of stress to a lower level so they can think clearly," Clarke says, "because once your heart rate goes over a certain percentage cognitive ability is quite limited. The quicker you can drop your heart rate, the quicker you can think clearly."

So, for instance, the England players now practise breathing protocols to help them recover before the next effort of ball-in-play.

What is Eddie Jones watching? For him, a key indicator on player performance is how long it takes them to get up off the ground. What every coach wants to know is when a player's tank is about to run on empty and also, therefore, when the stresses of the game will make them more vulnerable to injury, and therefore when the coach should make a substitution. Clarke says: "A lot of teams are going crazy on GPS and are creating their own algorithms to see if their players are at risk (of injury)."

Conversely, there is also a belief that, at some point, the science has maxed out. Jones and his coaching team have all the numbers at their fingertips, yet they still back their experience and intuition above the data on a laptop.

Professionalism in the men's game has now got to the point where one pack of forwards in a Premiership game is never going to be far different in weight to another. This is a physical plateau that the women's game hasn't yet reached, although it is not far behind.

This is Luke Woodhouse, who ran the strength and conditioning for the England women's team from 2015 to 2020: "The raw physical capabilities of players, over my time, was one of the biggest changes I saw. When I started, they were not muscular and strong enough, in upper body strength in particular. We have definitely seen a shift in the emphasis on physical development and preparation, because it is the survival of the fittest."

Over his five years, the average weight of an England international forward rose from 80-82kg to closer to 90kg average. This overall rapid physical development has triggered a change in the type of game the modern England women's team now brings to the field.

"It used to be a more linear game," Woodhouse says, "with emphasis on spinning the ball and trying to get round outside teams. But now you

A delighted Emily Scarratt celebrates winning the 2020 Grand Slam

see better defences in the female game and more kicking. With that, you get more stopping and starting as opposed to just constant running, more really explosive accelerating and decelerating, sidestepping, moving into different positions, resetting defence, up, back, up, back. It is the characteristic of the movement rather than the distance. This has changed hugely."

Dynamism and intensity – 150 years after international rugby started both men's and women's squads are aiming at roughly the same thing. They can't be doing too badly because, at the time of writing, they are both Six Nations champions. Where does it go from here? Here are three predictions:

One: Jones and his staff, and their peers around the world, will never let up in the search for improvement.

Two: Sports psychologists will become more prevalent. We often say that, at the very top, the difference between winning and losing is in the mind. In which case teams probably need more than one sports psychologist (often not even that) to help them win.

Three: In another 30 years' time, the game will look very different to how it does today. This game is moving so fast, it might be unrecognisable.

ENGLAND MEN'S CAPS 1871-2020

1871

AG Guillemard
A Lyon
RR Osborne
W MacLaren
JE Bentley
JF Green
F Tobin
RH Birkett
BH Burns
JH Clayton
CA Crompton
A Davenport
JM Dugdale
AS Gibson
AStG Hamersley
JH Luscombe
CW Sherrard
F Stokes
DP Turner
HJC Turner

1872

FW Mills
WO Moberly
H Freeman
S Finney
P Wilkinson
T Batson
JA Body

JA Bush
FI Currey
FBG d'Aguilar
FWR Isherwood
F Luscombe
JEH Mackinlay
WW Pinching

1873

CHR Vanderspar
CW Boyle
S Morse
EC Cheston
WRB Fletcher
HA Lawrence
H Marsh
MW Marshall
CH Rickards
ER Still

1874

JM Batten
MJ Brooks
WE Collins
WH Milton
HA Bryden
CW Crosse
FL Cunliffe
JSM Genth
E Kewley

S Parker
WFH Stafford
R Walker

1875

AW Pearson
L Stokes
AT Michell
EH Nash
FR Adams
EC Fraser
HJ Graham
WHH Hutchinson
ES Perrott
LH Birkett
WAD Evanson
JE Paul

1876

SHM Login
CR Gunner
CWH Clark
JV Brewer
CC Bryden
AM Bulteel
JDG Graham
W Greg
EE Marriott
EB Turner
CL Verelst

AH Heath
TS Tetley
WC Hutchinson
WH Hunt
FH Lee
WCW Rawlinson
GR Turner

1877

AN Hornby
PLA Price
RH Fowler
G Harrison
CJC Touzel
HWT Garnett
AF Law
R Todd

1878

HE Kayll
JM Biggs
FD Fowler
H Fowler
ET Gurdon
GT Thomson
GF Vernon
WJ Penny
HJ Enthoven
JL Bell
AH Jackson

T Blatherwick
AJ Budd
EF Dawson
HP Gardner

1879

H Huth
HH Taylor
GW Burton
NF McLeod
S Neame
HC Rowley
HH Springman
WE Openshaw
HT Twynam
HD Bateson

1880

TW Fry
R Hunt
S Ellis
C Gurdon
B Kilner
ET Markendale
JW Schofield
E Woodhead
CM Sawyer
RT Finch
CH Coates
C Phillips

1881

WR Richardson
CWL Fernandes
WW Hewitt
J Ravenscroft
JI Ward
H Vassall
CP Wilson
FT Wright

1882

E Beswick
WN Bolton
HG Fuller
JT Hunt
BB Middleton
A Spurling
JH Payne
PA Newton
WM Tatham

1883

AS Taylor
CG Wade
AM Evanson
Alan Rotherham
RSF Henderson
RS Kindersley
G Standing
CS Wooldridge

EJ Moore
RM Pattisson
HB Tristram

1884
CE Chapman
CJB Marriott
EL Strong
CH Sample
H Fallas
HJ Wigglesworth
H Bell
A Teggin
A Wood

1885
JJ Hawcridge
AE Stoddart
ED Court
AT Kemble
FJS Moss
HJ Ryalls
CH Horley

1886
AR Robertshaw
F Bonsor
WG Clibborn
CH Elliot
PF Hancock
RE Inglis
GL Jeffery
E Wilkinson
N Spurling
EB Brutton

1887
S Roberts
J Le Fleming
RE Lockwood
HC Baker
CR Cleveland
JH Dewhurst
JL Hickson
RL Seddon
ARStL Fagan
MT Scott
FE Pease

1889
AV Royle
JW Sutcliffe
WM Scott
C Anderton
H Bedford
JW Cave
F Evershed
D Jowett
FW Lowrie
A Robinson
HJ Wilkinson
W Yiend

1890
WG Mitchell
PH Morrison
J Valentine
FH Fox
JF Wright
RTD Budworth
JH Rogers
SMJ Woods
JW Dyson
RL Aston

E Holmes
JT Toothill
FW Spence

1891
FHR Alderson
P Christopherson
J Berry
WRM Leake
WE Bromet
T Kent
EHG North
JJ Richards
RP Wilson
LJ Percival
E Bonham-Carter

1892
WB Thomson
GC Hubbard
A Briggs
C Emmott
A Allport
E Bullough
W Nichol
J Pyke
S Houghton
JH Marsh
EW Taylor
A Ashworth
T Coop
H Varley
H Bradshaw

1893
E Field
RFC de Winton
H Marshall

T Broadley
JH Greenwell
FC Lohden
P Maud
T Nicholson
H Duckett
FP Jones
CM Wells
JJ Robinson
F Soane

1894
JF Byrne
SJ Morfitt
CA Hooper
F Firth
J Hall
H Speed
WE Tucker
R Wood
WJ Jackson
AE Elliott
W Walton

1895
H Ward
JHC Fegan
EM Baker
FA Leslie-Jones
RHB Cattell
GM Carey
HW Finlinson
F Mitchell
FO Poole
C Thomas
TH Dobson

1896
EF Fookes
LF Giblin
J Pinch
J Rhodes
A Starks
JW Ward
W Whiteley
RW Poole
JH Barron
GE Hughes
E Knowles

1897
T Fletcher
FA Byrne
W Ashford
PJ Ebdon
F Jacob
RH Mangles
RF Oakes
WB Stoddart
FM Stout
WL Bunting
JT Taylor
GC Robinson
S Northmore
OG Mackie
James Davidson
HW Dudgeon

1898
PG Jacob
H Myers
JH Blacklock
R Pierce
F Shaw
CE Wilson

WN Pilkington
PMR Royds
PW Stout
Arthur Rotherham
GT Unwin
HE Ramsden
JF Shaw
RO'H Livesay

1899
HT Gamlin
R Forrest
J Daniell
J Davidson
GR Gibson
CH Harper
W Mortimer
SW Anderson
AJL Darby
JH Shooter
JC Matters
RO Schwarz
AO Dowson
RFA Hobbs

1900
ET Nicholson
AT Brettargh
GW Gordon-Smith
SF Coopper
GH Marsden
FJ Bell
RW Bell
J Baxter
W Cobby
A Cockerham
JW Jarman
S Reynolds
CT Scott
JC Marquis
H Alexander
AF Todd
AFCC Luxmoore

1901
JW Sagar
EW Elliot
EJ Vivyan
CA Smith
EJ Walton
NC Fletcher
COP Gibson
D Graham
A O'Neill
EW Roberts
CJ Hall
RD Wood
NS Cox
PD Kendall
B Oughtred
CS Edgar
BC Hartley
HTF Weston

1902
PL Nicholas
JE Raphael
DD Dobson
GWF Fraser
JH Jewitt
LR Tosswill
TH Willocks
SG Williams
PF Hardwick
T Simpson

1903
JH Miles
RH Spooner
FC Hulme
R Bradley
J Duthie
VH Cartwright
WG Heppell
BA Hill
EIM Barrett
WV Butcher

1904
EW Dillon
PS Hancock
GH Keeton
JG Milton
NJNH Moore
CJ Newbold

1905
SH Irvin
FH Palmer
WTC Cave
TA Gibson
JL Mathias

WLY Rogers
CF Stanger-Leathes
HE Shewring
J Green
WM Grylls
G Vickery
AD Stoop
CEL Hammond
SH Osborne
EJ Jackett
HM Imrie
RE Godfray
AE Hind
J Braithwaite
DR Gent
RF Russell
GE Summerscales

1906
A Hudson
RA Jago
GEB Dobbs
HA Hodges
TS Kelly
AL Kewney
WA Mills
JE Hutchinson
CH Milton
JRP Sandford
JGG Birkett
J Peters
R Dibble
CH Shaw
TB Hogarth
FG Brooks
A Alcock

1907
H Lee
TB Batchelor
D Lambert
TG Wedge
FJV Hopley
WMB Nanson
LAN Slocock
FS Scott
AS Pickering
WC Wilson
G Leather
AW Newton
SP Start
GD Roberts

1908
AE Wood
WN Lapage
GV Portus
HJH Sibree
F Boylen
EL Chambers
H Havelock
RH Williamson
RJT Gilbert
HH Vassall
GHd'O Lyon
J Davey
WL Oldham
FB Watson
T Woods

1909
BB Bennetts
EW Assinder
FN Tarr
ER Mobbs

AH Ashcroft
JG Cooper
PJ Down
FF Knight
ADW Morris
SH Penny
H Archer
FG Handford
ED Ibbitson
WA Johns
RW Poulton
F Hutchinson
CA Bolton
AC Palmer
CCG Wright
HJS Morton
AJ Wilson
HC Harrison

1910
WR Johnston
FE Chapman
B Solomon
LE Barrington-Ward
H Berry
L Haigh
CH Pillman
DF Smith
LW Hayward
CS Williams
AA Adams
H Coverdale
ALH Gotley
RHM Hands
JAS Ritson
ES Scorfield
NA Wodehouse
PW Lawrie

FM Stoop
GR Hind

1911
SH Williams
AD Roberts
JA Scholfield
LG Brown
JA King
WE Mann
RO Lagden

1912
H Brougham
JA Pym
JH Eddison
D Holland
AH MacIlwaine
RC Stafford
ME Neale
JE Greenwood
WB Hynes

1913
CN Lowe
VHM Coates
WJA Davies
WI Cheesman
SEJ Smart
FE Steinthal
JAG Ward
AJ Dingle
AE Kitching
FE Oakeley

1914

JHD Watson
FM Taylor
GW Wood
J Brunton
AG Bull
AF Maynard
AL Harrison
RL Pillman
FLeS Stone
ARV Sykes

WORLD WAR I

1920

BS Cumberlege
HLV Day
EDG Hammett
JA Krige
CA Kershaw
JG Holford
FW Mellish
LPB Merriam
JR Morgan
WW Wakefield
WHG Wright
H Millett
AM Smallwood
WM Lowry
GS Conway
F Taylor
E Myers
SW Harris
AT Voyce
AF Blakiston
T Woods

1921

ER Edwards
ER Gardner
QEMA King
R Cove-Smith
LJ Corbett

1922

VG Davies
JS Tucker
RCW Pickles
MS Bradby
RFH Duncan
JE Maxwell-Hyslop
HL Price
JA Middleton
IJ Pitman
PBRW William-Powlett

1923

FG Gilbert
WGE Luddington
FW Sanders
TE Holliday
HM Locke

1924

BS Chantrill
HC Catcheside
HP Jacob
AT Young
A Robson
RH Hamilton-Wickes
CKT Faithfull

1925

JW Brough
JC Gibbs

HJ Kittermaster
RJ Hillard
EJ Massey
R Armstrong
HG Periton
RRF MacLennan
RG Lawson
DC Cumming
SGU Considine

1926

HC Burton
AR Aslett
TES Francis
JRB Worton
RJ Hanvey
E Stanbury
Sir TG Devitt
LW Haslett
WE Tucker
JWG Webb

1927

KA Sellar
HCC Laird
TJ Coulson
J Hanley
KJ Stark
PH Davies
WCT Eyres
DE Law
WE Pratten
JNS Wallens
W Alexander
RA Buckingham
CC Bishop

1928

WJ Taylor
CD Aarvold
JV Richardson
D Turquand-Young
TM Lawson
GV Palmer
RHW Sparks
FD Prentice
TW Brown

1929

RW Smeddle
GM Sladen
GS Wilson
H Whitley
RT Foulds
JWR Swayne
H Wilkinson
AL Novis
SSC Meikle
EE Richards
TWW Harris
H Rew
JSR Reeve
RS Spong
SA Martindale
E Coley
CHA Gummer

1930

JG Askew
FWS Malir
M Robson
WH Sobey
AH Bateson
DA Kendrew
BH Black

JW Forrest
PD Howard
A Key
JC Hubbard
CC Tanner
PWP Brook

1931

LL Bedford
DW Burland
MA McCanlis
TJM Barrington
EB Pope
MS Bonaventura
RF Davey
DH Swayne
AC Harrison
GJ Dean
GG Gregory
PC Hordern
PE Dunkley
EH Harding
ECP Whiteley
JA Tallent
TC Knowles

1932

RJ Barr
RA Gerrard
AD Carpenter
DJ Norman
RGS Hobbs
CSH Webb
JMcD Hodgson
AJ Rowley
LE Saxby
NL Evans
W Elliot

BC Gadney
RS Roberts
A Vaughan-Jones
RJ Longland

1933

LA Booth
ADS Roncoroni
R Bolton
EH Sadler
CL Troop
WH Weston

1934

HG Owen-Smith
AL Warr
P Cranmer
GWC Meikle
J Dicks
JC Wright
HA Fry
CF Slow

1935

HJ Boughton
J Heaton
R Leyland
PL Candler
JL Giles
ES Nicholson
AJ Clarke
AG Cridlan
DT Kemp
AT Payne
JR Auty

1936
AS Obolensky
HS Sever
EA Hamilton-Hill
HF Wheatley
H Toft

1937
AG Butler
TA Kemp
RE Prescott
TF Huskisson
AA Wheatley
DWI Campbell
DLK Milman
EJ Unwin
FJ Reynolds
JG Cook

1938
HD Freakes
BE Nicholson
GW Parker
RM Marshall
AA Brown

1939
RH Guest
GE Hancock
RSL Carr
GA Walker
P Cooke
DE Teden
JTW Berry
JK Watkins
EI Parsons
J Ellis

WORLD WAR II

1947
A Gray
NO Bennett
EK Scott
DW Swarbrick
NM Hall
WKT Moore
GA Kelly
AP Henderson
HW Walker
J Mycock
SV Perry
MR Steele-Bodger
BH Travers
DF White
MP Donnelly
CB Holmes
JO Newton-Thompson
JT George
RHG Weighill
SC Newman
GA Gibbs
VG Roberts

1948
RJP Madge
JH Keeling
E Evans
DB Vaughan
HF Luya
R Uren
I Preece
MF Turner
TW Price
LB Cannell
AC Towell
PW Sykes

1949
WB Holmes
JA Gregory
CB Van Ryneveld
T Danby
G Rimmer
MJ Berridge
GRd'A Hosking
EL Horsfall
B Braithwaite-Exley
RD Kennedy
JM Kendall-Carpenter
JH Steeds
JRC Matthews

1950
MB Hofmeyr
JV Smith
B Boobbyer
IJ Botting
WA Holmes
HA Jones
JJ Cain
HD Small
SJ Adkins
JP Hyde
JL Baume

1951
EN Hewitt
CG Woodruff
LFL Oakley
VR Tindall
TH Smith
RV Stirling
JT Bartlett
DT Wilkins
PBC Moore

GC Rittson-Thomas
JM Williams
EMP Hardy
BA Neale
WG Hook
DW Shuttleworth

1952
JE Woodward
AE Agar
CE Winn
AO Lewis
EE Woodgate
PJ Collins
RC Bazley

1953
M Regan
NA Labuschagne
J Butterfield
DS Wilson
WPC Davies

1954
I King
JP Quinn
DL Sanders
PG Yarranton
PD Young
R Higgins
N Gibbs
EF Robinson
JF Bance
VH Leadbetter
JE Williams

1955
DGS Baker
GWD Hastings
DStG Hazell
WJH Hancock
PH Ryan
PJ Taylor
H Scott
FD Sykes
IDS Beer
NSD Estcourt

1956
DF Allison
PH Thompson
PB Jackson
MJK Smith
REG Jeeps
CR Jacobs
JD Currie
RWD Marques
PGD Robbins
A Ashcroft

1957
RM Bartlett
R Challis

1958
JP Horrocks-Taylor
RE Syrett
JGG Hetherington
MS Phillips
JRC Young
JSM Scott
AJ Herbert

1959
ABW Risman
SR Smith
StLH Webb
JAS Wackett
GJ Bendon
BJ Wightman
JW Clements
HO Godwin

1960
D Rutherford
MP Weston
J Roberts
RAW Sharp
SAM Hodgson
TP Wright
WGD Morgan

1961
WM Patterson
LI Rimmer
MN Gavins
RJ French
JG Willcox
J Price
DP Rogers
VSJ Harding

1962
AM Underwood
MR Wade
PE Judd
ACB Hurst
JM Dee
TA Pargetter
SJ Purdy

1963

SJS Clarke
NJ Drake-Lee
JD Thorne
BA Dovey
AM Davis
JE Owen
DC Manley
KJ Wilson
DG Perry
RW Hosen
JM Ranson
VR Marriott

1964

RD Sangwin
RE Rowell
PJ Ford
TJ Brophy
CM Payne
DFB Wrench
TGAH Peart

1965

EL Rudd
GP Frankcom
DWA Rosser
CP Simpson
AL Horton
SB Richards
N Silk
PW Cook
AW Hancock

1966

TG Arthur
KF Savage
J Spencer

JV Pullin
DL Powell
RB Taylor
CW McFadyean
RC Ashby
WT Treadwell
JRH Greenwood
RD Hearn
TC Wintle
GA Sherriff

1967

PB Glover
CR Jennins
MJ Coulman
PJ Larter
JF Finlan
RDA Pickering
J Barton
DEJ Watt
JN Pallant
DM Rollitt
RE Webb
RH Lloyd
WJ Gittings

1968

RB Hiller
DH Prout
BW Redwood
BW Keen
MJ Parsons
PJ Bell
DJ Gay
BR West
TJ Brooke

1969

KJ Fielding
DJ Duckham
JS Spencer
KE Fairbrother
NE Horton
TJ Dalton
KC Plummer
PM Hale
IR Shackleton
NC Starmer-Smith
CB Stevens
AL Bucknall
CS Wardlow

1970

MJ Novak
MP Bulpitt
BS Jackson
AM Jorden
MM Leadbetter
GF Redmond

1971

PA Rossborough
JPAG Janion
ID Wright
JJ Page
BF Ninnes
RC Hannaford
A Neary
AR Cowman
FE Cotton
CW Ralston
RN Creed
PJ Dixon

1972

MC Beese
AGB Old
JG Webster
MA Burton
A Brinn
AG Ripley
PM Knight
LE Weston
NO Martin
GW Evans
SA Doble
AJ Morley
PS Preece
JA Watkins

1973

PJ Warfield
WF Anderson
SJ Smith
RM Uttley
PJ Squires
MJ Cooper
DFK Roughley

1974

K Smith
WH Hare

1975

WB Beaumont
PJ Wheeler
WN Bennett
PE Butler
AW Maxwell
P Kingston
BG Nelmes
ND Mantell

AJ Wordsworth
AJ Hignell
RM Wilkinson

1976

BJ Corless
MS Lampkowski
M Keyworth
DA Cooke
DM Wyatt
MAC Slemen
GJ Adey
CG Williams

1977

CP Kent
M Young
RJ Cowling
M Rafter

1978

JP Scott
PW Dodge
JP Horton
RJ Mordell
DWN Caplan
MJ Colclough
AM Bond

1979

GS Pearce
RM Cardus
CE Smart
J Carleton
NJ Preston
L Cusworth

1980

PJ Blakeway
CR Woodward

1981

DH Cooke
A Sheppard
GH Davies
NC Jeavons
R Hesford
WMH Rose
GAF Sargent
AH Swift
SGF Mills
JH Fidler

1982

PJ Winterbottom
NC Stringer
JP Syddall
S Bainbridge

1983

SB Boyle
DM Trick
NG Youngs
C White
PD Simpson

1984
JP Hall
B Barley
R Underwood
SP Redfern
PAG Rendall
AF Dun
JA Palmer
MD Bailey
RJ Hill
M Preedy
CJS Butcher
SE Brain
GW Rees
RAP Lozowski
S Barnes
ND Melville
GJ Chilcott
NC Redman

1985
ST Smith
KG Simms
CR Andrew
RM Harding
J Orwin
WA Dooley
CR Martin
MC Teague
JLB Salmon
ME Harrison
RP Huntsman

1986
SJ Halliday
GL Robbins
FJ Clough
D Richards

1987
RGR Dawe
DA Cusani
PN Williams
BC Moore
JM Webb

1988
WDC Carling
JA Probyn
MG Skinner
C Oti
J Bentley
DW Egerton
BJ Evans
RA Robinson
AT Harriman
CD Morris
PJ Ackford
JRD Buckton

1989
SD Hodgkinson
JC Guscott
SM Bates
MS Linnett
AR Mullins

1990
NJ Heslop
D Pears
J Leonard
D Ryan
CJ Olver

1991
MC Bayfield

1992
TAK Rodber
I Hunter
T Underwood
VE Ubogu
BB Clarke
PR de Glanville

1993
MO Johnson
JEB Callard
KPP Bracken

1994
NA Back
SO Ojomoh
MJ Catt
PA Hull

1995
GC Rowntree
RJ West
JA Mallett
DP Hopley
MP Regan
LBN Dallaglio
PJ Grayson
MJS Dawson

1996
JM Sleightholme
GS Archer
TRG Stimpson
AA Adebayo
ACT Gomarsall
SD Shaw
CMA Sheasby
RJK Hardwick

PBT Greening
ND Beal

1997
RA Hill
AS Healey
DJ Garforth
DJ Mallinder
NJJ Greenstock
KP Yates
SM Haag
ME Corry
AJ Diprose
R Cockerill
MS Mapletoft
DJ Grewcock
AD King
MB Perry
DL Rees
WJH Greenwood
AE Long
WR Green

1998
DE West
PJ Vickery
JP Wilkinson
SP Brown
SCW Ravenscroft
S Benton
B Sturnham
RJ Pool-Jones
S Potter
DE Chapman
OJ Lewsey
PH Sanderson
TD Beim
D Sims

JJN Baxendell
RJ Fidler
PC Sampson
DD Luger

1999
N McCarthy
B-J Mather
SM Hanley
TJ Woodman
JPR Worsley

2000
MJ Tindall
BC Cohen
IR Balshaw
JM White
DL Flatman
LD Lloyd

2001
JT Robinson
SW Borthwick
JD Noon
ME Stephenson
DJH Walder
BJ Kay
LW Moody
WRS White-Cooper
MB Wood
FHH Waters
OJ Barkley
TP Palmer
TMD Voyce
CC Hodgson
A Sanderson

2002
SG Thompson
NS Duncombe
HR Paul
MJ Horak
GN Appleford
JB Johnston
PD Christophers
AJ Codling
JD Simpson-Daniel

2003
RJS Morris
OJ Smith
MA Worsley
DGR Scarbrough
SR Abbott

2004
CM Jones
MJH Stevens
MR Lipman
AJ Titterrell
TAN Payne
MJ Cueto
AR Hazell
AJ Sheridan
HD Vyvyan
HA Ellis

2005

MJ Tait
J Forrester
AJ Goode
DSC Bell
MC Van Gisbergen
LP Deacon
PT Freshwater
LA Mears
TW Varndell

2006

PC Richards
AT Brown
MB Lund
GS Chuter
NPJ Walshe
PH Sackey
AO Allen
SA Perry
TGAL Flood

2007

OC Morgan
AD Farrell
T Rees
NJ Easter
D Strettle
SJJ Geraghty
JAW Haskell
SC Turner
MN Brown

DF Schofield
DE Crompton
RAM Winters
MI Cairns
BD Skirving
NJ Abendanon
DJ Hipkiss

2008

LJ Narraway
LPI Vainikolo
DJ Cipriani
REP Wigglesworth
TR Croft
PK Hodgson
TO Ojo
DS Care
DJ Paice
J Hobson
DA Armitage
RJ Flutey
UCC Monye
NJ Kennedy
DM Hartley
JS Crane

2009

SE Armitage
BJ Foden
TA May
MA Banahan
DG Wilson
SB Vesty
CDY Robshaw
AO Erinle
CL Lawes
PPL Doran-Jones

2010

DR Cole
MJ Mullan
BR Youngs
CJ Ashton
SE Hape
DMJ Attwood
CH Fourie

2011

TA Wood
AR Corbisiero
EM Tuilagi
C Sharples
MJ Botha
JPM Simpson

2012

BM Barritt
OA Farrell
PDA Dowson
GMW Parling
J Turner-Hall
LAW Dickson
BJ Morgan
RW Webber
JWG Marler
TA Johnson
JBA Joseph
TR Waldrom
AD Goode
TN Youngs
MN Vunipola
JO Launchbury
FS Burns

2013

WWF Twelvetrees
C Wade
MB Kvesic
KO Eastmond
VML Vunipola
HM Thomas
JJ May
M Yarde
SJ Myler
JA Tomkins

2014

JT Nowell
LD Burrell
GT Ford
JA Gray
CJ Pennell
K Brookes
S Rokoduguni
GEJ Kruis
AKC Watson

2015

HJH Slade
S Burgess
CT Clark
LA Cowan-Dickie
JE George

2016

JA Clifford
OM Itoje
PO Hill
EF Daly
T Harrison
E Genge
OJ Devoto

TWJ Taylor
NWJ Hughes
BJ Te'o
KNJS Sinckler
CJ Ewels

2017

AJ Lozowski
HAH Williams
ME Wilson
TM Curry
D Solomona
PG Francis
WStLW Collier
DW Armand
NA Isiekwe
JA Maunder
SG Underhill
SD Simmonds

2018

AW Hepburn
BDF Shields
BT Spencer
B Moon
ZI Mercer
RJ Cokanasiga
E Hill

2019

DJ Robson
WA Heinz
LW Ludlam
J Marchant
JH Singleton
RL McConnochie

2020

GA Furbank
WJ Stuart
BA Earl
JP Hill
OA Thorley
OF Lawrence
TG Dunn

Up to 1 November 2020

ENGLAND WOMEN'S CAPS 1986-2020

1986/1987
K Almond
P Atkinson-Kennedy *née* Spivey
S Cockerill
D Francis *née* MacLaren
C Gurney
C Isherwood
P King *née* Moore
S Lamb *née* Hill
J Pauley
N Ponsford
S Robson
S Treadwell *née* Purdy
C Vyvyan *née* Williets
J Watts
E Whalley
D Mills
P O'Brian *née* Harris

1987/1988
A Jenkinson
E Mitchell
J Ross
H Sykes
C Stennett

1988/1989
G Burns
M Forsyth *née* Schofield
J Mitchell
F Reynolds *née* Barnet
H Thompson
J Shapland
H Stirrup
S Wenn

1989/1990
J Coats *née* Mangham
S Wachholz-Dorrington

1990/1991
S Ewing
F Hackett
G Mather *née* Prangnell
M Edwards

1991/1992
J Edwards
V Blackett
A Cole

1992/1993
J Chambers
G Duhigg *née* Shore
J Jones *née* Byford
H Harding
A O'Kelly

1993/1994
J Gregory
J Potter
P George
C Bronks
E Garbutt *née* Scourfield
K Garson *née* Jenn
K Henderson

1994/1995
S Appleby
H Clayton
H Hulme
J Molyneux
A Wallace
S Dale *née* Portlock
T Siwek
L Mayhew

1995/1996
J Twigg
G Jew
S Thomas

1996/1997
C Green
J Watkinson *née* Smith
S Robertson *née* Denham
N Coffin
C Diver
K Knight
A O'Flynn

1997/1998
L Uttley
N Crawford *née* Brown
S Day
A De Biase
C Frost
J Poore
C Antcliffe *née* Sanderson
S Harris
T O'Reilly
G Stevens
T Collins
J Yapp

1998/1999
T Bowden *née* Andrews
V Huxford
C Bradley
E Cooke *née* Feltham
J Lyne *née* Phillips

1999/2000
N Drinkwater *née* Jupp
S Rudge
J Sutton
A Garnett
N Meston
P Ramsey
J Foster
F Penfold *née* Britten

2000/2001
S Marsh
A Palmer-Norrie
S Rae
K Andrew
A Rowley
N Goodwin
S Buckingham
E Smith

2001/2002
S Whitehead
E Knowles *née* Cribb

2002/2003
H Durman
A Pilkington
H Street *née* Flippance
D Waterman
R Clark
M Alphonsi

2003/2004
K Shaylor
V Gray
C Spencer
K Jones
R Murphy *née* Vickers
S Baker

2004/2005
C Barras
V Massarella *née* McCormack
M Staniford
L Moulding
A Turner
K Merchant
C Purdy

2005/2006
K Oliver
A Richardson-Watmore
H Robinson *née* Dawson
T Taylor
S Vetch

2006/2007
K Storie
R Burford
C Allan
S Hemming
J McGilchrist
S Beale
E Croker *née* Layland
S Hunter
K Daley-Mclean *née* Mclean
A Penrith

2007/2008
J Leonard
G Gulliver *née* Rozario
G Sharples
S Reeve *née* Dale
G Roberts
N Binstead
R Crowley
V Jackson
F Matthews
M Packer
F Pocock

2008/2009
E Scarratt
R Burnfield
R Essex
C Lee
O Poore

2009/2010
H Fisher
LT Mason

2011/2012
J Brightmore
V Fleetwood
N Hunt
L Keates
K Wilson
S McKenna
A Matthews
H Gallagher
I Noel-Smith
C Large
H Millar-Mills
E Braund
R Laybourn
K Newton
L Thompson
S Tuson
L Cattell
F Davidson
F Fletcher

2012/2013
A Reed
J Richardson-Watmore
A Chamberlain
E Scott
M Goddard
J Hope
M Foy
J Lucas
Z Saynor
C Keane

2013/2014
K Hancock
L Riley
A Wilson Hardy
S Acheson
N Brennan

2014/2015
A Brown
H Field
S Gregson
A Ward *née* Scott
B Blackburn
V Cornborough
K Mason
A Cokayne
H Kerr
L Davies
R Lund

2015/2016
C Clapp
B Dawson
P Cleall
L Demaine
C Gill
P Leitch
M Wood
S Bern
Z Aldcroft

2016/2017
M Jones

2017/2018
A Dow
J Breach
H Botterman
S Brown
C Mattinson
Z Harrison
E Kildunne
C O'Donnell
J Brown
L Tuima
C Pearce
K Smith

2018/2019
C Williams
T Heard
E Perry
S Beckett
C MacDonald
L Attwood
B Cleall
R Galligan
C Neilson
C Edwards

2019/2020
R Marston
A Harper
D Harper
M Venner
M Talling
H Rowland

Up to 1 November 2020

AUTHORS

Phil McGowan is the Curator at the World Rugby Museum. He was born and raised in Rochdale and graduated from University College London with an MA in 2007. He authored *Twickenham: Home of England Rugby* in 2014, *One Of Us: England's Greatest Rugby Players* in 2015 and *Doing their Duty: How England's rugby footballers helped win the First World War* in 2017.

Richard Steele is a professional musician and arts administrator who has had a life-long love of sport. A committee member and researcher at the World Rugby Museum at Twickenham since 2005, he is compiling and digitising the history and statistical details of major rugby union internationals between 1871 and 2020.

ACKNOWLEDGEMENTS

The information contained in this book is accurate according to the sources available to the authors in November 2020. If anyone has new or contradictory information, please send to museum@rfu.com. This particularly applies to the statistics around the England women's team. There are 16 fixtures between 1990 and 2004 for which only partial records are known to exist.

The authors received great support in preparing this publication. They would like to thank the following individuals and all the staff and volunteers at the World Rugby Museum for their help in researching and finding extra documentation for this book:

Phil Atkinson, Jeffrey Blackett, Gill Burns MBE, James Corsan, Doug Cheeseman, Tony Collins, Stephen Cooper, Sue Day MBE, Niamh Field, Stuart Farmer, Keith Gregson, John Griffiths, Tom Heeks, Frédéric Humbert, Carol Isherwood OBE, Chris Kelly, Richard Lowther, Deborah Mason, Mai, Jake and Alice McGowan, Emma Mitchell, Lewis Moody MBE, Patricia Mowbray, Peter Owens, Gwyn Prescott, Tony Price, Amy Rolph, Ray Ruddick, Caroline Steele, Bill Sweeney

In addition the publishers would like to thank:
Phil McGowan, Richard Steele, Patricia Mowbray, Jane Barron, Tom Heeks, Kathryn Williamson, Catherine Stewart, Emily Liles, Verity Williams, Caroline Steele, Niamh Field, Paul Morgan and Tim Buttimore. Special thanks must also go to Gill Burns MBE for her invaluable input and access to her personal archive, as well as Janis Ross, Garvin Davies, Frédéric Humbert, Matt Emery, Rocky Clark MBE, Jason Leonard OBE, Amanda Heathcote, Emily Scarratt, Luke Woodhouse, Jon Clarke, Eddie Jones, Simon Middleton, Katy Daley-Mclean MBE, Martin Johnson CBE, Lewis Moody MBE, Maggie Alphonsi MBE and Sue Day MBE

BIBLIOGRAPHY

The research for this book has involved the reading of around 200 books related to the development of English rugby over the last 150 years. The list below contains some of the principal sources consulted, but it does not include the many biographies, club and tour histories which were a valuable source of information and anecdotes:

Football – The Rugby Union Game, Marshall Rev F
Rugby Union Football 1870-1912, Holden LM
The History of the Rugby Football Union, Owen OL
Centenary History of the RFU, Titley UA & McWhirter R
The Barbarians 1890-1976, Starmer-Smith NC
The Book of English International Rugby 1871-1982, and
The Phoenix Book of International Rugby Records, Griffiths J
Running with the ball, Macrory J
The Carling Years – England Rugby 1988-96, Cleary M
England – The Official RFU History, Woolgar J
Sweet Chariot – The Rugby World Cup 2003, Robertson IG
Twickenham – The Official History, Harris E
The Lions – The complete history, Walmsley D
A Century of the All Blacks in Britain & Ireland, Fox D, Bogle KR & Hoskins M
English Rugby – Player by Player, Farmer S & Morgan P
Sweet Chariot 2 – Heroes and Heartbreak – Rugby World Cup 2007, Robertson IG
One among Equals – England's International Captains, Lewis S
100 Years of Twickenham & the 5/6 Nations Championship, Cleary M & Rhys C
A Social History of English Rugby Union, Collins T
The Red and the White – England v Wales Rugby, Richards H
Behind the Rose – Playing rugby for England, Jones S & Cain N
The King's Cup 1919, Evans H & Atkinson P
Thorny Encounters (England v All Blacks), Elliott M